PAPER DOLLS

of the
1960s, 1970s, and 1980s

Identification & Value Guide

Carol Nichols

cb

COLLECTOR BOOKS

A Division of Schroeder Publishing Co., Inc.

Cover design by Beth Summers
Book design by Joyce A. Cherry

COLLECTOR BOOKS
P.O. Box 3009
Paducah, Kentucky 42002-3009
www.collectorbooks.com

The current values in this book should be used only as a guide. They are not
intended to set prices, which vary from one section of the country to another.
Auction prices as well as dealer prices vary greatly and are affected by condition
as well as demand. Neither the author nor the publisher assumes responsibility
for any losses that might be incurred as a result of consulting this guide.

Searching For A Publisher?

We are always looking for people knowledgeable within their fields. If you
feel that there is a real need for a book on your collectible subject and have a
large comprehensive collection, contact Collector Books.

Contents

Dedication

This book is dedicated to my better half, James Garmon; without his support, endless hours of research, proofreading, organization, and writing skills, this book would not have been possible. James, thanks for keeping life stable and on track. You are the best!

Acknowledgments

I have several people to thank for their help in making this book become a reality. When you take on a project like this, you just cannot do it alone.

James, for his research and help in writing this book, providing some great advice along the way, hanging in there day after day as I talked only of paper dolls and this book, and never complaining as I dragged him to antique malls to search for a paper doll find. He is a trooper!

Jesse Reiner, who photographed over 1,000 pictures for this book and did a phenomenal job. (Didn't she?) She was always a pleasure to work with. Jesse was with child throughout all of our photographing sessions, so we must thank Jack, her unborn son, for hanging in there through all the bending and squatting.

Edna Corbett, who sent me many dolls from her own personal paper doll collection so that I could have them photographed for this book. She sent them all the way from the East Coast so that others could enjoy them. She also gave me many words of encouragement in all the stressful times, was always there to answer endless questions, and allowed me to glean from some of her incredible knowledge of paper dolls.

Julia Krug, who covered for me at work, allowing me to take extra days off to finish this book, and for being a great friend who always supports and encourages me in my endeavors.

"The kids," Michele, Jordan, Raven, Justin, Brandon, and ("the baby") Miss Lexy, along with the grandkids, Cyrus and Jonas, who fill our lives with laughter, joy, and sometimes major chaos.

I must thank my family, who has nurtured and encouraged my love of dolls along the way. Shirley Hanna, my mom, who affirmed and indulged my love for paper dolls by buying me anyone I wanted (I had quite a collection); you always seemed to understand my obsession. Nick Nichols, my dad, who made sure that every birthday and Christmas I had a new doll and paper dolls to play with. Glenda Walls and Cheryl Soto, who passed all their dolls on to me when Cheryl outgrew them. These are great memories. Papa-Jack Nichols, for being a loving and supportive person in my life. You gave me some of my best childhood memories. Jim Hanna, my stepdad, you were not around to see my young obsession with dolls, but you have witnessed my adult obsession, you always have had encouraging words to help me along the way, and you have loved me like your own daughter.

I appreciate each one of you who influenced my life, each of you having a part in molding me into who I am today. Thanks!

About the Author

My introduction into the doll world was in 1962. Yes, I was only two years old. However, those memories are still with me today. I played with my dolls like they were my children, feeding, dressing, and mothering them. At the age of four or five I found paper dolls. My mom tells stories of me in my room playing with my paper dolls for hours upon hours, and I remember cutting and punching out the dolls and their wardrobes, dressing them, and creating lives for all of them as I played. I could hardly sleep on Christmas Eve night, dreaming about the new doll and paper dolls I would find under the tree Christmas morning.

I have talked with many women who share the same love for dolls I do, and they express the same fond memories. What an impact paper dolls have had on all of us. As an adult, my love for dolls returned. I started making porcelain dolls. Soon, I began teaching classes, selling my dolls at doll shows, and participating in competitions all over the states. As I became a skilled dollmaker, other opportunities opened for me. I began writing for *Doll Maker's Workshop* and *Doll Crafter Magazine*. As my hobby grew, it took me in a different direction.

One day, as I thought about my childhood friends and the good times I had had playing with my dolls, I thought to myself, "I would love to possess those treasured toys I once loved so much..."

But I had no idea how to find them... Then I thought, "eBay! They have everything! Right?" I did a search for my

favorite doll, Tubsy — and there she was! I paid $177.00 for her, and she was worth it. When she came in the mail, all those memories came rushing in, and I was so excited that I had to keep looking. Well, I started searching on eBay for the paper dolls that I had as a child, and there they were in living color! That is when I got hooked and started my own collection.

I had almost every paper doll you could imagine in the '60s. Every time my mother and I would go to the store, I would plead with her to buy me the newest paper doll I didn't yet have. Most of the time she gave in, and my childhood collection grew. I took my current favorite with me wherever I went, and in most all of my childhood pictures I am holding a paper doll. I even begged a cameraman to let me hold my paper doll in a picture that they were taking for a newspaper article representing Smokey the Bear and the fire department. As I look back, I just can't believe that cameraman let me hold my paper doll. I must have been very persuasive.

As I started receiving my auction-won paper dolls in the mail, it was an incredible feeling to see and hold my old childhood treasures and reminisce about the hours of fun I had shared with them. I looked and looked for a book that would have all the different paper dolls that I had enjoyed as a child. I found a wonderful book, *Tomart's Price Guide to Lowe* and *Whitman Paper Dolls,* by Mary Young. (This along with eBay,

B-6   THE SAN DIEGO UNION   Monday, July 25, 1966

SMOKEY THE BEAR IDEA
Children Taught Fire Perils

By PETER BROWN

EL CAJON — Smokey the Bear has nothing on El Cajon Firemen Al Petree and Roy Creamer.

Like the fictional bear, they figtt fires with a psychological approach, and like Smokey, they aim at the younger generation.

The two men form the city's active Fire Prevention Bureau which, fighting an educational battle, has to keep one jump a head of potential fire conditions.

Getting back to the kids — they are the biggest headache to the two-man bureau which calculates little children set at least one fire a day during the summer months.

'MINIMUM FIGURE'

"One a day is just a minimum figure," Fire Marshal Petree said. "Of course, most of the blazes are caught in time."

Some fires can do a lot of damage in a short time the two firemen said. Petree cited the case of a young ster who set off a flare in a women's dress shop causing $1,500 in damage. The problem is, the firemen say, to reach the young potential arsonists on their own level.

"You have to realize," Creamer said, "that 99 per cent of the fires are caused by ordinary kids playing with matches.

GREAT SUCCESS

"It is all psychological. If you talk to the kids, and show them fire damage, they catch on pretty fast."

The El Cajon Fire Preven-

tion Bureau, which emphasizes parental counciling rather than criminal prosecution, can claim 95 per cent success in its program.

"We hardly ever have a repeater," Petree said. "But there are always new ones cropping up."

Meanwhile, the summer

fires are running in a heavy cycle.

"We expect one a day, most of them grass fires," he said, "but threre are days when the total reaches as high as 15."

In a single day last month, Creamer confiscated 1,500 fire crackers.

The two men spend most of their time promoting educa-

tional programs and child-parental counciling sessions.

"That is the only way to get to them," Petree said. "Tell them about fires and they will cease to think of them as a plaything."

Parents could do the same thing and save us a lot of trouble, he said.

—Bob Crosby Photo

El Cajon fire inspector Roy Creamer tells Steve Nichols, 4, and sister Carol, 6, of fire dangers as they stand near area burned by matches.

is where I have gotten a lot of my information for this book.) But *Tomart's* is out of pring and hard to get. I felt there was a need for a current book with many pictures that would show paper doll lovers now and in the future what the 1960s had, and what the values of those dolls are currently.

That brings me to the present. I have since spent countless hours researching and collecting paper dolls and enjoying every

all the different paper dolls that I had enjoyed as a child. I found a wonderful book, *Tomart's Price Guide to Lowe* and *Whitman Paper Dolls,* by Mary Young. (This along with eBay,

minute of it, and I hope you will get as much joy out of reading this book as I did from writing it.

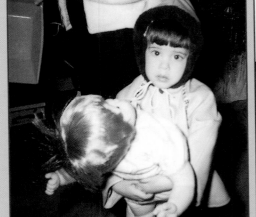

Introduction

Paper dolls have consistently been an inexpensive way for little girls to pretend and play.

As for myself, I could spend all day in my room cutting out clothes, dressing my paper dolls, and make-believing that my Barbie paper doll would bring over a fresh cherry pie to Wilma Flintstone. (I had to find the perfect dress for Barbie to wear so Wilma would be impressed!)

Paper dolls brought me so much joy as a young girl that these fond memories are etched in my mind forever, and I know many of you reading this book have your own treasured memories.

As more and more households owned television sets in the 1960s, '70s, and '80s, paper dolls changed with the times. Many were created in the likenesses of favorite celebrities, whether musicians or actors on popular television shows. Others were created in the likenesses of favorite fashion dolls, and some paper dolls were re-created favorites of past decades. The sets for little girls to choose from were endless, and parents loved paper dolls because they were a fraction of the cost of a vinyl baby doll. Most little girls could have several different sets of paper dolls, never getting bored.

The exciting thing in our world today is having the ability we do to purchase our childhood treasures. Vintage paper dolls were much harder to find in the past. You may have been able to find them at flea markets, garage sales, or maybe estate sales. Now, with eBay, we can find whatever treasures we want (for a price 100 times greater than what we paid in the 1960s, '70s, or '80s. With more and more antique stores and antique malls popping up, we have many ways to find and own our favorite childhood paper dolls. It may take a bit of looking and some tedious hours of searching and bidding. However, one thing is for sure — if we keep looking and persevere, we can own and enjoy those special paper dolls we treasured as childern.

Paper Dolls of the 1960s, 1970s, and 1980s is a comprehensive guide for the paper doll lover and collector. This book will include a price guide with descriptions, and photographs of approximately 395 different paper dolls of the 1960s, '70s, and '80s. All pricing is based on mint and uncut condition. The publisher will be noted, along with the owner of the trademark for the featured paper doll; for example, Publisher: Whitman (publisher)/Mattel (trademark owner).

Each chapter deals with a different decade, providing you, the collector, with an easy way to identify and value your own collection or future collection.

Each paper doll set will have two to five pictures of the cover or box front, the dolls themselves and a sampling of clothes, and, sometimes, the inside of the folder.

The price guide is based on research I have done primarily through eBay and several books, including Mary Young's books *Tomart's Price Guide to Saalfield and Merrill Paper Dolls* and *Tomart's Price Guide to Lowe and Whitman Paper Dolls*. I have also used other books, including *A Collector's Guide to Barbie Paper Dolls*, *Schroeder's Collectible Toys Antique to Modern Price Guide*, and *Liddle Kiddles Identification and Value Guide*. In addition, I have relied on my own personal experience finding and buying for my collection through the years. The prices listed in this book are only a guide and are not meant to set current values; no one is obligated to buy, sell, or trade according to the values listed in the book.

A Kaleidoscope of Paper Dolls

I can't really say that I collect a specific kind of paper doll, simply because my collection is a mélange of any and every type that tickles my fancy. The main body of my collection is centered on the era in which I grew up, the 1960s. However, it would be silly for you or me to limit ourselves to just one particular genre or era when there is a diverse world of paper dolls out there. *Paper Dolls of the 1960s, 1970s, and 1980s* is filled with all kinds. Take a look.

Fashion paper dolls

Fashion has played an important role in the production of paper dolls, just as it has in the production of 12" dolls. I think manufactures have always realized that every young girl likes to play dress-up, and that all women, young and old, love to keep up with the latest rage in the world of fashion. From the long, frilly dresses of the Victorian age to the miniskirts and go-go boots of the '60s and the leg warmers and designer jeans of the '80s, fashion paper dolls have remained in step with the times.

Small Baby & Child paper dolls

This was one of the most beloved categories of paper dolls for little girls and collectors in the past and still is today. These paper dolls had major appeal for me as a child. I would dress my babies and toddlers and play Mom! I loved the way the artist could capture the angelic faces, too, Those babies and tots were so realistic looking, and the clothes! Oh boy, it was like Christmas every time I got a new paper doll book. I would carefully press or cut out each piece and spend hours dressing and re-dressing my dolls. Some of my favorite artists who could capture the look of a baby or child were Louise Rumely, with her Babyland; Queen Holden, who gave me perhaps my favorite childhood paper doll, Baby Anne Smiles and Cries; Neva Shultz, with her Lovable Babies; Betty Campbell, with her Magic Mary's; the Myers, with their Baby Go Along; and Belle Benoit, with her Sunbeam Babies. These are just a few of the talented artists that made my childhood so much fun.

Toy Doll paper dolls

As popular as the vinyl dolls themselves, these were some of my favorites as a child, and they still are. Likenesses of Chatty Cathy, Barbie doll, Frankie doll, Crissy doll, Betsy Wetsy, Baby Go Bye-Bye, and Big Jim (for the fellas) appeared soon after their 12" or 18" counterparts hit the shelves. I can remember going shopping with my mother or on vacation, and in my little carrying case were most of my favorite dolls — not the plastic or vinyl ones, but the paper dolls.

Animated Character paper dolls

When you folks were younger, did you ever bring out your Disney character paper dolls?

Did you, in addition, create your very own Magic Kingdom? Or did you, on Saturday morning, ever re-create your favorite cartoon? Sure, you did. Paper dolls of animated characters from Disney, Warner Bros., and other companies have always been a mainstay of the paper doll industry. Alongside children's stories and coloring books, they continue to have a successful run.

Celebrity paper dolls

I actually become a fan of celebrity paper dolls when I was about nine or ten years old. I was outgrowing my dolls and stuffed toys (sort of), so they were regulated to the little table in the corner of my room. I cleared off the top of my dresser and made room for paper dolls in the likenesses of Keith Partridge and the Partridge Family, Donny and Marie Osmond, Patty Duke, Haley Mills, and the Beverly Hillbillies. Collecting celebrity paper dolls of popular TV and movie personalities is part of the whole memorabilia collecting craze, and is just as big as collecting celebrity posters, dolls, cups, plates, or lunchboxes.

Fantasy & Sci-Fi paper dolls

America has always had a love affair with fantasy and science fiction. Why? No one really knows. It may come from the need to explore the unknown, or from our love of mysteries; who can say? This genre has found a niche in paper dolls. The gamut is wide ranging, from mermaids to pixies, Greek heroes to King Arthur, and Star Trek to Star Wars. These types of paper dolls truly let us play make-believe.

You may be a history buff, love movie or television shows, like cartoon and animated characters, or enjoy fashions from a certain period in time.

It really doesn't matter, because out there in the Land of Paper Dolls, you are sure to find what piques your interest. There's a kaleidoscope of paper dolls.

Cut or Not? It's up to you!

Have you ever looked at your paper dolls and said, "Should I cut or not?" It can be so much fun to cut out all those adorable outfits and try them on your dolls. Depending on the type of collector you are, you will have strong views either way.

Some collectors love to display their paper dolls in a cabinet or frame them on acid-free matting. Some want to cut and dress their paper dolls, while other collectors want to keep their books mint and intact. Whatever kind of collector you are, some things are important to know before you decide.

A paper doll book in mint condition will be worth two to three times (if not more) the value of a paper doll book that has been cut. For paper doll books that are cut, the value will be based on the condition of the dolls, clothes, and folder.

For example, if a doll has tape or creases anywhere, a set's value is significantly diminished. The same goes for missing pieces and poorly cut out clothing. If a paper doll book has been cut, but the doll or dolls are in excellent condition, all clothes and accessories are accounted for, the cutting is precise, and the folder has very little shelf wear, a set's value can still be very good. However, keep in mind that nothing compares to the uncut mint paper doll set as far as value goes.

Value will also depend on the production era. As with most collectibles, the earlier the decade, the higher the value. For instance, paper dolls of the '60s will typically have a higher value then those of the '70s, and so on. The reason, in our area of collecting, is mainly due to the difficulty of finding paper dolls, cut or uncut, in excellent to mint condition.

Value is also determined by the rarity and popularity of the paper doll itself. I have seen mint condition paper dolls go for hundreds of dollars, because they were considered rare; their rarity made them highly sought after and collectible.

So, remember that to cut or not it is really up to you. My choice...Well, I go both ways, displaying some of my absolute favorites fully decked out in their best duds. Other favorites stay in their mint condition and are displayed that way.

Whatever you decide, remember to have fun and enjoy your collection.

Preserving and Caring for Your Paper Dolls

You've started your collection, you display it in a glass case or maybe some sort of (do I dare say?) clear plastic sleeve...now what? You treasure your collection, hoping to keep it around for years, maybe passing it on to sons, daughters, or grandchildren.

Well, this is where a little understanding of paper preservation comes in handy. Now, you won't have to be a chemist or have a PhD in paper conservation, but having some knowledge of the adverse effects that certain elements can have on paper and paper products could save you a few headaches, and even a fewer heartaches, down the road. In this section, I will try to give you some helpful hints concerning preservation and maintenance of your paper dolls, and will discuss what to be on the lookout for; that is, the leading causes of deterioration of paper doll collections.

Okay, here we go.

What is paper preservation? Simply put, it is the protection of paper cultural property, through processes that minimize the chemical and physical damage and/or deterioration.

Whew, didn't I say that you don't have to have a PhD? Okay, okay, so maybe I spoke too soon. That's alright, let's move on. Sometimes people confuse the word *preservation* with the word *conservation*. Before we go any further, I'd like to clear up any misconception. Preservation is the process of prolonging the existence of cultural or societal property, and conservation is the actual process or physical treatment of items that are in distress or have begun to show signs of damage.

As we search and scour the Internet, flea markets, and antique stores, we've all noticed some items that appear fragile, brittle, faded, discolored, or even sticky (yuck!). What could cause such damage? "Officer Preservation, could bring you in bring in the lineup?" Staring at the far left, we have bad guy #1, physical handling; next up is light, and after that comes temperature, humidity, improper storage, tiny unseen pests, and poor manufacturing. You see, folks, there are a number of culprits that love to get their grubby little paws into anything made of paper, including our beloved paper dolls. But let's start with the top seven on the Most Wanted list. I know you are all reading this and starting to feel a dark cloud form above your heads, and rest assured that I once felt the same way, but wait — all is not lost, and there is a silver lining in that dark cloud. Once you have become aware of the culprits involved in paper deterioration, I'm sure you will all feel and sleep a little more soundly. Well, you might not have lost any sleep, but you will, like me, pay a little more attention to the care of your paper dolls.

When you acquire a set of paper dolls for your collection, the natural thing to do is pick it up and flip through the pages, and if you've found a set that has the dolls already punched out, you may have a slight urge to play dress-up. I'm a kid at heart also, and that's all fine and dandy, but pay careful attention to the manner in which you handle your collection. You see, our skin secretes a protective covering known as the "acid mantle," which is a fine film with a slightly acid pH that acts as a barrier against disease and the natural elements. Paper, like most everyday items in our lives, does not react well when confronted with acid. Another natural occurrence is the secretion of oil from our fingertips. This oil acts like a magnet, attracting dust, dirt, and microscopic pests, and when it gets on paper, it stays on. So when handling your collection, remember to avoid direct contact such as picking up, holding, or turning the pages using the pincer-type grasp imbedded in the DNA of every creature that has opposable thumbs and a forefingers. Instead, use the tip of your finger or fingernail, and use the palm of your hand to cup or cradle your paper doll or the pages (this may seem awkward and a little extreme). Use care when touching your paper doll if your hands have lotion, hand cream, or any type of perfume applied to them. The key focus here is to maintain our collection in prime condition.

All of us like to display our paper doll collections out where they can be seen, and we know they are best seen in daylight, but hold on before you let the sunshine through or place a 120-watt floodlight in your display case. Be on the lookout for light degradation (too much of a good thing, remember?). Light degradation is the culprit responsible for turning those clear, colorful, glossy pages of paper dolls into dull, yellow, or darkened images of, what's the word? Oh yeah — BLAHH!!! Most paper contains products or chemicals that are light activated and often acidic, and most light, be it natural or artificial (such as fluorescent), produces ultraviolet rays. If you have ever been out in the sun for too long, you know how these can cause a very nasty burn. For skin and paper products alike, light is double-edged sword. In order to halt or at least slow down the degradation process, try using cold lights with UV filters. These can be picked up at most hardware or lighting stores and cost a little more than regular light bulbs. As an alternative, you might simply decrease the period of time that you leave the light on in your display case. Always use acid-free material and avoid any materials with acetate.

Some of you say, "Carol, I like my collection out in the open, not behind glass in a display case," and I respond to that by fainting. Sure, you want to let your paper dolls breathe, so you put them on a shelf, pages fanned out, high out of the reach of small children or grandchildren. But remember, air carries pollutants such as dust, soot, smoke, mold, and dust mites.

If you do have your collection displayed behind glass, then from time to time do a quick check of the air inside your case by taking a whiff with the old reliable. I'm talking about the old olfactory, the nose, that is. If the air inside appears stale or moldy, it may be a signal that some unpleasant and unwanted guests have or are about to take up residence on or within the folds of your paper doll books. An increase in air circulation should do the trick; just open the doors of your case for a few minutes every other day or carefully fan through the pages. What I've found works is to place a small electric fan, set on low, in the door of the display case, and to run it for 10 – 15 minutes every two to three days. It's great for circulating the air.

This airing-out process can also be an all-in-one method to control other conditions, like the aforementioned humidity and temperature. Mold and mildew love dark, damp, and cool locations, which are also prime breeding grounds for what is known as foxing. Foxing is the brownish mold stains that appear in either small bull's-eye or big snowflake-like patterns, or as flyspecks that resemble dark, small, glossy spots on the surface of the paper. A good rule to keep in mind is the 68/35 rule. When storing most paper products, including paper dolls, in an enclosed space, keep temperature at 68° F and the humidity at approximately 35% (any level between 30% and 40% is acceptable.)

There are many other factors that can wreak havoc on our paper doll collections to take into account. I've only tried to list the most destructive. Other considerations include where the doll or paper was made, how long it was kept in storage and under what conditions, and how and with what it was treated during manufacturing. The list is endless if you stop and think about it. But as I have learned and continue to learn, care and handling are the two most important considerations when trying to preserve our paper dolls. Preservation is important not solely for the investment aspect; more important, for me at least, is the preservation of the memories I had when I was young and the treasures that I hope to pass on to my children and grandchildren.

Seek — and Ye Just Might Find

Well, it looks like someone may have caught a bit of the collecting bug, or maybe you've recently taken a trip down memory lane and want to reclaim a piece of your childhood. Whatever your reason for seeking paper dolls, here are a few tips on where to look.

eBay

I am a huge fan of eBay, and if you ask my significant other, and he might say that I'm a fanatic. Feeling weak, must log on, find auction. Okay, that's his opinion. But honestly, eBay has become the premier auction site, and if you need it (or don't need it, but want it), then this is the place to come. Organized, easy to navigate, and full of goodies, new and vintage, right at your fingertips. Most of you already know this.

Some of you might disagree with me. I've heard from a few who have had a run-in with a scoundrel who took a payment and "sent it, but it must have gotten lost in the mail," or said, "I'm sorry, it's sitting on the table, I just keep forgetting to ship it." If you are deceived, you have a number of options to help address this type of situation. Let eBay know about the circumstances, and please, please make sure that you send that person a *negative feedback*. It will alert others to what type of seller or bidder they are dealing with. For more tips on how to protect yourself against fraud, check out eBay's Safeharbor section. If you are a buyer and have already sent or made a payment through Paypal, Bidpay, etc., then you may be able to file a report with the United States Postal Service. Now some of you who have written me felt that the prices were too high, which can be true at times. In this case, you have to ask yourself, "How bad do I need it?" or "Can I afford to wait and see if another one shows up sometime down the road?" One thing you need to remember about eBay is that it should be fun, so don't let one or two bad experiences spoil your adventure.

I do concede that one major drawback, however, has been fraud. We all know that if there is a will, then anyone with a lesser degree of morals will find a way, but don't let this deter you from taking full advantage of this great site. This past summer, the folks at eBay initiated a range of new safeguards and precautionary measures to insure that the unscrupulous out there have a more difficult time trying to scheme and scam us serious bidders and collectors out of our rightfully-won treasures.

Antique Malls

You gumshoe types who love a good hunt should head out to one of these organized yet sometimes dusty treasure troves and look through the various dealer booths. Some antique malls have mailing lists and will send out announcements of pending sales, new additions, etc., on a monthly basis. This can have its ups and downs, though. While you are informed, so are others, and it's a race; on the other hand, one person's junk may be another person's goldmine.

Other antique malls provide a members' guestbook, in which you can leave your name, number, and even jot down specific items that you are looking for. This is where talking to and building friendly relations with the people there can really pay off; they remember you and call as soon as they have something you are looking for. I've lucked out a few times by networking. One piece of advice before you head out: check local listings in the phone book or log onto the web and look in the Internet directory for antique malls in your area. It's a time saver.

Flea Markets

Put on the sunscreen and some comfortable walking shoes. There's nothing like a flea market when the weather is good. Here is another place where one person's junk is another person's goldmine, and shopping at a flea market can pay off big for you. Whether it's paper dolls, vinyl dolls, action figures, or Hot Wheels cars, flea markets will have something for everyone. Two things to remember: 1) Study up on what you will be looking for; e.g., serial numbers, place of origin, manufacturer, and special features, all of which are used to determine if that item you find is vintage or not, and 2) Don't be afraid to barter. The seller may have a price tag on the item or may just tell you a price, but believe me, it's usually not set in stone, especially if it comes down

to a choice between getting rid of the item or repacking it and lugging it back home.

Garage Sales

I call these neighborhood flea markets. They are just as good and fun to check out as the regular flea markets. Most garage sales are held by families who have moved or are moving and want to make room for new things that they are buying or get rid of stuff that they don't want to pack and move. What I look for are the sales in the older parts of Denver, where a held by family has lived in the same house for years and years. The kids are all grown and on their own, so bedrooms, attics, basements, and storage areas are cleared out. Out go the old dolls, toys, games, furniture, and so forth.

Local Newspaper and *Thrifty Nickels*

The classified sections of newspapers can hold a wealth of information. Many newspapers have deadlines for sellers to get their new listings in by; most new listings appear every Wednesday or Thursday. What can you find in the classifieds? Look for auctions (estate sales, or sales by storage companies when renters have failed to return for their things or pay storage fees), antique and collector shows, or garage sales. Monthly *Thrifty Nickels* are other good sources; items are listed by categories and reasonably priced. However, items that have already been sold are not withdrawn until the next month's issue.

Word of Mouth

Searching can take you near and far, and if you're the type of person who gets a little sick and tired of going to the same places over and over — What, are you mad? — then the next time you are out and about, searching high and low, drop off a homemade business card or leave a flyer with your contact information and what you are seeking at a dealer's counter. Once again, networking and building relationships can help.

Whatever, your particular method of collecting, just be an *educated buyer.* Whether you collect vintage paper dolls, toys, marbles, action figures, clothing, or jewelry, know the specifics that make items unique and valuable now or in the future. Bidding, bartering, and collecting should be *fun* experiences. For me personally, the satisfaction from collecting paper dolls comes from the history and the art as much as it does from making that winning bid or seeing that special find.

1960s

1960

Debbie Reynolds   Year: 1960   #1956

Debbie Reynolds was born Mary Frances Reynolds, in El Paso, Texas, on April 1, 1932. She got her start by winning a Burbank beauty contest at the age of 16. Reynolds had small roles in several films before she got the lead female role in Gene Kelly and Stanley Donen's musical comedy *Singin' in the Rain.* Reynolds had no professional dance training and did not know how to tap dance prior to being chosen for the role. Her performance was praised, and the movie became her big break. She continued to make movies at MGM and was known for such films as *The Unsinkable Molly Brown* and *The Singing Nun,* to name just a couple. Her career is alive and well even today; she recently starred in a favorite movie of mine, *Mother.* She was great in that role! I laugh every time I see it.

This fabulous set includes one medium-weight cardboard Debbie Reynolds doll and a 33-piece cut-out wardrobe with tabs.

Publisher: Whitman Publishing Company/Debbie Reynolds
Original Price: 29¢   Value: $70.00 – 85.00

Magic Stay-on Dresses, Carol   Year: 1960   #4626

An adorable little tyke, Carol is a statuette doll made from heavyweight cardboard. This set includes approximately 57 outfits and accessories, all ready to cut out. Rub the clothing briskly over the doll and, like magic, the clothes stay on.

Publisher: Whitman Publishing Company
Original Price: 79¢   Value: $18.00 – 25.00

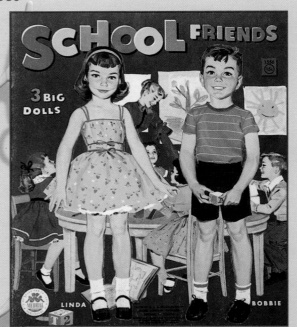

School Friends   Year: 1956/1960   #1556

I love this set! It is brightly colored and wonderfully illustrated by Barbara Briggs. It was released in 1956 and again in 1960. It is a reprint of #1548, Kitty Goes to Kindergarten, also released in 1956.

In this set, you will find three die-cut dolls, Linda, Bobbie, and Diane, along with 46 cut-out outfits and accessories with tabs.

Publisher: Merrill
Original Price: 15¢   Value: $35.00 – 55.00

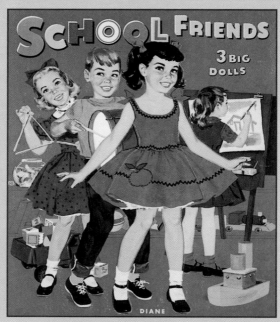

Six Sisters **Year: 1955/1960** **#2582**

Big N' Little Six Sisters, 6 and Sweet 16 is the title of this set, which Maxine MCCaffrey beautifully drew with vivid colors and expressive faces. This set was published in 1955 and again in 1960, and includes six die-cut dolls. Three of the sisters are sweet 16 — Jane, Sue, and Katie — and three of the sisters are six — Jill, Sally, and Kerry. Three pets are also included. In addition, there are 55 outfits and accessories to cut out; each tab has the name of the doll that the outfit belongs to.

Publisher: Merrill
Original Price: 29¢ **Value: $40.00 – 65.00**

Cindy and Mindy   Year: 1960   #1974

   Beautifully drawn by the Myers, this darling set features Cindy and Mindy, the turn-about twins. These little cuties have a front and back to them, allowing them to display their clothing from either side. The set includes the two die-cut twins and 20 cut-out outfits and accessories with tabs; each outfit has a front and a back. You can dress each twin by slipping the tabs on her clothing between her front and her back.

Publisher: Whitman Publishing Company
Original Price: 29¢   Value: $20.00 – 35.00

Courtesy of Edna Corbett

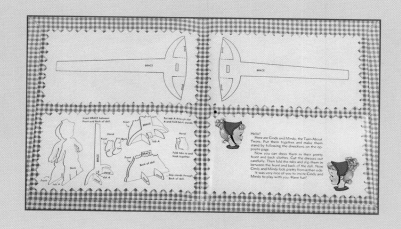

A Dozen Cousins   **Year: 1960**   **#2090**

A Dozen Cousins is an adorable set drawn by the Myers, and includes 12 die-cut dolls named Allen, Babs, Chuck, Debbie, Ellen, Fred, George, Heidi, Ida, Jean, Kerry, and Larry. There are 146 cut-out outfits and accessories with tabs. The tabs have the first letter of the name of each doll, to identify to whom the outfit belongs.

Publisher: Whitman
Original Price: 15¢   **Value: $20.00 – 30.00**

Courtesy of Edna Corbett

Baby Kim   Year: 1960 – 1962   #1969

Baby Kim is a statuette doll and is dressed in her little red sunsuit, shoes, and socks. She comes with her carry tote and 28 outfits and accessories with tabs.

Publisher: Whitman
Original Price: unknown   **Value: $15.00 – 25.00**

Baby Bonnie   Year: 1960   #1970

Baby Bonnie is a large statuette doll who looks very similar to Baby Kim. She shares the same pose, but has some minor differences. Baby Bonnie is about an inch larger and wears ruffled panties, shoes, and socks. She has soft red curls instead of Baby Kim's thick blonde curls.

The inside of Baby Bonnie's cover doubles as a storage tote, as well as a Bathinette and baby buggy into which you can slip her. Also included are 17 outfits and accessories with tabs.

Note: Both Baby Bonnie and Baby Kim have their own unique outfits and accessories.

Publisher: Whitman
Original Price: 29¢   **Value: $15.00 – 25.00**

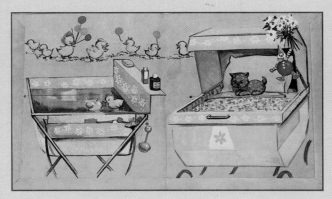

Ballerina   **Year: 1960**   **No number**

Ballerina is not only a paper doll set; it also includes a storybook. It consists of four die-cut little girls named Tamara, Denise, Marie, and Ariane. Each doll has featured costumes from popular ballets, such as the *Nutcracker*, *Coppelia*, and *Swan Lake*.

There are a total of 46 outfits and headpieces to cut out. The tabs on each costume show the name of the doll the costume belongs with.

To top it off, there are two three-dimensional stage sets; each one can create a scene from a famous ballet.

A storybook tells the story of the little ballerinas and has slits the dolls can fit into and become an interactive part of the story.

Publisher: Golden Press
Original Price: $1.00   **Value: $45.00 – 65.00**

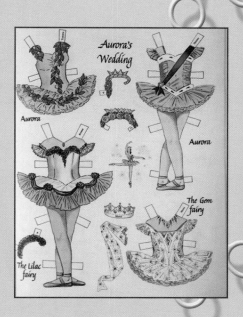

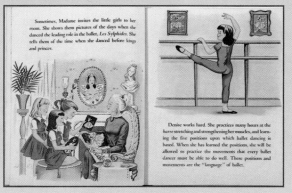

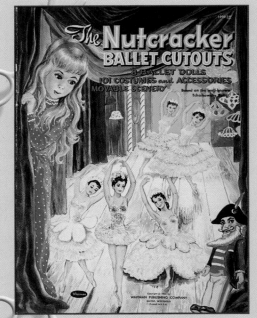

The Nutcracker Ballet   Year: 1960   #1990

I love this Christmastime ballet. Originally based on the story *The Nutcracker and the King of Mice,* written by German writer E. T. A. Hoffman, the ballet was accompanied by the music of Tchaikovsky; the music was known as the *Nutcracker Suite*.

In the story, the young Clara is given a nutcracker doll by Drosselmeyer, her godfather, a clock maker and inventor of mechanical toys. The godfather, while working at the palace, invented a trap that killed most of the mice population. As revenge, the King of Mice turns Drosselmeyer's nephew into a nutcracker doll. To break the spell, the Nutcracker must kill the King of Mice, and does so after saving Clara and leading the Toy Soldiers in a great battle against the mice. In the end, he is sent along with Clara through the Land of Snow to the Kingdom of Sweets, to be entertained by the Sugar Plum Fairy.

The Nutcracker debuted in Russia on December 17, 1892, and a shortened version debuted in the US in 1940.

In this beautifully illustrated set, there are eight die-cut dolls (only seven of the dolls are shown below), with 101 cut-out costumes and accessories with tabs. The tabs have numbers that match numbers on the base of each doll. The folder opens to create a scene from *The Nutcracker*.

Publisher: Whitman Publishing Company
Original Price: 59¢   Value: $55.00 – 65.00

Santa's Workshop   **Year: 1960**   **#1989**

A charming and delightful set drawn by the Myers, it is jam-packed with holiday fun, from roly-poly Santa Claus to his adorable little elves busily making toys for Christmas. The set is not an easy find, especially complete and in mint condition.

Santa's Workshop features Mr. and Mrs. Santa Claus, three of Santa's trusty elves, four reindeer, six dolls, several pieces of furniture, and approximately 50 cut-out outfits and accessories with tabs.

The folder is tri-fold. When opened, one can create Santa's Workshop, complete with a candy cane ladder, curtains, workbenches, and lots of toys!

Publisher: Whitman
Original Price: 59¢   **Value: $125.00 – 175.00**

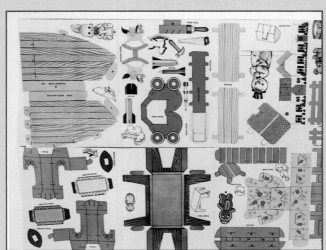

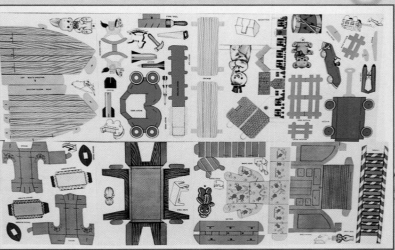

One Hundred and One Dalmatians   Year: 1960   #1954

Written by Dodie Smith and first published in 1912, *The Hundred and One Dalmatians* launched the literary career of its English author. A student of the dramatic arts at the Royal Academy of Dramatic Art, she would also go on to write novels for adults.

In the story, a man named Roger lives alone with his dog Pongo, a dalmatian. Roger is lonely and seeks a wife. One days he meets and falls in love with a beautiful woman named Anita, who herself owns a dalmatian named Perdita. Soon Roger and Anita are married.

Enter Cruella, an old acquaintance of Anita's, who wants one thing — the fur coats of dalmatians. Knowing that the couple's two dogs will soon have puppies, she waits for the day that the litter is born. When Perdita gives birth to her puppies, Cruella sends two henchmen to kidnap them. With their litter missing, Pongo and Perdita begin the search to rescue their offspring from Cruella. Helped by Colonel, an old dog, and Tibbs, a cat, they find the puppies as well as many other dalmatians. From there it's a mad rush to save all the dogs from becoming Cruella's new fur coat and to get back to Roger and Anita.

This is one in a long list of classic stories adapted and animated by Disney. It was released in 1960, and was the first film created with the Xerox Photographic Process.

A truly delightful set that features many of the characters from this popular film, this set includes 25 stand-up figures and 15 costumes, all with tabs and ready to cut out. The try-fold folder opens to re-create scenes from the movie.

Publisher: Whitman/Walt Disney Productions
Original Price: 59¢   Value: $80.00 – 150.00

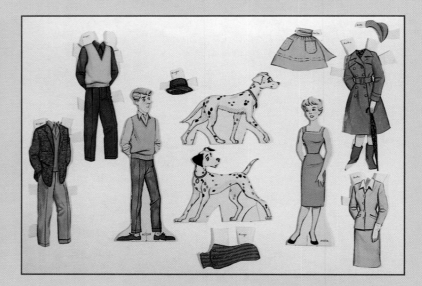

10" Little Theater Paper Dolls   Year: 1960   #1365

This set is a reprint from #4444 the Old Woman Who Lived in the Shoe, dated 1960. There is no date on this set. However, many reprints were done around the same time period, so I chose to display this set with the others of 1960. There are 10 die-cut dolls, including the old woman, and 51 cut-out costumes and hats. Each tab has a number to match the number on the doll.

Publisher: Saalfield
Original Price: 29¢   Value: $10.00 – 20.00

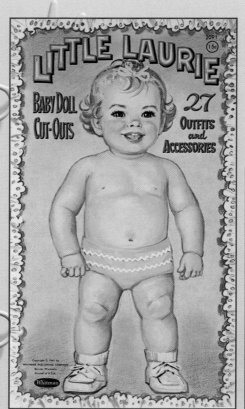

Little Laurie   **Year: 1961**   **#2091**

Little Laurie's set features a darling die-cut toddler, Laurie, along with 27 outfits and accessories to cut out. Also included are four of Laurie's toys (pictured on the back cover) to press out, a duck, rabbit, rattle, and baby cup.

Publisher: Whitman Publishing Company
Original Price: 15¢   Value: $18.00 – 30.00

Sally and Susie Magic Dolls   **Year: 1961**   **#4701**

In this set, you will find two magnetic statuette dolls, Sally and Susie. By attaching a metal magnet to the clothing pieces with scotch tape, you can make the clothes stay on the dolls like magic. There are over 50 outfits and accessories to cut out.

Publisher: Whitman Publishing Company
Original Price: unknown   Value: $35.00 – 50.00

Carol Heiss   **Year: 1961**   **#1964**

Olympic figure skating champion Carol Heiss began skating at the age of five. At the age of seven, she began taking lessons from Pierre Brunet of the Skating Club of New York. Pierre confidently told Carol's mother, "In ten years, your daughter can be the best in the world," and within five years Carol won the US Novice title. The following year, she brought home the US Junior title.

Beginning in 1953, she would win four consecutive silver medals in the US Figure Skating Championships, following in the shadow of Tenley Albright. Carol would later say, "I was beginning to wonder if I was always going to be the bridesmaid and never the bride." Fortunes changed when she finally succeeded in beating Albright at the 1956 World Championships in Garmisch, West Germany, the first of five consecutive World titles for Heiss. She also went on to win four consecutive US titles and two North American Championships before winning the gold in 1960 by delivering one of the most polished performances in Olympic figure skating history, earning all nine first-place votes from the judges.

Her paper doll set includes one medium-weight cardboard doll, Carol Heiss, and 70 cut-out costumes and accessories with tabs. Her folder doubles as a carry tote with handles.

Publisher: Whitman Publishing Company
Original Price: 29¢   Value: $35.00 – 55.00

National Velvet   Year: 1961   #1958

Many paper dolls were inspired because of popular movies. This set is no exception, and is based on the MGM movie *National Velvet*, starring Mickey Rooney and Elizabeth Taylor. *National Velvet* was 11-year-old Elizabeth Taylor's first starring role, and it made her a star.

This paper doll set includes one statuette doll, Velvet, made of heavyweight cardboard and with 32 cut-out costumes and accessories with tabs. The folder folds out to create a beautifully illustrated stable.

Publisher: Whitman Publishing Company
Original Price: 29¢   Value: $45.00 – 65.00

Candy and Her Cousins   **Year: 1961**   **#2581**

A wonderfully charming set drawn by Elizabeth Gartrell Voss, with dolls that are both adorable and delightful printed in vivid colors, and a wardrobe that is magnificently detailed, which makes this set a favorite with collectors.

Candy and Her Cousins includes four die-cut dolls, Candy, Mimi, Patti, and Gigi, and with 52 outfits and accessories to cut out. Each tab has the first initial of the doll the outfit belongs to.

Publisher: Merrill Publishing Company
Original Price: 29¢   Value: $40.00 – 65.00

White House Party Dresses   **Year: 1961**   **#11550**

This set features glamorous dresses of famous women who attended White House parties; some of the ladies who wore these dresses and stand out are Martha Washington, Dolly Madison, Mary Lincoln, and Eleanor Roosevelt, to name a few. This set includes two die-cut beauties, along with 25 exquisite dresses and accessories, all with tabs and ready to cut out.

Publisher: Merrill Publishing Company
Original Price: 15¢   **Value: $30.00 – 55.00**

Peter and Pam   Year: 1961   #1974

This is another adorable front and back set drawn by the Myers. Peter and Pam have 24 cut-out costumes and accessories. There are detailed instructions printed inside the folder to help you stand up your front and back dolls.

You will notice that Peter and Pam resemble the earlier dolls by the Myers called Cindy and Mindy (also in this book). The differences between the two are that Peter and Pam have different hairstyles, one of these twins is a boy, and the clothes of the two sets are totally different.

Publisher: Whitman
Original Price: 29¢   Value: $25.00 – 35.00

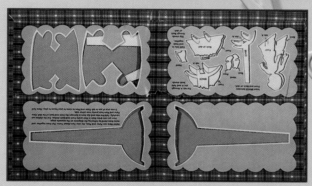

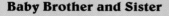

Baby Brother and Sister   Year: 1961   #1956

A truly charming and beautifully illustrated set drawn by Alice Schlesinger. There are two heavyweight cardboard statuette toddlers, Baby Brother and Baby Sister. The two of them have a 50-piece wardrobe with tabs and are ready to cut out. The folder doubles as a gorgeous brightly colored playroom complete with loads of toys.

Publisher: Whitman Publishing Company
Original Price: 29¢   Value: $30.00 – 50.00

Bride and Groom   **Year: 1961**   **# 2755**

This is a wonderful bride and groom set, drawn by George and Nan Pollard. This set comes in a large folder/book with four bridal party die-cut dolls. and 36 cut-out outfits and accessories with tabs, including a 1960s-style wedding dress and tuxedo.

Publisher: Lowe James & Jonathan, Inc.
Original Price: 29¢   Value: $20.00 – 40.00

Courtesy of Edna Corbett

Platter Party   **Year: 1961**   **#3730**

This is a fabulous and hard-to-find set published by Dell; it includes four die-cut dolls, Mona, Moira, Dan, and Dave, with 26 outfits and accessories to cut out. Each outfit has a name written on the tab that matches the appropriate doll. This extraordinary set comes with a die-cut record player. The player has a hole in which to insert a pencil. The pencil holds one of seven records on the player. In addition, a record holder with slots allows you to store the records when they are not on the player.

Publisher: Dell-Western
Original Price: 35¢   **Value: $35.00 – 65.00**

Courtesy of Edna Corbett

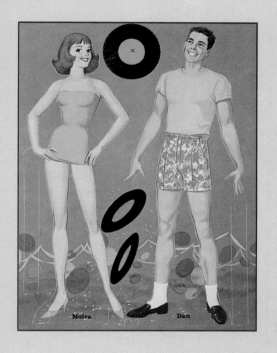

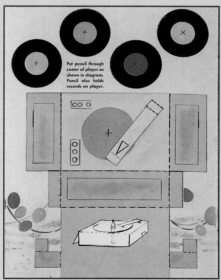

Little Ballerina   **Year: 1961**   **#1963**

Little Ballerina features two adorable little girls ready to do their ballet recital. Bonnie and Becky are made from heavyweight cardboard and come with loads of adorable ballet costumes and accessories, all with tabs and ready to cut out.

Publisher: Whitman Publishing Company
Original Price: 29¢   **Value: $15.00 – 25.00**

1962

Magic Mary   **Year: 1962**   **#R4010-1**

I love this Magic Mary set! Betty Campbell beautifully drew the doll's features to match those of a real little girl. The fashions are those of the 1960s era.

This particular set comes from Canada, by Somerville Industries Limited, in London Ontario.

There are many variations of Magic Mary, including Magic Mary Lou and Magic Mary Jane, to name just two. I have shown many models in this book.

Mary's clothing stays on by means of a magnet taped to the back of it. This set includes one statuette doll, Mary, made of heavyweight cardboard, and approximately 15 outfits and accessories to cut out.

Publisher: Milton Bradley
Original Price: unknown   **Value: $20.00 – 35.00**

Magic Mary Ann   Year: 1962   #4010-2

I love all the Magic Mary paper doll sets. In my opinion, the idea of a magnetic doll and magnets that tape on to the back of her clothes is pure genius!

In this set, you will find one heavyweight cardboard statuette doll, Mary Ann, and approximately 10 outfits, plus magnets to tape on Mary Ann's clothing.

Publisher: Milton Bradley
Original Price: unknown   **Value: $25.00 – 45.00**

Sweetheart Paper Dolls   Year: 1962   #2737

Sweetheart Paper Dolls is a reprint of the 1962 set You Are a Doll, #6160, drawn by Jeanne Voelz. Sweetheart does not have a date printed on the book; however, most reprints are done within a similar time frame as the first printing, so I included this set in the 1962 section to correspond to the first set.

SweetHearts has two large die-cut dolls and 25 outfits and accessories, including an autograph dog and a frame to hold a photo of your best friend.

Publishing Company: Saalfield
Original Price: 15¢   Value: $20.00 – 35.00

Gina Gillespie   **Year: 1962**   **#1331**

Gina Gillespie is a beautifully illustrated set that includes four die-cut dolls dressed in ballet costumes. It has 70 outfits and accessories to cut out. Each outfit has a number printed on the tab that corresponds to a number on the doll.

Publisher: Saalfield-Artcraft
Original Price: 29¢   **Value: $40.00 – 50.00**

Ginny Tiu Year: 1962 #2089

This child prodigy turned actress enjoyed a brief career on television and the big screen in the 1960s. Ginny made guest appearances in *Make Room for Daddy* and *The Danny Thomas Show*, starred with Elvis Presley in *Girls, Girls, Girls* (1962) and *It Happened at the World's Fair* (1963), and also played piano on an episode of *The Ed Sullivan show* (1965).

Since turning back to her musical talents in the 1970s, Ginny has performed at Buckingham Palace and Carnegie Hall, and has played for world dignitaries and US presidents. She still enjoys celebrity status in Hawaii as the feature performer at some of the premier entertaining venues in Honolulu.

If you are a fan of Ginny's, then you may be able to find audio/video recordings that she has done. She has recorded as Ginny Tiu and The Little Tius for Perry Como's Kraft Music.

This is a beautifully illustrated set, featuring one die-cut doll, Ginny Tiu, and a 33-piece cut-out wardrobe and accessories set (which includes Ginny's little dog) with tabs.

Publisher: Whitman
Original Price: 15¢ **Value: $25.00 – 40.00**
Courtesy of Edna Corbett

National Velvet Year: 1962 #1948

This National Velvet paper doll set was modeled after the television series, *National Velvet*, which starred Lori Martian. Martian took over the role of Velvet for the television series; Elizabeth Taylor was the star of the beloved movie classic of the same name.

In this 1962 set of paper dolls, Lori Martian's Velvet is the featured doll. The set includes one die-cut doll, 12-year-old Velvet, and her 42 outfits and accessories with tabs, ready to cut out.

Note: Elizabeth Taylor's Velvet was the featured doll in the 1961 National Velvet paper doll set.

Publishing Company: Whitman Publishing Company
Original Price: 29¢ **Value: $40.00 – 50.00**

Lennon Sisters   Year: 1962   #4798

The talented Lennon Sisters — Dianne, 16; Peggy, 14; Kathy, 12; and the youngest, 9-year-old Janet — from Venice, California, made their television debut on *The Lawrence Walk Show* in 1955. That night, as they sang "He" a cappella, America fell in love with these four little girls and their smooth harmonies and angelic voices. The Lennon Sisters became part of the cast of *The Lawrence Welk Show,* performing every Saturday night for the next 13 years, until they left to start their own variety/musical show for ABC, called *Jimmy Durante Presents the Lennon Sisters Hour.*

The sisters not only became television stars, but with the help of Mr. Welk, they were able to land a contract with Coral Records. They sang their first singles, "Hi to You" and "Mickey Mouse Mambo," during an appearance on *The Mickey Mouse Club.*

In 1956, they had their first hit with the single "Tonight You Belong to Me," which reached number 15 on the charts.

Through the 1970s and 1980s, the sisters made appearances on *The Andy Williams Show* and took to the road to perform at entertainment shows in Las Vegas and Atlantic City. In 1994, the Lennon Sisters came out of semiretirement to star in *The Lawrence Welk Show* revue in Branson, Missouri. To this day, the group performs up to two shows a day, six days a week. They still remain America's Sweethearts.

This wonderful set features three heavyweight cardboard statuette dolls, Kathy, Peggy, and Janet. The box doubles as a traveling case with a plastic handle, and includes 42 outfits and accessories to cut out. Each outfit has the name of the sister that the outfit belongs to.

Publishing Company: Whitman
Original Price: unknown   Value: $45.00 – 65.00

Dorothy Provine   Year: 1962   #1964

Born January 20, 1937, in Deadwood, South Dakota, Dorothy Michele Provine started her career while attending the University of Washington. The bouncy blonde actress appeared in some 35 amateur and professional stage productions, and was co-host of a Seattle TV quiz program. At the ripe age of 20 Provine headed to Broadway, but she soon found herself in Hollywood, where she really began to shine. She was given star billing in such low-budget films as *The Bonnie Parker Story* (in 1958) and *The 30 Foot Bride of Candy Rock* (in 1959); she then was signed to a Warner Brothers contract in 1959. Provine starred in two hour-long television series, *The Alaskans* and *The Roaring 20s*. Both programs gave Provine the opportunity to display her singing and dancing talents, as did her cameo in the 1965 Blake Edwards hit movie *The Great Race*. She also proved to be a comedian in films such as *It's a Mad Mad Mad Mad World* (in 1963), in which she played alongside such greats as Spencer Tracy, Sid Caesar, Milton Berle, Ethel Merman, Jonathan Winters, Jimmy Durante, and Buddy Hackett, to name a few. She also appeared in films like *Good Neighbor Sam* (in 1964) and *Who's Minding the Mint?* In 1967, Dorothy Provine married cinematographer Robert Day, and she retired from movies in 1968.

Her paper doll set consists of one statuette doll, Dorothy Provine, made of heavyweight cardboard and with 53 cut-out costumes and accessories with tabs.

Publisher: Whitman
Original Price: 29¢   **Value: $40.00 – 60.00**

Courtesy of Edna Corbett

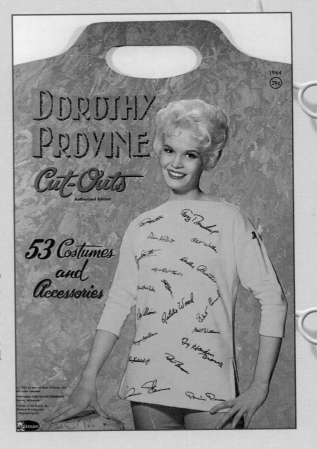

Annette Funicello   Year: 1962   #1958

Annette Funicello may be best known as a member of the Mickey Mouse Club and the star of early 1960s beach movies.

At 13 years old, she was spotted by Walt Disney in Burbank, California, while dancing the lead in *Swan Lake* at the Starlight Bowl, and was invited to audition for the *Mickey Mouse Club*. She would be one of the most popular Mouseketeers.

After leaving the Mickey Mouse Club in 1957, Annette remained under contract to Disney and went on to appear in the television show *Zorro*. She starred in the Disney's *The Shaggy Dog*, *Babes in Toyland*, *The Misadventures of Merlin Jones*, and *The Monkey's Uncle*. As she entered her late teens, Annette starred in a series of beach party movies, teaming up with Frankie Avalon and even finding success as a recording star with hits such as "Tall Paul," "How Will I Know My Love," and "Pineapple Princess."

Annette founded the Annette Funicello Teddy Bear Company in 1992, after announcing that she had been fighting multiple sclerosis since 1987. Proceeds from her company and sales from her line of perfume help fund the Annette Funicello Research Fund for Neurological Disease.

This set features one statuette doll, Annette, along with a 35-piece cut-out wardrobe with tabs. The wardrobe includes beachwear, date ware, formal wear, and more.

Publisher: Whitman Publishing Company
Original Price: 29¢   Value: $30.00 – 50.00

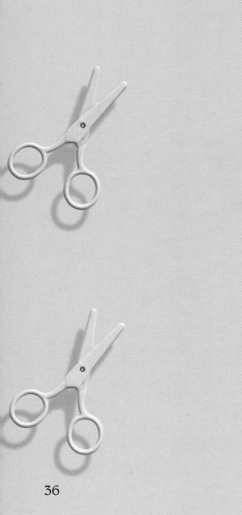

This is Susie, Here is Jo Ann   Year: 1962   #1560

This is Susie is a reprint of an earlier set from 1954 called B is for Betsy and C is for Carol, #1561, a delightfully charming set with wonderful illustrations. This set includes two die-cut dolls, Susie and Jo Ann, and a 50-piece wardrobe, with tabs and ready to cut out.

Publishing Company: Merrill Publishing Company
Original Price: 15¢   Value: $40.00 – 55.00

Jack and Jill   Year: 1962   #1561

Jack and Jill, a reprint of an earlier, 1955 set called In Peter Pumpkin's House, #1563, is brightly illustrated. It comes with six die-cut dolls. Four are children; the other are the children's pet pussycat and pet bunny rabbit.

There are 45 cut-out outfits and accessories with tabs, including costumes for the pussycat and bunny rabbit. Tabs on the costumes have numbers to match the numbers of the coordinating dolls.

Publisher: Merrill Publishing Company
Original Price: 15¢   Value: $25.00 – 35.00

1963

Dolls from Storyland   **Year: 1963**   **#1562**

Dolls from Storyland, drawn by Vivian Robbins, is a reprint of the 1948 set with the same name, #1554. This set includes seven die-cut dolls and 45 costumes to cut out representing famous nursery rhyme characters such as Mary (of "Mary Had a Little Lamb"), Yankee Doodle, Little Boy Blue, and Jack and Jill, just to name a few.

Publisher: Merrill
Original Price: 15¢   **Value: $25.00 – 50.00**

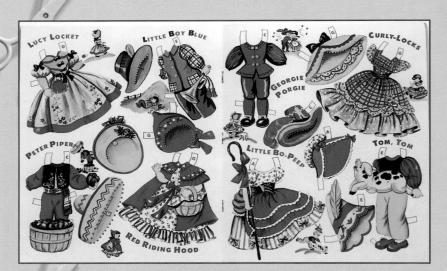

Bride and Groom   Year: 1963   # 2070

The bride and groom are featured in this wedding set and have 25 cut-out outfits with tabs, including a 1960s-style wedding dress, a tuxedo, honeymoon outfits, and, for the wedding night, nighties.

Publisher: Whitman Publishing Company
Original Price: 19¢   Value: $20.00 – 30.00

Courtesy of Edna Corbett

The Lennon Sisters   Year: 1963   #1995

There were many sets produced of the Lennon Sisters in the 1960s, and here is another wonderful set that includes three statuette sisters and 84 outfits and accessories to cut out.

The tri-fold folder has illustrations of the Lennon Sisters enjoying a day at the fair, and in handwriting on the front of the book reads, "'Hi' from the Country Fair! 'The Lennons.'"

Note: Read more about the Lennon Sisters in the 1962 section.

Publisher: Whitman/Teleklew Productions, Inc.
Original Price: 59¢   Value: $45.00 – 70.00

Courtesy of Edna Corbett

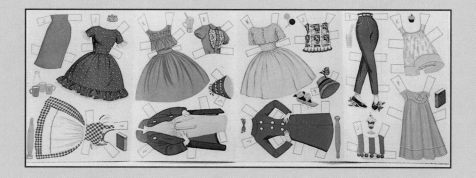

The Nurses   Year: 1963   #1975

Some of you may remember this show as *The Nurses* (1962 – 1964) or as *The Doctors and The Nurses* (1964 – 1965). It first aired in CBS in September 1962.

Taking place at the fictitious Alden General Hospital, this medical drama basically centered on two nurses, Liz Thorpe, played by Shirl Conway, and Gail Lucas, played by Zina Bethune. Miss Ayres (Hilda Simms), Dr. Anson Kiley (Edward Binns), and Dr. Ned Lowry (Stephen Brooks) made up the rest of the permanent characters. *The Nurses* not only took on the moral and ethical issues of the time, but also explored the personal lives of the show's main characters.

For the sake of ratings, maybe to draw in the female audience, the show's title was changed in 1964 to *The Doctors and The Nurses*, and the characters of Dr. Alex "Ski" Tazinski, played by Michael Tolan, and Dr. Ted Steffen, played by Joseph Campanella, were added to the series. The new additions could not keep the series going, and in May 1965, the last episode aired.

This is a wonderful set featuring two statuette dolls made of heavyweight cardboard, Mrs. Thorpe and Gail Lucas. It has a 52-piece cut-out wardrobe with tabs. The folder doubles as a carry tote.

Publisher: Whitman/Columbia Broadcasting System, Inc.
Original Price: 29¢   Value: $40.00 – 65.00

Sandy and Sue   Year: 1963   #1956

This set includes two die-cut dolls, Sandy and Sue, and lots of adorable outfits and accessories, all with tabs and ready to cut out.

Publisher: Whitman
Original Price: 29¢   Value: $10.00 – 20.00

Bonnets and Bows   Year: 1963   #1339

   Drawn by Ann Barkdoll, this gorgeous set includes four die-cut dolls, Linda, Holly, Bonnie, and Judy, along with 16 die-cut bonnets and bows, Kitty the Cat, and 69 cut-out outfits and accessories with tabs.

Publisher: Saalfield-Artcraft
Original Price: 29¢   Value: $55.00 – 75.00

Kewpie Dolls   Year: 1963   #6088

This is my favorite set of Kewpie Dolls and was drawn by Jeanne Voelz. The adorable boxed set comes with six heavyweight statuette Kewpies and 56 costumes to press out; the clothes are made to stay on by means of a stick of scribble glue included in the set. The directions on the scribble glue read, "Scribble over the back of a costume, place it on the doll, press down and rub lightly. The costume will stay in place until it is lifted off."

Publisher: Saalfield-Artcraft
Original Price: $1.00   Value: $50.00 – 80.00

Baby Pat   Year: 1963   #2072

Baby Pat is a darling red-headed baby drawn by Neva Schultz. The set includes one die-cut Baby Pat and 17 outfits, plus several accessories, to cut out. The inside of the folder has a baby buggy to slip Baby Pat into or to store her and her clothes in when not in use.

Publishing Company: Whitman
Original Price: 19¢   Value: $15.00 – 25.00

Baby Anne Smiles and Crys   Year:1963   #2749

Baby Anne is one of my personal favorites! You will find a picture in this book of a newspaper article and the photograph that accompanied it. I posed for that photograph when I was five years old.

Because I took Baby Anne with me everywhere, I insisted that I hold her when the picture was taken. The photographer must have had kids, because he seemed to understand the attachment I had to my doll, and he allowed me to hold her up in the picture.

One of Baby Anne's most notable features is the unique hologram-type face that appears to change expressions; the doll appears to either smile or cry, depending on how your hold her. The complete Baby Anne set includes a beautifully illustrated Baby Anne and an adorable 47-piece cut-out wardrobe with tabs.

Note: Baby Anne was drawn by Queen Holden, one of the most beloved paper doll artists of all time.

Publisher: Lowe/James & Jonathan, Inc.
Original Price: 29¢   Value: $45.00 – 60.00

Courtesy of Edna Corbett

Baby Doll Factory Sheet   Year: 1963

A factory sheets is a pre-production paper doll. The doll has not been pre-cut, and the sheet has no staples. Sometimes factory sheets differ in size and/or appearance from the finished set.

Created by the Samuel Lowe publishing company.

Pebbles Flintstone   Year: 1963   #1997

Pebbles Flinstone, possibly the cutest cartoon baby of all time, was a character on the popular cartoon *The Flintstones*, created by Hanna-Barbera Productions.

In this set, there is one die-cut doll, Pebbles, her toys (including her stuffed Dino), and a Stone Age playpen and baby buggy. She has 44 punch-out outfits and accessories with tabs.

Publisher: Whitman/Hanna-Barbera
Original Price: 59¢   Value: $30.00 – 50.00

Nursery　　　**Year: 1963**　　　**#4284**

This set drawn by Louise Rumely features the most beautifully illustrated babies and toddlers. This set was a favorite of mine growing up and originates from set #1341 Baby. There are many variations of Baby, including Babyland and Babes in Fairyland (pictured). All sets have identical wardrobes.

This set features four die-cut dolls, Christine, Ann, Jimmy, and Harvey, and four nursery rhyme characters. Nursery rhymes are printed throughout a book that doubles as a doll stand, with rhymes such as "Mary Had a Little Lamb," "Little Miss Muffet," "Jack Be Nimble," and "Little Boy Blue." There are 29 cut-out outfits with tabs. Each tab has the first initial of the doll the outfit belongs to.

Publisher: Saalfield
Original Price: 39¢　　　**Value: $35.00 – 55.00**

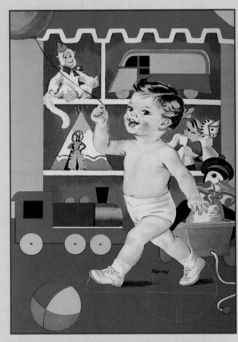

Babyland   Year: 1963   #N3964

This is another variation of Baby, and as I mentioned before, many variations of this fabulous set exist. Babyland has the same children as the Nursery set, the only difference being that the names have changed to Cathy and Hugh (the toddlers) and Jerry and Amy (the babies). The outfits are identical to those in the Nursery set and are ready to cut out.

Publisher: Saalfield
Original Price: 49¢   **Value: $25.00 – 50.00**
Courtesy of Edna Corbett

Babes in Fairyland   **Year: 1963**   **#4494**

    Here we have another variation of Baby, this time with a Fairyland theme. The name of the dolls in this set are the same as in Babyland — Amy, Jerry, Cathy, and Hugh, and the wardrobe is identical to the preceding two sets.

    Note: This set was reprinted in 1968.

Publisher: Saalfield
Original Price: 29¢   **Value: $35.00 – 55.00**

Chatty Baby   Year: 1963   #1972

In 1962, Chatty Cathy got an adorable baby sister, Chatty Baby. Chatty Baby was met with instant success, and became as well loved as her big sister. She was naturally smaller then Chatty Cathy, being the baby and all, and had a chubbier, more baby-like body stature. Like her sister, she had a pull string and could recite 11 phases, such as "doggie bow-wow" and "nice baby."

Because Chatty Baby was so popular, Mattel released an African American Chatty Baby. She is rare and quite sought after today, and can go for a hefty price.

This Chatty Baby paper doll set came on the scene shortly after the vinyl doll was released and includes one 11" die-cut cutie, Chatty Baby (blonde), along with 49 press-out outfits and accessories with tabs. The clothing in this set is exactly like original Chatty Baby outfits.

Publisher: Whitman/Mattel
Original Price: 59¢   Value: $30.00 – 45.00

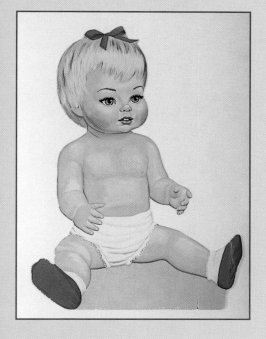

Tiny Thumbelina   Year: 1963   #1885E

Tiny Thumbelina features a darling and beautifully illustrated set that includes two die-cut babies, both named Thumbelina, 30 outfits and accessories, and 16 toys and flowers, all ready to cut out.

Note: Both dolls can wear all clothing pieces.

Publisher: Watkins Strathmore Co./Western
Original Price: 29¢   Value: $20.00 – 35.00

Courtesy of Edna Corbett

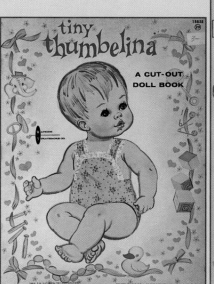

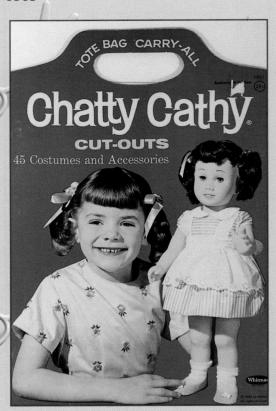

Chatty Cathy   **Year: 1963**   **#1961**

In 1960, Mattel introduced 20" Chatty Cathy, perhaps the most beloved doll of its time. Innovative for the period, Chatty Cathy was given a pull string mechanism. For the next 30 years, pull strings would allow many dolls and toys to speak.

Little girls now had a completely different world open to them; they not only had a doll, they had a friend to converse with. By pulling Chatty's string, a girl could make her speak 11 different phrases, such as "I love you," "Do you love me?" "I'm so tired," and "Give me a kiss." By 1962, Chatty had more phrases added to her vocabulary, for a total of 18. They included "Let's have a party" and "Let's play school." In addition, in an attempt to ensure the doll's continued popularity, in 1962 Mattel added more variety to Chatty's line. Hair was now available blonde or brunette, and eyes were now available in blue or brown. Mattel also added an African American version to the Chatty line. Few African American Chattys were produced, so they are highly collectible and somewhat hard to find, selling for astronomical prices, usually in the hundreds but sometimes in the thousands of dollars.

This wonderfully illustrated paper doll set includes one heavyweight cardboard statuette doll and 45 delightful outfits and accessories to cut out. Chatty Cathy's folder has handles and doubles as a carry tote.

Publisher: Whitman/Mattel
Original Price: 29¢   **Value: $45.00 – 55.00**

Tiny Chatty Twins   Year: 1963   #1985

This set is based on the popular 1960s dolls. Tiny Chatty Twins are a scaled-down version of their sister, Chatty Baby. In this set, you will find two large die-cut dolls, Tiny Chatty Baby and Tiny Chatty Brother, and 25 press-out outfits and accessories.

Publisher: Whitman/Mattel
Original Price: 59¢   Value: $30.00 – 45.00

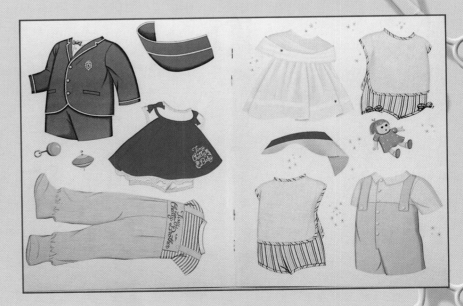

Barbie Doll   Year: 1963   #1962

Elliot Handler was the co-owner of Mattel toys. One day in 1959, as his wife Ruth was watching her daughter Barbara play with her paper dolls, she thought it would be marvelous to have a three-dimensional doll for little girls to play with. A girl could dress it and fantasize about being a fashion model or a career woman, or imagine going to her high school prom. The result of Ruth's idea was the Barbie doll, the most popular doll of all time. I am sure Ruth, even in her wildest imagination, could not have predicted that her Barbie doll would become an American icon.

Barbie doll was 11½" tall, with red lips, eyes with white irises and black pupils, V-shaped eyebrows, and a pert blonde or brunette ponytail.

In 1961, Barbie changed her image with a sort of bouffant hairstyle called the bubble cut, which Al Anderson beautifully illustrates in this set that includes one brunette die-cut Barbie doll and comes with 48 original Barbie doll cut-out fashions with tabs.

Publisher: Whitman/Mattel
Original Price: 29¢   Value: $95.00 – 125.00

Barbie, Ken, and Midge   Year: 1963   #1976

In 1961, Mattel introduced Ken doll, the steady boyfriend of Barbie doll. He has become something of a star himself, passing the test of time just as Barbie doll has.

At the time of his debut, he was 12" tall, with short hair and dazzling blue eyes. Ken brought romance and adventure into the lives of little girls and opened a new door to their imaginations. In 1963, Mattel introduce Barbie doll to Midge doll. They quickly became best friends. Like Barbie dolls, Midge doll was 11½" tall, and she had a freckled face, soft features, and the popular flip hairstyle.

This fantastic set features three die-cut dolls, Barbie, Ken, and Midge dolls, and 52 press-out outfits and accessories with tabs.

Note: Barbie and Midge can share outfits.

Publisher: Whitman Publishing Company/Mattel
Original Price: 59¢   Value: $60.00 – 85.00

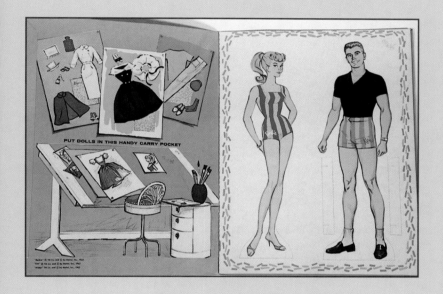

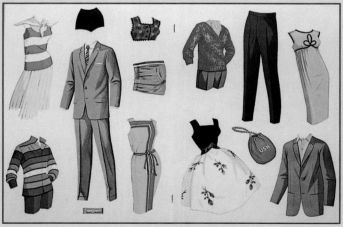

Dolls of Other Lands   **Year: 1963**   **#2074**

 Drawn by the Myers, this set includes six die-cut dolls representing their own countries and cultures, and 42 cut-out outfits with tabs, representative of the clothing of the dolls' native lands.

Publisher: Whitman
Original Price: 19¢   **Value: $10.00 – 25.00**

Buttons and Billy   Year: 1963/1967   #1818-4

Another adorable set drawn by the Myers, this includes two die-cut dolls, Buttons and Billy, and 31 cut-out outfits with tabs. Buttons and Billy was also produced by Whitman Publishing Company in 1963, as #2071, and was given a different cover.

Publisher: Watkins-Strathmore Co./Western
Original Price: 29¢   Value: $10.00 – 25.00

Charmin' Chatty   **Year: 1964**   **#1959**

Charmin' Chatty came on the scene in 1963; she was perhaps the most celebrated Chatty of all time. She made doll history with her appearance on the cover of the *Saturday Evening Post* in the Dec. 7, 1963, issue, and for years she had a prominent spot in the doll section of the *World Book Encyclopedia*.

She was very different from other Chattys; she stood 25" tall, and had an impish grin, a slightly cocked head, long gangly legs, and glasses. She was not what you would call beautiful.

Like her predecessor Chatty Cathy, she could be made to talk by pulling a string on her back. She had one small difference, however. A slot on the side of her body housed a small record; though she normally spoke 12 phrases, extra records could be purchased, giving Charmin' a vocabulary of 120 phrases! In addition, she spoke seven different languages. Today she is a favorite of collectors.

Often a popular play doll will produce a beautiful paper doll, and Charmin' Chatty was no exception. This set includes one die-cut Charmin Chatty and a 57-piece wardrobe, with tabs and ready to press out.

Publisher: Whitman Publishing Company/Mattel
Original Price: 29¢   Value: $40.00 – 65.00

Charmin' Chatty paper doll activity book
Year: 1964   #GF237

Jam-packed with Charmin' Chatty fun is this activity book featuring Charmin' Chatty home on the range. The complete activity book includes one die-cut Charmin', along with 23 outfits and accessories, with tabs, to color and cut out. Also included are a die-cut horse, saddle, and chuck wagon to press out and assemble so that Charmin' can enjoy the great outdoors. You will also find games and a wonderful story to read about Charmin' Chatty's adventure at the ranch.

Publisher: Golden Press/Mattel
Original Price: 29¢   Value: $35.00 – 60.00

56

Chatty Cathy   **Year: 1964**   **#1961**

This is another favorite of mine. This beautifully illustrated Chatty Cathy set includes one die-cut Chatty Cathy and a 50-piece cut-out wardrobe with tabs.

Note: Read more about Chatty Cathy in the 1963 section.

Publisher: Whitman Publishing Company/Mattel
Original Price: 29¢   Value: $35.00 – 60.00

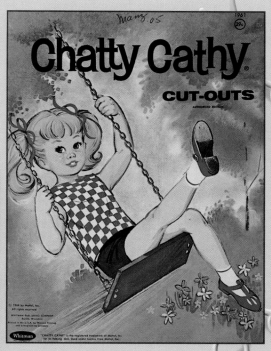

Front and Back Dolls and Dresses   **Year: 1964**   **#2766**

Front and Back Dolls sets are unique, because they show fronts and backs of the dolls and their clothing. This set includes two die-cut dolls, Jan and Fran, and 20 outfits and hats printed on lightweight cardboard. The clothing fits on the dolls by slipping over their heads. The outfits fold at the shoulders; there are no tabs.

Publisher: Lowe/James & Jonathan, Inc.
Original Price: 29¢   Value: $8.00 – 15.00

Mimi   Year: 1964   #2766

Another adorable little girl drawn by Queen Holden. This set includes one statuette doll, Mimi, and approximately 20 cut-out outfits and accessories with tabs. Mimi is one of three in the Keepsake Folio series; the other two dolls are Emily and Trudy.

Publisher: Lowe/James & Jonathan, Inc.
Original Price: 29¢   Value: $20.00 – 35.00

Trudy   Year: 1964   #2424

Trudy is number three in the Keepsake Folio collection. This set includes one statuette doll and 23 cut-out outfits and accessories with tabs.

Publisher: Lowe/James & Jonathan, Inc.
Original Price: 29¢   Value: $20.00 – 35.00

Dollies Go Shopping   Year: 1964   #2753

Many of Queen Holden's paper dolls are reprinted and combined to create new sets, which may have some minor differences between them. In this set, Mimi and Emily's arms are posed differently in this set than they are in the Keepsake series sets.

Dollies Go Shopping includes two die-cut dolls, Mimi and Emily, and 50 outfits and accessories to cut out.

Publisher: Lowe/James & Jonathan, Inc.
Original Price: 29¢   **Value: $35.00 – 55.00**

Cute Quintuplets   Year: 1964   #1818-5

Alice Schlesinger drew this set of "Cute Quintuplets." It includes five die-cut dolls, Timmy, Debby, Bobby, Susy, and Jacky, and 14 pets and toys. It also has a whopping 73 outfits and hats, all ready to cut out. Each tab has the name of the doll the outfit belongs to.

Publisher: Watkins Strathmore Co./Western
Original Price: 29¢   Value: $15.00 – 30.00

Connie Darling and Her Dolly **Year: 1964** **#6092**

This unique set was cutting edge at the time it was issued. Connie Darling and her Dolly had life-like wavy hair. The dolls were made of heavyweight cardboard with 36 outfits to cut out. Each tab has either the letter "C" for Connie or the letter "B" for Baby.

Publisher: Lowe
Original Price: unknown   **Value: $20.00 – 30.00**

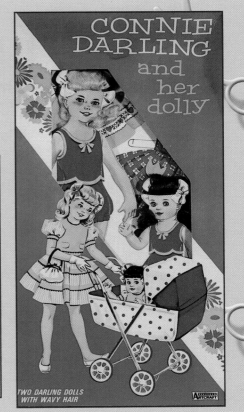

Wendy Dress-a-Doll Storybook   **Year: 1964**   **#3945**

This angelic doll has piercing blue eyes and a cute rosebud mouth. It was drawn by Queen Holden, and is a paper doll and storybook in one. Wendy is a large statuette doll with eight outfits that change as the pages of the book are turned. Each page tells a story about Wendy and the outfit she is wearing. Also included are several accessories, such as hats, shoes, and a bunny, that are ready to cut out. Wendy originally comes from set #9048, and her clothes are from set #2915.

I loved this paper doll as a little girl; I could change her clothes and not lose all the pieces.

Note: The picture in this book does not show the complete set.

Publisher: Lowe
Original Price: unknown   **Value: $15.00 – 30.00**

Pebbles and Bamm-Bamm   **Year: 1964**   **#1983**

Pebbles and Bamm-Bamm come from the hit cartoon *The Flinstones,* and they remain as popular today as they were in the 1960s. In this set, you will find two large die-cut dolls, Pebbles and Bamm-Bamm, and lots of Stone Age outfits and hats to punch out. The folder is beautifully illustrated and has slits for storing Pebbles and Bamm-Bamm.

Publisher: Whitman/Hanna-Barbera Productions, Inc.
Original Price: 59¢   **Value: $30.00 – 45.00**

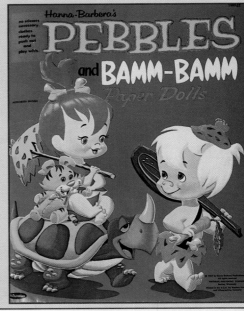

Pebbles and Bamm-Bamm   **Year: 1964**   **#4791**

This is a boxed set of Pebbles and Bamm-Bamm. The dolls are dressed and posed slightly differently in this set then they are in the one above.

In this set, you will find two statuette dolls, Pebbles and Bamm-Bamm, and 55 outfits and accessories to cut out. Two plastic stands and a pair of scissors complete the set.

Publisher: Whitman/Hanna-Barbera Productions, Inc.
Original Price: unknown   **Value: $35.00 – 55.00**

The Beverly Hillbillies **Year: 1964** **#1955**

"Come and listen to a story 'bout a man named Jed..." Okay, you know the rest. If at some point in your life you found yourself singing this show's catchy song, don't worry, it's happened to the best of us. *The Beverly Hillbillies* first aired in black and white, on CBS in September of 1962.

While out hunting for food, Jed missed his target (which I think was a rabbit), but hit something more valuable. "Oil that is, black gold, Texas tea." He sold his land to the OK Oil Company for $25 million, and Cousin Pearl convinced him to move his immediate family and her son Jethro to Beverly Hills. The characters included Jed Clampett (Buddy Ebsen), Daisy "Granny" Moses (Irene Ryan), Milburn Drysdale (Raymond Bailey), Jethro Bodine (Max Baer), Elly May Clampett (Donna Douglas), Jane Hathaway (Nancy Kulp), and Pearl Bodine (Bea Benaderet).

The series came to an end in September of 1971. For nine years, the backwoods family from the Ozarks kept us all laughing as they made a new life in the land of swimming pools and movie stars. On Sunday, July 6, 2003, Buddy Ebsen (who I'm told is a distant cousin of mine) passed away. He was 95.

The Beverly Hillbillies comes complete with four die-cut dolls, Jed, Granny, Jethro, and Elly May, and a 24-piece cut-out wardrobe with tabs.

Publisher: Whitman/Filmways TV Productions, Inc.
Original Price: 29¢   **Value: $65.00 – 85.00**

Petticoat Junction   Year: 1964   #1954

I have fond memories of sitting and watching *Petticoat Junction* with my mother and her girlfriends. Shown on CBS from 1963 to 1970, this comedy told the story of Kate Bradley (played by Bea Benaderet) and her three daughters, Billie Jo (Gunilla Hutton), Bobbie Jo (Pat Woodell, 1963 – 1965, and Lori Saunders, 1965 – 1970), and Betty Jo (Linda Henning). Kate ran the Shady Rest Hotel in the farming community of Hooterville. The hotel owed its existence to the Cannonball, a train that ran right through town and usually stopped a short distance from the Shady Rest.

Kate certainly hand her hands full. Running a business, raising her daughters, and putting up with the manly gentlemen callers each one had, plus having to deal with the not-too-capable man of the house, Uncle Jo (Edgar Buchanan), who would sometimes act as repairman at Shady Rest, usually had Kate running every which way. She would fit right in with today's modern woman, don't you think? In 1967, Kate married Steve (Mike Minor), the local crop duster, and they had a daughter named Kathy Jo (Edna Hubbell).

This set has four die-cut dolls, Bobbie Jo, Betty Jo, Billie Jo, and Kate. It comes with 66 cut-out outfits and accessories with tabs.

Publisher: Whitman/Wayfilms
Original Price: 29¢   Value: $45.00 – 65.00

Lucy   Year: 1964   #1963

Who could forget that loveable, wacky redhead, Lucy Ricardo? Her comic brilliance entertains millions of us through reruns even today. *I Love Lucy* aired in 1951 and ended in 1961. In 1962, Lucille Ball went on to star again in her own television show, as Lucy Carmichael in *The Lucy Show.* Lucy Carmichael was a widow sharing a house with her divorced best friend (Vivian Vance) and raising three kids; we embraced Lucille Ball once again, and the show aired until 1968. Lucy will always remain a huge part of Americana — sort of like apple pie! This set includes one die-cut doll, Lucy, along with 25 glamorous cut-out outfits with tabs.

Publisher: Whitman/Desilu Productions, Inc.
Original Price: 29¢   Value: $65.00 – 85.00

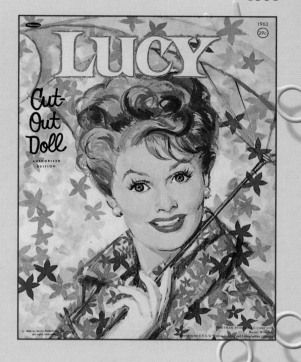

Mary Poppins   Year: 1964   #4700

The Mary Poppins set is based on the Walt Disney motion picture of the same name about a family named Banks. After the incorrigible children run off another nanny, Mr. Banks puts an ad in the paper for a new one. However, a series of events helps Mary Poppins (Julie Andrews) find her way to the Banks household, and she becomes their new nanny. Mary Poppins is stern with the children, but she is also loving and fun. Therefore, the children begin to love her, and the three share many unique adventures together.

In this set, there are three statuette dolls, Mary Poppins and the children, Jane and Michael. The set also has over 55 outfits and hats to cut out.

Publisher: Whitman/Walt Disney Productions
Original Price: $1.00   Value: $35.00 – 45.00

Hello, Dollies   Year: 1964   #2768

Hello, Dollies is a darling set drawn by Queen Holden. It features two die-cut dolls, Marilyn and Dolly. Marilyn comes from the set #2424, and Trudy (also shown in this book) and Dolly can be found in Queen Holden's sets Betsy #9118 and Betsy #6918.

There are 33 press-out outfits and accessories, with tabs and made of lightweight cardboard.

Publisher: Lowe, James & Jonathan, Inc.
Original Price: 29¢   Value: $15.00 – 25.00

Two Little Girls   Year: 1964   #9045

"Big" is an understatement when describing this charming set of paper dolls. The book measures 18½" tall! These two little cuties (or should I say big cuties, at 13½" tall?) made their debut as Wendy and Nancy in this set; however, their clothing came from two of Queen Holden previous sets, #2904 and #2015.

With these two tots, Queen Holden captured an endearing innocence that only a child could possess. The girls' wardrobes were also wonderfully illustrated. This hard-to-find set is a real favorite of mine, and I feel fortunate to have one in my collection.

Currently, you can find a reprint of this set. Published by B. Shackman & Co., Inc., the book is smaller at 15" tall, Wendy and Nancy are 10½". The wardrobe is identical to the original set with the exception that the clothes are printed on paper as opposed to lightweight cardboard. The reprint is a fraction of the price of the original set, which appeals to some collectors. However, in my humble opinion, nothing can beat original vintage paper dolls.

The *Big, Big Doll Book,* as this reads on the cover, has two charming die-cut tots, Wendy and Nancy, along with a 38-piece press-out wardrobe with tabs. The dolls come with a unique easel stand.

Publisher: Lowe/James and Jonathan, Inc.
Original Price: $1.00   Value: $40.00 – 65.00

Tammy and Her Family   **Year: 1964**   **#1997**

The Tammy and Her Family set has five die-cut dolls, Dad, Mom, Tammy, Ted, and Pepper, along with 50 outfits and accessories to press out. The inside of the folder doubles as a bedroom and family room, for hours of paper doll play.

Note: Read more about Tammy and Pepper in section 1966.

Publisher: Whitman Publishing Company
Original Price: 59¢   Value: $25.00 – 50.00

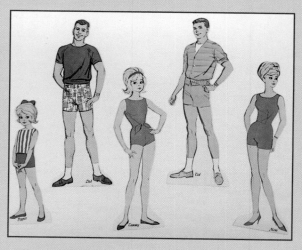

Barbie and Skipper Dolls   **Year: 1964**   **#1957**

In this set, you will find two die-cut dolls, Barbie doll and her little sister Skipper doll, along with six pages of over 40 outfits and accessories to cut out. All of Barbie doll and Skipper doll's outfits match one another and reflect the clothing of the original sets.

Publisher: Whitman/Mattel
Original Price: 29¢   Value: $45.00 – 65.00

Baby Doll   Year: 1964   #1895C

Baby Doll's set includes one die-cut doll and 19 cut-out outfits and accessories with tabs.

Publisher: Watkins-Strathmore Co./Western
Original Price: 10¢   Value: $8.00 – 15.00

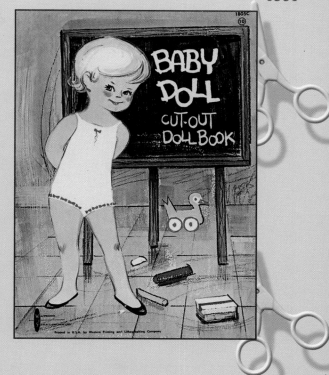

Sandy   Year: 1964   #1805D

Sandy includes one die-cut doll, Sandy, and 19 cut-out outfits and accessories with tabs.

Publisher: Watkins-Strathmore Co./Western
Original Price: 10¢   Value: $8.00 – 12.00

Magic Princess   **Year: 1964**   **#1010**

Magic Princess was the first paper doll set that came with its own record, which allowed little girls to hear the voice of her paper doll and helped to create hours of fun. This set features one large statuette, Princess, and several magical outfits that stay on with the touch of a wand. (Wand is included in the set.)

Publisher: Magic Wand Corporation
Original Price: $1.29   **Value: $35.00 – 60.00**

This is the front and back of the fold-out pamphlet that came in all of the Magic Wand paper doll sets.

Kim   **Year: 1964**   **#6503**

Kim is a large pre-teen fashion doll, with a Shapely-Shape body, and her set includes a 21-piece wardrobe to cut out, a Rub'n Stay stick could be used to color the back of Kim's clothing, but when rubbed on the doll, it allowed her clothing to stick. The clothing could then be peeled off and reapplied repeatedly. The A Rub'n Stay stick helped provide hours of play.

Publisher: Merry Manufacturing Co.
Original Price: $1.00   **Value: $8.00 – 16.00**

Cinderella   Year: 1965   #1992

This set is based on the Walt Disney version of the familiar fairy tale, which was based on the French version of the story, written by Charles Perrault. Cinderella is tormented by her stepmother and two stepsisters and forced to become a servant in her late father's home. Cruel, dreadful, and seemingly jealous of Cinderella, the stepmother allows her only brief glimpses of the outside world, keeping her busy catering to the whims and whines of the spoiled stepsisters. When the king decides to hold a royal ball in the hope of finding a bride for his son, the prince, all the eligible maidens in the kingdom are invited, including Cinderella. As she makes preparations to attend, Cinderella must help her stepsisters get ready and then finish her chores before her stepmother will allow her to go. However, her stepmother has no intention of actually letting Cinderella go, and her dress is ripped apart by her stepsisters.

Cinderella is deeply saddened and feels so alone, but her Fairy Godmother appears to transform her into the truly beautiful maiden that she is. Cinderella attends the ball, where under the envious eyes of everyone, she wins the heart of the prince. When the clock strikes midnight, she races home to be changed back to her everyday self, leaving behind her glass slipper. The next day, Prince Charming sets out to find the young maiden, and the slipper is tried on the foot of every young woman in the kingdom, until finally it is placed on the foot of the Cinderella. It is a perfect fit, and the couple is married and live happily ever after.

This wonderfully enchanting set includes five die-cut dolls, Cinderella, Prince Charming, the Wicked Stepmother, and the two Wicked Stepsisters, with lots of press-out outfits and accessories with tabs.

Publisher: Whitman Publishing Company/Walt Disney
Original Price: 59¢   Value: $30.00 – 55.00

Little Miss Christmas and Holly-Belle   **Year: 1965**   **#2968**

This set, drawn by Elizabeth Anne Gartrell Voss. is another favorite of mine, because of its bright colors and whimsical style. Included are two die-cut dolls, Little Miss Christmas and Holly-Belle, with 27 Christmas costumes to cut out. Each tab has either a printed snowflake, for Miss Christmas, or holly, for Holly-Belle.

Publisher: Merrill
Original Price: 29¢   **Value: $65.00 – 85.00**

Skooter Doll   Year: 1965   #1985

Skooter doll made her debut in 1965, as Skipper doll's best friend. She was the same size as Skipper doll, so the dolls could actually wear each other's clothing. Barbie doll and her family kept growing in popularity, so more paper dolls were produced to imitate the original dolls and their clothing.

In this set you will find three die-cut Skooter dolls with three different hair colors: red, blonde, and brunette. It has 34 outfits and accessories to press out. Inside the folder, there is a dressing screen and a steamer trunk to store the Skooter dolls and their clothes in when they are not in use.

Publisher: Whitman/Mattel
Original Price: 59¢   Value: $45.00 – 65.00

Wishnik   Year: 1965   #6503

Trolls were popular with kids in the 1960s mainly because of their whimsical look and brightly colored hair. Here we have a fantastic set that includes four die-cut dolls with colored hair and a variety of different costumes to cut out.

Publisher: Whitman/Uneeda Doll Company
Original Price: 29¢   Value: $15.00 – 25.00

Patty Duke   Year: 1965   #1991

Patty Duke started as a child star; at the age of 12, she won an Oscar for her 1962 role as the young Helen Keller.

She starred in the ABC TV sitcom *The Patty Duke Show* from 1963 to 1966. In it, she played a dual role: Patty the outgoing, perky, American teenager with a thirst for excitement and knack for twisting simple matters into thorny situations, and Cathy, her identical cousin from Scotland, who was more reserved, intellectual, and sophisticated.

This show was a hit with teenagers, especially teen girls, mainly because it revolved around the lives of two high school girls who experienced the everyday ups and downs that they did too. Of course, cameo appearances by teen recording stars of the day such as Bobby Vinton and Frankie Avalon also helped boost the ratings.

Though she was "America's favorite teenager," Patty Duke had to overcome child abuse, poverty, addiction, and mental illness. Today Patty is an activist and strong supporter of the National Alliance for the Mentally Ill, as well being a mother, wife, and actress.

Inspired by the Patty Duke show, this paper doll set includes two die-cut dolls, Patty and Cathy, along with 43 press-out outfits and accessories with tabs.

Publisher: Whitman/Untied Artists Television, Inc.
Original Price: 59¢   Value: $25.00 – 45.00

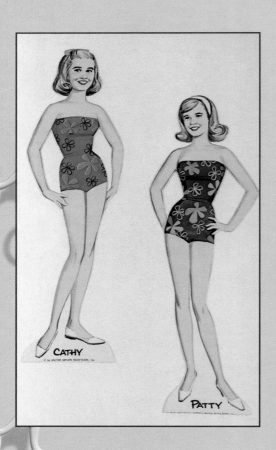

Hayley Mills, from *That Darn Cat*   **Year: 1965**   **#1955**

When it came to making family movies of the 1960s and 1970s, Disney was number one on the block. *That Darn Cat*, released in 1965, was one of my favorites. Starring Disney regulars Hayley Mills, Dean Jones, and Roddy MacDowall, it was one of the funniest of the year.

The plot involves a Siamese cat named DC, who has a wristwatch placed around his neck by a bank teller who has been taken hostage by bank robbers. On the watch, the teller has scratched a message for help. The cat's owner, played by Haley Mills, discovers the watch and the message and calls the FBI, which assigns the case to an agent played by Dean Jones. What make the storyline even more hilarious is that he is allergic to cats; still, he must follow DC in hopes of being lead to the bank robbers and their hostage.

Disney assembled the perfect cast for this movie. Ed Wynn makes a cameo appearance as a panicky jeweler, and he provides what is definitely one of the funniest moments in the movie.

This set, based on this very funny movie, includes one die-cut doll, Hayley Mills, along with 41 cut-out outfits and accessories with tabs.

Publisher: Whitman/Walt Disney
Original Price: 29¢   Value: $28.00 – 50.00

Courtesy of Edna Corbett

Baby First Step   Year: 1965   #1997

The first issue of Mattel's vinyl doll Baby First Step was released in 1965. This doll stood 18" tall. She was a battery-operated mechanical walking doll. When her switch was in the "on" position, she would walk across the floor with little baby steps. She had an adorable face and her hair was multiple shades of blonde. Later, Mattel released Baby First Step with her own pair of roller skates.

The popularity of the doll led to the paper doll set, also released in 1965. The paper doll is just as cute as the original doll, and includes one die-cut toddler, Baby First Step, with her very own wagon and rocking horse. It also includes 19 press-out outfits with tabs.

Publisher: Whitman/Mattel
Original Price: 59¢   Value: $35.00 – 55.00

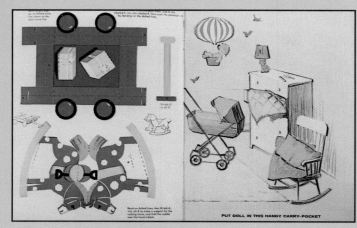

Drowsy   Year: 1965   #1986

In 1965, Mattel introduced the talking baby doll Drowsy. She was instantly popular despite her somewhat homely looks. She had a vinyl head with sleepy eyes and an adorable plush body that made her look like she was wearing flannel sleepers.

This set of paper dolls is dated "1965," and has one die-cut Drowsy and 23 flocked cut-out outfits and accessories with tabs.

The folder doubles as a nursery scene, and Drowsy fits into her die-cut rufled bassinet.

Publisher: Whitman/Mattel
Original Price: 59¢   Value: $20.00 – 30.00

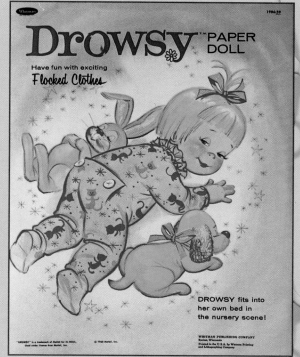

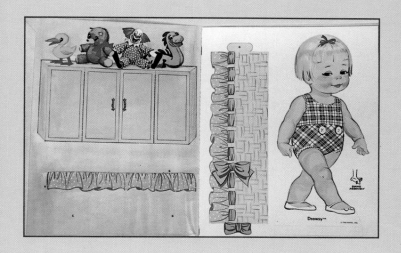

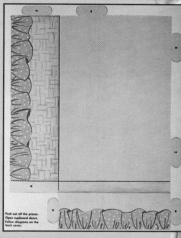

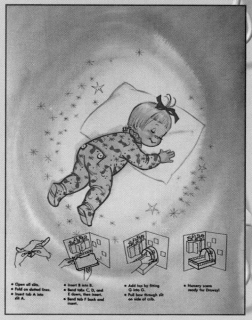

Storybook Dolls   Year: 1965   #1962

Patty and Pam have adorable faces that were drawn by the Myers. Those faces made this set popular among little girls in the 1960s.

In this set you will find two die-cut dolls, Patty and Pam, with ten die-cut storybook toys such as Bo-Peep's sheep, Cinderella's coach, and Miss Muffet's spider. The set also includes 23 popular storybook cut-out outfits, with tabs, that either doll can wear.

Publisher: Whitman/Western
Original Price: 29¢   Value: $18.00 – 25.00

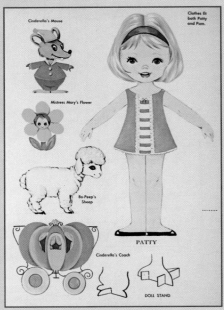

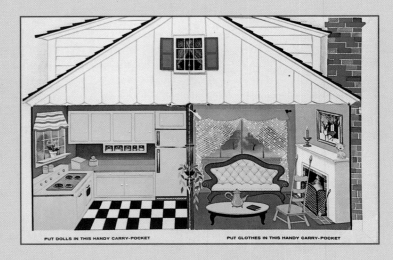

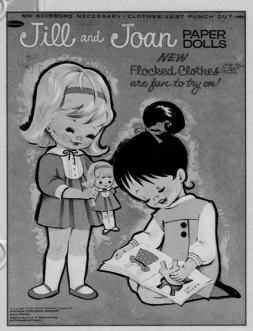

Jill and Joan   Year: 1965   #1995

Jill and Joan have the same faces as the Storybook Dolls, but have redrawn hairstyles that are also drawn by the Myers. You will find these same faces with different names in many of the Myers' sets. Included in this set are two large die-cut dolls, Jill and Joan, and lots of flocked punch-out outfits with tabs.

Publisher: Whitman/Western
Original Price: 59¢   Value: $18.00 – 25.00

Pretty Belles   Year: 1965   #1961

On this page, I have shown two similar sets of paper dolls, both named Pretty Belles. The dolls and clothing are identical; the differences are in the folder illustrations. The first set features a folder that reads, "A collection of fun-time fashions for Karen and Kathy." Inside it you will find two die-cut dolls and 35 cut-out outfits and accessories. Clothes with pink tabs fit Karen, and those with blue tabs fit Kathy.

Publisher: Whitman/Western
Original Price: 39¢   Value: $15.00 – 25.00

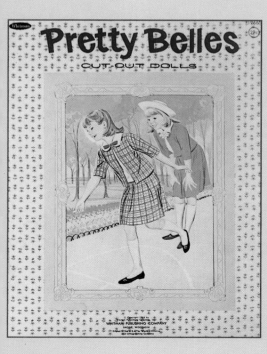

Pretty Belles   Year: 1965   #1966

In this set, the folder shows Karen and Kathy playing hopscotch. Inside you will find a beautifully illustrated picture of the girls feeding birds at the park. As in the above set, there are two die-cut dolls, Kathy and Karen, and 35 outfits to cut out (identical to those in the above set). The tabs are pink and blue, to coordinate with each doll.

Publisher: Whitman/Western
Original Price: 29¢   Value: $15.00 – 25.00

1966

Mod Fashions Featuring Jane Fonda   Year: 1966   #4469

Many of us know Jane Fonda from her many movies, such as *Coming Home*, for which she won an Oscar, *Barefoot in the Park*, or *On Golden Pond*. Or, we may have exercised our way to a better body through her videos. She has done so many things in her life, but one thing is certain: Jane Fonda has been an influential woman in America for many decades. This paper doll set features two die-cut Jane Fonda dolls and a 40-piece, tabbed, cut-out wardrobe.

Publisher: Saalfield/Artcraft
Original Price: 29¢   Value: $45.00 – 65.00

Magic Mary Lou   Year: 1966   #4010-4

Magic Mary Lou is another magnetic paper doll set in which magnets are taped to the backs of the outfits.

In this set, you will find one heavyweight cardboard statuette doll named Mary Lou, lots of outfits to cut out, and the magnets that help provide the hours of fun.

Publisher: Milton Bradley
Original Price: unknown   Value: $35.00 – 65.00

Raggedy Ann and Andy   Year: 1966   #1979

In 1915, Johnny Gruelle stumbled upon an old rag doll in his attic. Gruelle drew a new face on the doll and gave it to his daughter. After careful thought, he decided to name the doll Raggedy Ann. He then used Raggedy Ann as a model for a cartoon he drew for the *New York World*; he soon wrote a book called *Raggedy Ann Stories*. As the book grew in popularity, Gruelle decided to create a companion for Raggedy Ann. He named him Raggedy Andy.

Raggedy Ann and Andy's popularity is still going strong today, and the dolls are still being produced.

Their cute shoe-button eyes, red yarn hair, striped socks, and hearts on their chests that say "I love you" have made them favorites of children for more then 75 years.

This set of Raggedy Ann and Andy paper dolls, drawn by the Myers, includes two die-cut dolls and 17 punch-out outfits with tabs.

Publisher: Whitman/The Bobbs-Merrill Company, Inc.
Original Price: 59¢   Value: $13.00 – 20.00

Tammy and Pepper   Year: 1966   #1953

Tammy and Pepper made their debuts in 1962. These popular dolls were made by Ideal. Tammy was known for her sweet face, which captured an innocence and charm that her rival Barbie doll didn't possess. Also, her body reflected the proportions of a real teen, which was appealing to many mothers at the time. Later, family members Mom and Dad, and best friend Dodi, were added to the Tammy line.

In this set, you will find two die-cut dolls, Tammy and Pepper, and 48 cut-out outfits and accessories. Tammy's wardrobe has pink tabs, and Pepper's has blue.

Publisher: Whitman/Ideal Toy Corporation
Original Price: 29¢   Value: $30.00 – 45.00

Dodi   Year: 1966   #1965

Dodi is part of the Tammy collection and is Pepper's bubbly redheaded friend. This set includes one die-cut doll, Dodi, and a 53-piece cut-out wardrobe with tabs.

Publisher: Whitman\Ideal Toy Corporation
Original Price: 29¢   Value: $30.00 – 45.00

Dolly Darlings   Year: 1966   #1963

In 1965, Dolly Darlings came on the scene as 4" dolls made by Hasbro. The early Hatbox series dolls came with molded hair, but this changed to rooted hair in 1967. Several series of Dolly Darlings followed.

In this set, you will find six die-cut dolls, Cathy, Susie, John, Beth, Shary, and Karen, and over 55 cut-out outfits and accessories with tabs.

Publisher: Whitman/Hassenfeld Bro., Inc.
Original Price: 29¢   Value: $40.00 – 60.00

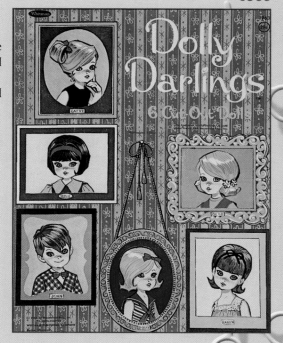

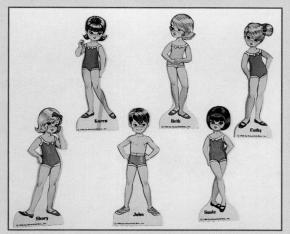

Heidi   Year: 1966   #1954

Heidi was a probably the most popular doll ever produced by Remco. She made her appearance in 1965 and had a button on her tummy that, when pushed, would raise her arm to wave.

She came in her own pocketbook carry case so that a girl could take her anywhere. Later, Remco came out with series of pocketbook dolls of Heidi's family and friends.

In this set, you will find one die-cut doll, Heidi, and 64 cut-out outfits and accessories with tabs.

Publisher: Whitman/Remco Industries, Inc.
Original Price: 29¢   Value: $30.00 – 45.00

Cheerful Tearful   Year: 1966   #4740

Cheerful Tearful paper dolls are based on Mattel's baby doll of the same name. When the original Cheerful's arm is up, she smiles, and when down, she pouts and cries real tears.

In this set, you will find two 7" Magic Stay-on Cheerful Tearful dolls made of heavyweight cardboard. One is smiling and one is crying. The set also includes a 28-piece wardrobe that stays on by briskly rubbing the pieces over the doll. Like magic, the clothes stay on!

Publisher: Whitman Publishing Company/Mattel
Original Price: $1.00   Value: $15.00 – 25.00

Cheerful Tearful   Year: 1966   #1993

This set is very similar to the above set. The die-cut dolls look identical to those above, but are much larger at 10½" tall. The wardrobe pieces all have tabs and are ready to press out.

Publisher: Whitman/Mattel
Original Price: 59¢   Value: $15.00 – 25.00

Lovable Babies   Year: 1966   #1978

This adorable set, drawn by Neva Shultz, features two die-cut toddlers named Kitty and Kelly. They come with their own stand-up playpen that they can slip into. There are 28 flocked outfits and hats to punch out. The outfits with green tabs belong to Kelly, and those with blue tabs belong to Kitty.

Publisher: Whitman/Western
Original Price: 59¢   Value: $20.00 – 30.00

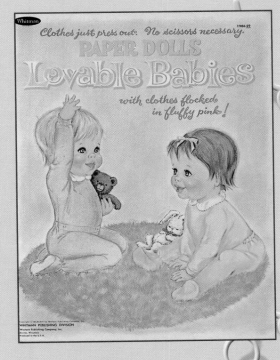

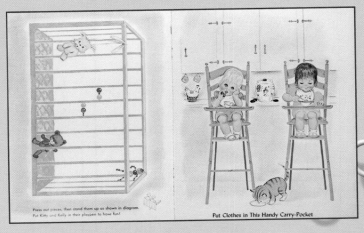

Toodles   Year: 1966   #1216

Toodles was a charming and innovative walking toddler; with the assistance of a leg disk, she could walk or run!

This adorable set includes two die-cut dolls, both of them Toodles, along with two leg disks made of medium-weight cardboard. The two walking disks each show a different pair of shoes. The first disk has walking shoes; the second has winter boots. Each leg disk is made to fit on the first toddler's body and turn in a circular motion, giving the illusion that the little sprite is on the go. The second Toodles is illustrated the same as the first; however, her legs are attached, allowing little girls to choose if they want Toodles to walk or not. To complete the set, there are 22 cut-out outfits and accessories with tabs.

Publisher: Saalfield
Original Price: 39¢   Value: $10.00 – 20.00

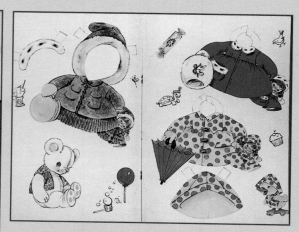

Toodles   Year: 1966   #N3962

Here is another toodles set, with a different book cover. It includes one die-cut doll identical to the first Toodles above, and a die-cut leg disk. It also has a leg disk made of paper. Both sets have identical clothing.

Publisher: Saalfield
Original Price: 49¢   Value: $10.00 – 20.00

Courtesy of Edna Corbett

Sunny   Year: 1966   #4401

Sunny is a familiar face drawn by the Myers. This boxed set comes with a 6" doll made of heavy-weight laminated cardboard and includes approximately 32 outfits to cut out. The clothing stays on when rubbed briskly against the doll.

Publisher: Whitman/Western
Original Price: 29¢   Value: $10.00 – 16.00

Gretchen   Year: 1966   #4613

Gretchen is a 9½" doll made of heavy cardboard and was drawn by the Myers. She has a 48-piece wardrobe that is flocked, and her clothes have tabs and are ready to press out.

Publisher: Whitman/Western
Original Price: unknown   Value: $15.00 – 20.00

Peg, Nan, Kay, Sue   Year: 1966   #1995

I love this set because each of the four die-cut dolls represents an ethnic group. Peg is a beautiful African American girl, Nan is a Caucasian girl, Kay is a Hispanic girl, and Sue is an Asian girl. There are 32 outfits and accessories to punch out. The outfits with pink tabs fit both Peg and Kay, and those with blue tabs fit Nan and Sue.

Publisher: Whitman/Western
Original Price: 59¢   Value: $45.00 – 65.00

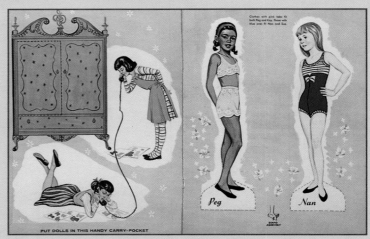

Terri and Tonya, the Duo-Tones   **Year: 1966**   **#1247**

Terri and Tonya are the mod and musical singing Duo-Tones, and originate from set 4469, Mod Fashions Featuring Jane Fonda (shown on page 80).

In this set, you will find two die-cut dolls, Terri and Tonya, their only differences being hair color and style.

There are 36 outfits and accessories to cut out that are identical to those in the Jane Fonda set.

Publisher: Saalfield
Original Price: 39¢   **Value: $15.00 – 25.00**

Baby Secret   Year: 1966   #1960

This paper dolls set is based on Mattel's 1965 talking doll called Baby Secret. She had a pull string, and when it was pulled, her lips would move as she whispered phrases like "My Name is Baby Secret," "Hold me close and whisper," "Will you tell me a story?" and many more.

In this set, you will find one die-cut doll, Baby Secret, and a 20-piece cut-out wardrobe with tabs.

Publisher: Whitman/Mattel
Original Price: 29¢   Value: $15.00 – 25.00

1967

Dolly Dears   Year: 1967   #4701

This is the boxed set of Dolly Dears. In 1968 section of the book you will find a similar Dolly Dears set, #1960.

There are two big-eyed statuette dolls named Carolyn and Cathy, with lots of mod clothes to cut out. Like magic, the clothes stay on without tabs when they are rubbed on the doll.

Publisher: Whitman/Western
Original Price: $1.00   Value: $15.00 – 25.00

Snow White   Year: 1967   #1987

This was a Brothers Grimm tale that was revised by Walt Disney. The movie this doll set was based on tells the story of a young princess who is betrayed by her evil stepmother — the Queen. A henchman is ordered to kill Snow White and bring her heart back to the Queen, but he cannot bring himself to commit such an act on the princess, and instead he begs her to run away and never return.

Fearing for her life, Snow White leaves behind her father, the King, and the life she has known. Frightened and lost, she falls asleep in the woods, only to be awakened by animals who lead her to a small cabin. Thinking it has been abandoned, she begins to clean and tidy up the place. Exhausted, Snow White falls asleep on one of the beds, and after some time, she awakes to see seven dwarves standing around her. It is at this point Disney breaks away from the original and not only names each dwarf — Happy, Sleepy, Sneezy, Grumpy, Dopey, Bashful, and Doc — giving them each their own personality, but also turns Snow White from a helpless victim into a strong heroine totally unlike the Brothers Grimm character.

Learning that Snow White is still alive, the Queen turns herself into an old woman, finds the princess at the cabin, and tricks her into taking a bite of poison apple. The seven dwarves return too late to save Snow White, and they place her body in a glass coffin.

A prince who has been looking for Snow White comes upon her coffin, opens the lid, and places a kiss upon her lips. She slowly opens her eyes, the Prince carries her to his horse, and they ride off into the sunset toward his castle, to live happily ever after.

Several Snow White paper doll sets were produced over the years; this particular set includes ten delightful die-cut dolls, Snow White, Prince Charming, the Wicked Queen, and the seven unforgettable Dwarves. The set came with approximately 25 press-out costumes and accessories with tabs.

Publisher: Whitman/Walt Disney Productions
Original Price: 59¢   Value: $45.00 – 75.00

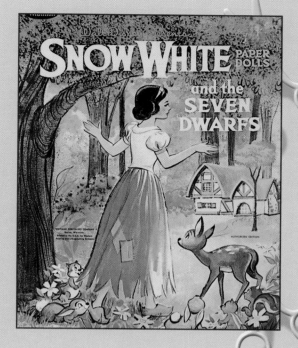

Tiny Tots   Year: 1967   #1983

This set of Tiny Tots was drawn by Alice Schlesinger, and includes two die-cut dolls, Cathy and Carolyn, along with eight animal toys. There are 30 punch-out outfits with tabs. Both dolls can wear each piece of clothing.

There is another, almost identical, set of Tiny Tots, #1977. The only difference between the two is that the clothing in the second set is flocked in red. Alice Schlesinger drew this set also.

There are many sets of paper dolls from this era that go by the name of Tiny Tots or have "Tiny Tots" in the title, so a helpful tip for identifying your set is to know the artist, publisher, and subtitle.

Publisher: Whitman/Western
Original Price: 69¢   Value: $40.00 – 65.00

Tina and Trudy   Year: 1967   #1952

Tina and Trudy are adorable redheaded twins drawn by Queen Holden's daughter Kathy Lawrence, who definitely has the same flair for drawing as her mother. Included in this adorable set are two die-cut dolls, Tina and Trudy, along with a 50-piece matching wardrobe to cut out. Trudy's outfits have pink tabs, and Tina's have green.

Publisher: Whitman Publishing Company
Original Price: 29¢   Value: $25.00 – 40.00

Courtesy of Edna Corbett

PeePul Pals   Year: 1967   #1984

This PeePul Pals paper dolls set was drawn by Leon Jason and is based on the dolls of the same name. They were popular around the mid-1960s and were created by Reuben Klamer. They include Nina the Nurse, Rock-a-bye Baby, Cinderella, Sally the Stewardess, and many other darling characters. They are not easy to find in excellent condition. However, I have seen them on eBay from time to time.

In this set, there are nine die-cut dolls: Betty Ballerina, Brenda Bride, Cinderella, Goldilocks, Mother Goose, Nina Nurse, Red Riding Hood, Rock-a-bye Baby, and Sally Stewardess. There are over 50 brightly colored outfits to press out. Each tab has a number that corresponds to the number on the doll.

Publisher: Whitman/Western (A Reuben Klamer Creation)
Original Price: 59¢   Value: $15.00 – 25.00

PeeWees   **Year: 1967**   **#1963**

This set is based on the 3½" pocket-size dolls with the chubby bodies. Each doll had the same face, but a different hairstyle and hair color.

This set includes four die-cut dolls and 74 outfits and accessories to cut out. The colored tabs match the panty color of a doll.

Publisher: Whitman/Western/Uneeda Doll Co., Inc.
Original Price: 39¢   Value: $15.00 – 25.00

Kewpie Kin   Year: 1967   #4413

Ever since these adorable Kewpies came on the scene in the early 1900, we haven't been able to get enough of them. Their elf-like faces and chubby bodies still capture our hearts just as they did in the early part of the century.

Kewpie Kin includes six die-cut Kewpie dolls and one Kewpiedoodle dog, along with 24 dresses, with armholes, to be cut out and wrapped around the dolls. There are no tabs on the clothing.

Publisher: Saalfield/Artcraft, Licensed by Cameo Doll Prod. Co.
Original Price: 29¢   **Value: $35.00 – 60.00**

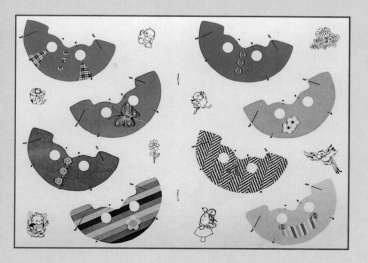

Baby Doll (My Very Own)   Year: 1967   #2761

Baby Doll is a variation of the 1963 paper doll set Baby Anne Smiles and Crys (also pictured in this book). Both sets were drawn by Queen Holden, but they have some differences. In this Baby Doll set, the face of the doll is drawn differently than in the 1963 set, but the body is posed the same. The clothes are identical in both sets, with the exception of one added coat and hat in the 1963 Baby Anne set.

This gorgeous set features one die-cut baby doll, along with 45 cut-out outfits and accessories with tabs.

Publisher: Lowe
Original Price: 29¢
Value: $50.00 – 65.00

Here Comes the Bride   Year: 1967   #1320

This lovely bride set includes two die-cut dolls, the bride and groom, and also features a garden trellis for the bride and groom to stand in front of. The set also has a wedding invitation, wedding cake, a bride and groom cake topper, a table (with bells that slip into it), the bride's bouquet, rings, the ring bearer's pillow, a bag of rice, gifts for the bride and groom (which tuck into slits on the flower cart), and (because we mustn't forget!) "something old, something new, something borrowed, and something blue."

To complete the set, there are 16 cut-out outfits with tabs, including a beautiful wedding dress, veil, and tuxedo.

Publisher: Saalfield
Original Price: 29¢   Value: $55.00 – 75.00

Liddle Kiddles   Year: 1967   #1981

In 1966, we were introduced to Mattel's Liddle Kiddles. They were beautifully painted little sprites with big eyes and small bodies one could pose. They were created with much attention given to detail, from their delicate, painted features to their clothing with tiny buttons. Each doll had high-quality accessories that matched a theme. The original series featured such cuties as Florence Niddle, Howard "Biff" Boodle, Liddle Diddle, Greta Griddle, Lola Liddle, Babe Biddle, Calamity Jiddle, Bunson Bernie, and Millie Middle. In 1967, the second Kiddle series made its debut. Each year thereafter, Mattel introduced a different series, including series like Storybook Kiddles, which reflected favorite children's stories; Kiddles in Lockets, with jewelry for little girls to wear; Cologne Kiddles, with scents; and Walking Skiddle Kiddles. Eventually, in 1968, Kiddles evolved into tiny 7/8" figures that came in pieces of jewelry such as lockets, rings, or bracelets. Those of us who grew up with these little cuties are often willing to pay hundreds of dollars to once again own and enjoy these delightful Liddle Kiddles.

This charming set includes nine die-cut dolls from the first and second series: Babe Biddle, Bunson Burnie, Freezy Sliddle, Lola Liddle, Sizzly Friddle, Soapy Siddle, Surfy Skiddle, Trikey Triddle, and Windy Fliddle. It also has a 60-piece press-out wardrobe with tabs. Each tab has the name of the doll that the outfit belongs to.

Publisher: Whitman/printed by Western/Mattel
Original Price: 59¢   Value: $30.00 – 50.00

Lucky Locket Kiddles   Year: 1967   #1993

Lucky Locket Liddle Kiddles were the rage in the mid-1960s. Each doll came with a locket that a child could wear around her neck or display with the doll.

I enjoyed hours of fun with my Locket Kiddles as a kid.

The folder is flocked, and there are 7" Locket pictures to punch-out and display. Also included are seven die-cut paper dolls, Lorna Locket, Lilac Locket, Liz Locket, Lou Locket, Lola Locket, Larky Locket, and Lois Locket, and 48 punch-out outfits and hats. There is a colored dot on each doll's base to match the colored tabs on her clothes.

Publisher: Whitman/Western/Mattel
Original Price: 59¢   Value: $35.00 – 60.00

That Girl   Year: 1967   #1351

This was a time in America when young women began to come into their own, and television networks were quick to reflect social changes. *That Girl* debuted on ABC and ran for five seasons, from September 8, 1966, until September 10, 1971.

Marlo Thomas played the lead role in this comedy about the life of an independent young woman. The show focused on the exploits of actress/model Ann Marie, who left her parents' home in upper New York state to make her way in the Big Apple. She was liberated, but at the same time dependent on her boyfriend, Donald, played by Ted Bessell, and her father, Lou, played by Lew Parker. The show's regular cast included future stars Ruth Buzzi, George Carlin, and Dabney Coleman, and featured an A-list of high-ranking guests such Milton Burle, Carl Reiner, and Marlo's real-life father, Danny Thomas.

Marlo was also on the show *Friends,* where she had a recurring role, and she is continuing her late father's charitable work for St. Jude's Children's Hospital.

This fabulous set of paper dolls includes three die-cut dolls, all of them depicting Ann Marie, along with 36 outfits and accessories to cut out.

Publisher: Saalfield/Daisy Productions
Original Price: 29¢   Value $45.00 – 75.00

The Mods   Year: 1967   #4727

I love this paper doll set because it is so reflective of the 1960s mod era. The two dolls are posed in a popular 1960s dance move. The outfits perfectly reflect the fashions for this time in history.

In this set, you will find two statuette dolls and 58 mod outfits and accessories to cut out. There is an adhesive stick included so that adhesive can be applied to the back of the clothing; if pressed on firmly, the clothing will then stick to the doll.

Publisher: Milton Bradley
Original Price: unknown   Value: $55.00 – 75.00

Twiggy   Year: 1967   #1999

Leslie Hornsby was born in north London on September 19th, 1949. At 16 years of age, Twiggy (who acquired her name for her stick-like figure) was the first model to become an international sensation. She was named "the face of '66" by the *Daily Express*, and adorned the cover of virtually every magazine of the time. Her modeling career was rather short, a mere four years, and she never walked a runway before leaving the industry behind to pursue an acting career.

Twiggy went on to film, stage, and television. Her first starring role, for which she received two Golden Globes (Best Actress in a Musical and Most Promising Newcomer), was in the film *The Boyfriend*. She continued her acting career in both the US and in England, taking parts in *Club Paradise*, *The Blues Brothers*, *The Little Match Girl,* and *Young Charlie Chaplin*. She has recorded albums of pop, rock, country, and show tunes, and has had two silver discs.

Never leaving a field completely behind for good, Twiggy made a very brief return to modeling during the Milan fashion week in 2002, strutting down her first catwalk.

This fashionable set has one die-cut doll, Twiggy, along with 43 mod outfits and accessories to press out. There is a pin-up picture of Twiggy to hang, along with a life size Plastilon dress that a little girl can cut out and wear like a paper doll outfit. The dress is durable and wipes off with a damp cloth, for hours of fun and play.

Publisher: Whitman/Western/Minnow Co., Ltd.
Original Price: $1.00   Value: $65.00 – 85.00

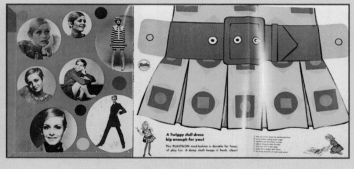

Twiggy Magic Paper Doll   **Year: 1967**   **#4704**

This is a boxed set featuring a second Twiggy, which includes one statuette doll and a "London-look" fashion wardrobe of more then 60 outfits and accessories to cut out. The clothing stays on like magic when you briskly rub the pieces on the doll.

There is also a photo album with different pictures of Twiggy.

Publisher: Whitman/Minnow Co. Ltd.
Original Price: $1.00   Value: $45.00 – 65.00

Barbie Has a New Look   Year: 1967   #1976

Barbie doll has a new mod look in this groovy set of paper dolls that includes two die-cut dolls fashioned after the Twist and Turn Barbie dolls that were so popular at the time. Also included are 33 press-out outfits from Barbie doll's original mod-era wardrobe, all with tabs. They have names such as Studio Tour, Fashion Shiner, Patio Party, and Sunflower.

Publisher: Whitman/Western/Mattel
Original Price: 59¢   Value: $35.00 – 75.00

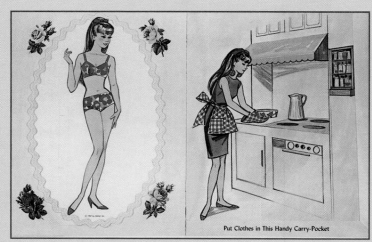

Francie and Casey Dolls Year: 1967 #1986

This set features Francie doll and her fun friend Casey doll, and includes four die-cut dolls, two Francie dolls and two Casey dolls, and 46 of their most popular mod outfits to punch out. The outfits have names such as Style Setters, Side-Kick, Iced Blue, and Bells. Each tab has a colored dot to match a dot on the base of the doll it belongs to.

Publisher: Whitman/Western/Mattel, Inc.
Original Price: 59¢ Value: $30.00 – 50.00

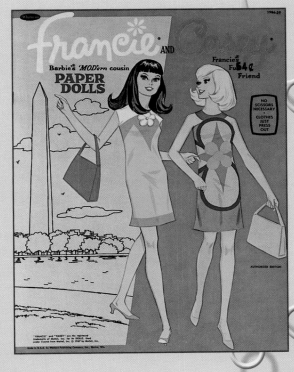

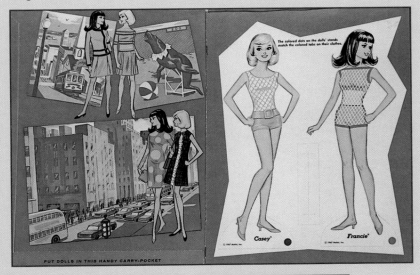

Baby's Hungry!   **Year: 1967**   **#4643**

In 1967, Mattel released an innovative doll for the times called Baby Hungry! She was battery operated, and when you put her spoon or bottle in it, her mouth would move up and down to imitate chewing or drinking. The Christmas of 1967 I found this fabulous doll under my tree, and I remember feeling like I was a real mom feeding and diapering Baby's Hungry!

This boxed set resembles the vinyl doll and includes one statuette Baby's Hungry with over 14 press-out outfits with tabs.

Publisher: Whitman/ Mattel, Inc.
Original Price: unknown   Value: $15.00 – 25.00

1968

Baby's Hungry!   **Year: 1968**   **#1978**

Here we have another set of Baby's Hungry! Though this set was published in 1968, the dolls in both sets are similar looking, but have some minor differences. The die-cut doll in this set has teeth and is posed in an opposite direction to the one above, which has no teeth. This die-cut doll is also larger. There are 21 outfits, all different from the boxed set above; all wardrobe pieces press out and have tabs. A rocking horse completes the set.

Publisher: Whitman/Western/Mattel, Inc.
Original price: 59c   Value: $15.00 – 25.00

Tubsy   Year: 1968   #1980

Tubsy, by Mattel, had an adorable smile that showed off her two bottom teeth. She came with a hooded towel, a diaper, and a toy. She was battery operated, and could sit in her bathtub moving her arms up and down to splash the water. After Tubsy's bath, her tub doubled as a changing table. Tubsy was my favorite doll as a little girl, I think because of her adorable expression. I loved to take her into the bath with me.

In this paper doll set, you will find one delightful 11½" die-cut baby, Tubsy, with her own stand-up bathtub that she can slip into. The set also includes an 18-piece press-out wardrobe and toys to press out. Tubsy's clothes stay on with tabs.

Publisher: Whitman/Ideal Toy Corporation
Original Price: 59¢   Value: $15.00 – 25.00

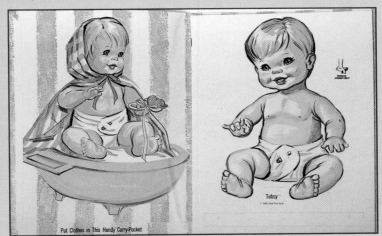

My Susie Doll Book   Year: 1968   #1971

Drawn by Alice Schlesinger, My Susie Doll Book set includes one adorable 12" die-cut doll, Susie, and 28 outfits, hats, and bows, all with tabs and ready to press out.

Publisher: Whitman/Western
Original Price: 39¢   Value: $15.00 – 20.00

Paper Doll Playmates   **Year: 1968**   **#1971**

This set is a reprint of set #4451, drawn by Ann Barkdoll, and includes three die-cut dolls, Penny, Scott, and Francie, and 23 cut-out outfits and accessories with tabs. Tabs have the first initials of the dolls the outfits belongs to.

Publisher: Saalfield
Original Price: 39¢   **Value: $15.00 – 25.00**

Chitty Chitty Bang Bang   Year: 1968   #1982

Chitty Chitty Bang Bang paper dolls are based on the famous movie of the same name starring Dick Van Dyke as Caractacus Potts. Potts saves a rusting motor car and restores it. Potts, with his two children and friend Truly Scrumptious, embarks on a great adventure with the flying car. In this set, you will find five die-cut dolls: Truly, Potts, Jeremy, Jemima, and Grandpa. This set has 34 outfits to punch out, and the color of each tab indicates the doll the outfit belongs to.

Publisher: Whitman/Western, Gildrose Productions, Ltd.
Original Price: 59¢   Value: $30.00 – 45.00

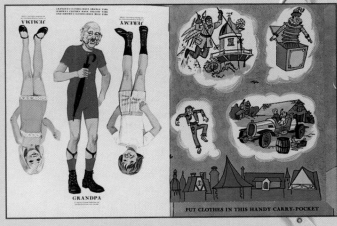

Betty   Year: 1968   #2777

Betty reflects an adorable African American girl with an infectious smile and big eyes, and includes one 11" die-cut doll, Betty, and 21 punch-out outfits and accessories with tabs, all made from lightweight cardboard.

Publisher: Lowe, James & Jonathan, Inc.
Original Price: 29¢   Value: $10.00 – 20.00

Peggy and Me   Year: 1968   #1980

Peggy and Me is a beginner's paper doll book and features Peggy and Patty. Each of the 14 pages has a different outfit; as you flip the pages the outfits change.

Publisher: Whitman/Western
Original Price: 39¢   Value: $8.00 – 12.00

Baby Go-along   Year: 1968   #1988

Baby Go-along can go with you anywhere! Drawn by Louise Myers, this darling set includes two 9½" die-cut babies, Mindy and Mary, and lots of animal toys, plus a 22-piece wardrobe to press out. Mindy's clothes have blue tabs, and Mary's have pink. The folder doubles as a carry tote with handles; it's converted by flipping the folder inside out. This set gave me hours of fun and was a favorite of mine when I was eight.

Publisher: Whitman/Western
Original Price: 59¢   Value: $15.00 – 25.00

Amy Magic Doll   Year: 1968   4618

Amy is a magic doll drawn by Ruth Ruhman. There is another set (#4618), named Vicki, with the same doll, but it is drawn with dark hair and a different hairstyle.

In this set, Amy is a statuette doll with red hair and green eyes. There are 34 outfits and accessories to cut out and rub briskly over the surface of the doll. Like magic, the clothes stay on. Two plastic stands and a pair of scissors are also included.

Publisher: Whitman/Western
Original Price: unknown   Value: $10.00 – 18.00

Raggedy Ann and Andy Magic Doll   Year: 1968   #4740

This is a boxed set of Raggedy Ann and Andy Magic Paper Dolls. As I have mentioned before, there were many Raggedy Ann and Andy sets drawn over the years, and each has its own special charm. In this set, there are two statuette dolls, Raggedy Ann and Raggedy Andy, with approximately 25 outfits and accessories to cut out and rub on the dolls. Like magic, the clothes stay on.

Publisher: Whitman/Western/The Bobbs-Merrill Company, Inc.
Original price: unknown   Value: $25.00 – 50.00

Lucky Locket Kiddles   Year: 1968   #4774

Lucky Locket Kiddles are based on the very popular Liddle Kiddle dolls. They came with their own locket, complete with a chain, that little girls could wear around their necks. This boxed set features four statuette dolls, Lois Locket, Lorelei Locket, Loretta Locket, and Lottie Locket, and 40 outfits and hats to cut out. There are no tabs; the clothes stay on like magic when rubbed briskly over a doll's surface. Also included are four plastic stands and a pair of scissors.

Publisher: Whitman/Western/Mattel, Inc.
Original Price: unknown   Value: $20.00 – 40.00

Baby PeeWee   Year: 1968   #4607

Uneeda Doll Co. produced Baby PeeWees, minidolls with a variety of hairstyles and outfits. The paper dolls have followed in their cute footsteps. The set includes four statuette Baby Pee-Wee dolls, along with over 30 press-out outfits with tabs.

Publisher: Whitman/Western/Uneeda
Original price: 59¢   Value: $12.00 – 25.00

Skediddle Kiddles   **Year: 1968**   **#4722**

This paper dolls set is based on the walking Skediddle Kiddles dolls, made by Mattel in the 1960s. It includes three statuette magic dolls, Shirley, Sheila, and Suki Skediddle, along with 57 outfits and accessories to cut out and rub briskly over a doll's body. The clothes magically stay on.

Publisher: Whitman/Western
Original Price: unknown   **Value: $25.00 – 45.00**

Barbie, Christie and Stacey Dolls   Year: 1968   #1976

This set is unique in that the paper dolls pose like fashion models. Perforations in the bases allow you to stand a doll with one leg in front of the other. This set of paper dolls is based on the 1968 versions of Barbie doll and her friends by Mattel. There are three die-cut dolls, Barbie doll, Christie doll, and Stacey doll, along with 34 press-out outfits and accessories that fit each doll. The outfits are replicas of original Barbie doll outfits, such as Extravaganza, Bermuda Holidays, Swirly Cue, and Togetherness, to name just a few.

Publisher: Whitman/Western
Original Price: 59¢   Value: $35.00 – 55.00

Tutti Doll   Year: 1968   #1991

In 1966, Barbie doll added a new member to her family. Tutti doll is the little sister of Barbie doll and Skipper doll. At the time she was first made, her body was different than those of her big sisters because she had a wire armature that allowed her arms and legs to be posed in a variety of positions.

This adorable paper dolls set includes two die-cut dolls (one doll not shown), along with approximately 20 outfits and accessories to punch out. The folder doubles as Tutti's bedroom; by pressing out the pieces and fitting the tabs into slits on the folder, you can create a bed and vanity for Tutti.

Publisher: Whitman/Western/Mattel, Inc.
Original Price: 59¢   Value: $25.00 – 55.00

Six Paper Doll Playmates   Year: 1968   #1964

Drawn by Neva Shultz, 6 Paper Doll Playmates includes six die-cut dolls, Christine, Diane, Jeanne, Maria, Nancy, and Sharon, and approximately 70 cut-out outfits and accessories with tabs. The tabs are colored to match the doll that the outfit belongs to.

Publisher: Whitman/Western
Original Price: 29¢   Value: $20.00 – 35.00

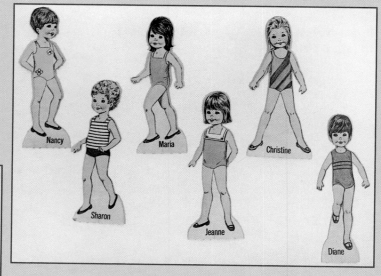

Ballet Paper Dolls   Year: 1968   #4719

This boxed set of Ballet Paper Dolls includes four statuette dolls, Andrea, Claudia, Emily, and Margot, along with 39 press-out costumes and accessories with tabs.

Publisher: Whitman/Western
Original Price: unknown   Value: $20.00 – 40.00

Family Affair   Year: 1968   #4767

This paper doll set is based on the television show *Family Affair*, which was on the air from 1966 to 1971. The premise of the show is that three children tragically lose their parents in a car accident. The children, Cissy, and her twin siblings, Jody and Buffy, are sent to live with their bachelor uncle. Uncle Bill lives in a luxurious 5th Avenue apartment in New York. Bill has a gentleman's gentleman named Mr. French, who is exasperated with his new role as the nanny. The children turn his life upside down. It's not long before the children charm their way into his heart, and they all become a family unit.

In this set, you will find five statuette dolls, Uncle Bill, Mr. French, Cissy, Jody, and Buffy, and over 30 outfits and accessories, including Mrs. Beasley (Buffy's favorite doll), to press out.

Publisher: Whitman/Western/Family Affair Company
Original Price: unknown   Value: $20.00 – 40.00

Julia   Year: 1968   #1335

The show *Julia,* starring Diahann Carroll as Julia Baker, was about a young African American woman working as a nurse. This was a significant premise because it left behind the stereotypical portrayal of black women. Julia was a widow whose husband had been killed in Vietnam. After his death, she found herself alone, trying to raise a young son, Cory (played by Marc Copage), and make a new life in L.A.

Running from September 1968 to May 1971, on NBC, *Julia* was the first sitcom to star an African American woman in the title role. Other cast members included Lloyd Nolan as Dr. Morton Chegley, Janear Hines as Roberta, Betty Beaird as Marie Waggedorn, and Michael Link as Earl J. Waggedorn.

For her performance, Diahann Carroll won a Golden Globe and received an Emmy nomination for Best Actress. *Julia* was one of the best shows of the late 1960s and early 1970s, and can be seen today in syndication on TV Land.

The Julia paper doll set includes five die-cut dolls: Julia, Cory, Marie, and two of Cory's friend Earl J. Waggedorn. It also includes 51 outfits and accessories to cut out. Each tab has the name of the doll the outfit belongs to.

Publisher: Saalfield Publishing Company
Original Price: 29¢   Value: $30.00 – 55.00

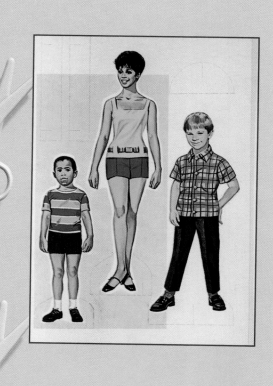

The Flying Nun   Year: 1968   #4417

The Flying Nun was a favorite television show that debuted in 1967 and enjoyed three seasons on the air. The show was never expected to have the popularity that it did, and it surprised all who were involved. *The Flying Nun* starred a young Sally Field as Sister Bertrille. The story was about a 90 lb. nun named Sister Bertrille, who was assigned to a convent and orphange in SanTanco, in San Juan, Puerto Rico. When those San Juan winds stirred up, Sister Bertrille could take flight by tilting her coronet.

She encountered many mishaps and adventures, joined by a good-looking playboy named Carlos Rameros, her fellow sisters, and the children of the orphange.

Included in the set, you will find nine die-cut dolls, Sister Bertrille, Carlos Rameros, Sister Sixto, Sister Jacqueline, Mother Superior, and four San Juan children, along with 30 cut-out outfits for Carlos and the children.

Publisher: Artcraft/Screen Gems, Inc.
Original Price: 29¢   Value: $18.00 – 40.00

Buffy Paper Doll Set **Year: 1968** **#1995**

Buffy and Mrs. Beasley paper dolls are based on the hit television show *Family Affair*. Buffy, played by Anissa Jones, had perhaps the most popular doll of all time. Mrs. Beasley won little girls' hearts with her intelligence and her listening skills, and she gave great advice! Every little girl wanted to have her own Mrs. Beasley doll (made by Mattel).

In this set, there are two die-cut dolls, Buffy and Mrs. Beasley, and over 30 outfits and accessories with tabs. Mrs. Beasley also has her own die-cut cradle that really rocks.

Publisher: Whitman/Western
Original Price: 69¢ **Value $35.00 – 45.00**

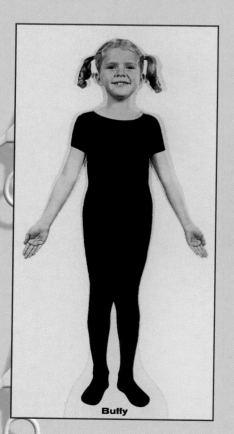

Buffy

Buffy Paper Doll   Year: 1969   #1985

With this 1969 Buffy set, by flipping the folder inside out you can create a tote to carry your dolls and wardrobes in when you are on the go. There is also a pint-size tote for Mrs. Beasley.

In this set, you will find two die-cut dolls, Buffy and Mrs. Beasley, along with 30 outfits and accessories, all with tabs and ready to press out.

Publisher: Whitman/Western
Original Price: 59¢   Value: $35.00 – 45.00

Pictured to the left are the Buffys from both the 1968 set and the 1969 set. You will notice the similarities between the dolls. They share the same pose and have been produced in a photographic style. However, they have different expressions on their faces. Their wardrobes are different as well; the 1968 set has a photographic style of clothing, and the 1969 set has a drawn style. Mrs. Beasley looks the same in each of the sets.

The 1968 doll is on the right and the 1969 doll is on the left.

Dollies Try on New Clothes   Year: 1969   #2780

Another adorable reprint using dolls and clothes drawn by Queen Holden. This set comes with two die-cut dolls, Vicky and Helen. Vicky is from set #2762, Vicky, and Helen is from set #2763, Dolly Gets Lots of New Clothes. There are 59 cut-out outfits and accessories with tabs. The outfits are a mixture of those in previous Queen Holden sets.

Publisher: Low/James & Jonthan, Inc.
Original Price: 29¢   Value: $30.00 – 45.00

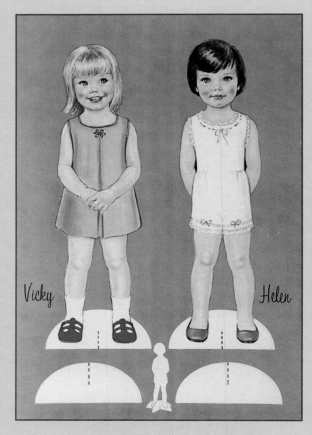

Tiny Tot Shop   **Year: 1969**   **1231965**

This set of paper dolls is drawn by Kathy Lawrence, and on the opposite page is a set drawn by her mother, Queen Holden. The similarities are amazing!

Both artists are incredibly skilled at capturing the beauty and innocence of little children. In this set, you will find three die-cut dolls and over 160 cut-out outfits and accessories with tabs. There are three of every style of outfit, in different sizes, to fit the appropriate doll.

Publisher: Whitman Book/Western
Original Price: 39¢   Value: $40.00 – 50.00

DollTime   **Year: 1969**   **#2783**

This set drawn by Nan Pollard has three die-cut dolls named Jill, Robin, and Wendy. These dolls are beautifully drawn, with big eyes and wonderful expressions. Also, there is a 47-piece cut-out wardrobe with tabs, for school, parties, and play.

Publisher: Lowe/James & Jonathan, Inc.
Original Price: 29¢   Value: $25.00 – 30.00

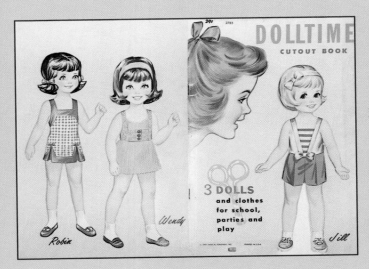

Dolly and Me   Year: 1969   #1323

Dolly and Me is a lovely set drawn by Athena Tsambon. It originates from set #4443 and includes two die-cut dolls, a cute little redheaded girl with pigtails and her baby doll, along with 22 punch-out outfits and accessories with tabs, made of medium-weight cardboard.

Publisher: Saalfield
Original Price: 29¢   **Value: $10.00 – 20.00**

Courtesy of Edna Corbett

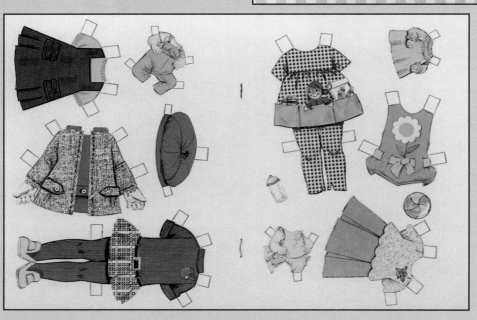

Tini Go-along   Year: 1969   #1977

Tini Go-along comes with an easy flip-fold tote. By turning the folder inside out and flipping up the handles, you and your paper doll are ready to go. Tini was a United Airlines travel promotion; the cover reads, "Come fly with me." The set includes two 11½" dolls, Lynn and Chris, along with 30 outfits and hats to press out. The tabs are pink or blue to match the swimsuit of the doll the outfits belong to. Both dolls have their own pint-size travel tote.

Publisher: Whitman/Western
Original Price: 59¢   Value: $15.00 – 25.00

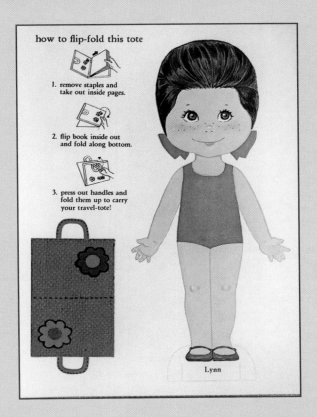

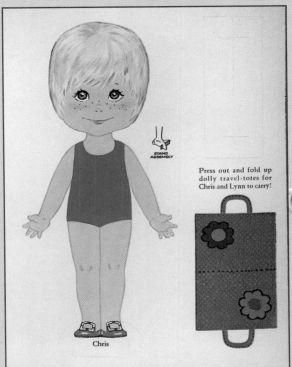

Swingy   Year: 1969   # 4780

Swingy was Mattel's 18" dancing doll; she would wiggle her hips. On her original box was a paper record so that Swingy could get her groove on. Later, Mattel came out with an 11" version called Tiny Swingy.

In this set, you will find one statuette doll, Swingy, along with 24 outfits to cut out and rub briskly over the doll. Like magic, her clothes stay on.

Publisher: Whitman/Western/Mattel
Original Price: $1.00   Value: $8.00 – 18.00

Winking Winny   Year: 1969   #4754

In 1968, Remco introduced a wonderful African American doll, Winking Winny. Both Winking Winny and the boxed set of paper dolls based on her are rare finds. She was a 15" vinyl doll that winked when you pushed the button on her tummy,

In the Winking Winny paper doll set, you will find one 9½" statuette doll, Winking Winny, and a 41-piece press-out wardrobe with tabs.

Publisher: Whitman/Western/Remco
Original Price: unknown   Value: $10.00 – 20.00

Flatsy   Year: 1969   #4756

In the late 1960s, the Ideal Toy Corporation introduced Flatsy dolls. These unique little dolls were made from a rubber-like material with a bendable wire armature and came flat as a pancake in a variety of sizes and styles, with beautifully painted features, long hair, and many accessories.

They enjoyed an instant popularity that continued well into the 1970s. Early Flatsys were packaged in a picture frame that included accessories. Later, they were sold in a clear plastic locket.

In this boxed set, you will find three statuette dolls, Sandy Flatsy, Candy Flatsy, and Filly Flatsy, along with 70 outfits and accessories to press out. The tabs on the outfits are colored to match the panties of the doll the outfit belongs to.

Note: Because all three dolls are posed identically, each can wear all clothing pieces.

Publisher: Whitman/Western/Ideal Toy Corporation
Original Price: unknown   Value: $15.00 – 25.00

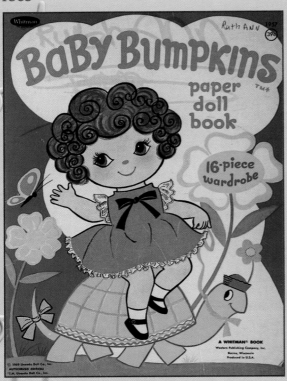

Baby Bumpkins   **Year: 1969**   **#1957**

This darling set includes one 10" die-cut doll, Baby Bumpkins, and a 16-piece cut-out wardrobe with tabs.

Publisher: Whitman/Western/Uneeda Doll Co., Inc.
Original Price: 39¢   Value: $9.00 – 20.00

Growing Sally   **Year: 1969**   **#4733**

Growing Sally was a vinyl doll made by Remo in 1968. She had a red yarn wig with pigtails, and freckles around her nose and cheeks. When she came out of the box, she was 6" tall, but her torso was made somewhat like a telescope, so when you gave her a tug, she grew to 6½" tall.

This boxed set, drawn by Judy Stang, includes two magic statuette dolls, 6" small Sally and 9" tall Sally, along with a 67-piece stay-on wardrobe. Briskly rub the clothes over a doll's body and, like magic, the clothes stay on!

Publisher: Whitman/Western
Original Price: unknown   Value: $15.00 – 20.00

Baby Doll   Year: 1969   #4220C

This set features an African American version of Baby Doll #2403 from 1957. The dolls are posed identically, but have a slight difference in their smile, and in this set, the doll is made from thick cardboard and has flocked black hair. In the Baby Doll set #2403, the doll is made from heavy cardboard and has painted hair.

Included in this set is a beautifully illustrated, medium-weight statuette doll and her 13-piece wardrobe to cut out.

Publisher: Lowe/James and Jonathan, Inc.
Original Price: 49¢   **Value: $18.00 – 30.00**

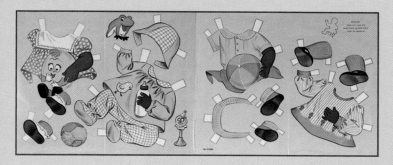

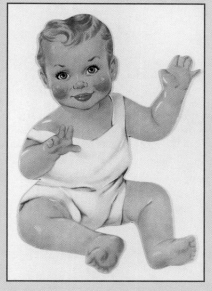 

The doll on the left is Baby Doll from set #2403. She is a 10" statuette doll made of heavyweight cardboard.

The doll on the right is Baby Sue from set #2786. She is a 10" die-cut doll.

Baby Sue   Year: 1969   #2786

This is another reprint of #2403, and is almost identical to set #4220C. In this set, there is one 10" die-cut doll (no flocking) and 13 of the identical outfits, shoes, and hair accessories as set #4220C. However, there is one small difference — the clothing in this set is made of lightweight cardboard, and the pieces press out.

Publisher: Lowe/James & Jonathan, Inc.
Original Price: 29¢   **Value: $8.00 – 15.00**

Newborn Thumbelina   **Year: 1969**   **# 1967**

In the early 1960s, Ideal Toys introduced one of its most beloved dolls, 15" Thumbelina. It was so popular that other lines were created to keep up with demand. In 1967, a 9" version with the name of Newborn Thumbelina, came on the scene and was instantly popular. She had a cloth body with vinyl head and vinyl limbs, and when you pulled her string, she would wiggle her head and body like a real newborn baby.

In this set, you will find one realistic die-cut doll, Thumbelina, along with 25 cut-out outfits and accessories with tabs.

Publisher: Whitman/Western/Ideal
Original Price: 39¢   **Value: $15.00 – 25.00**

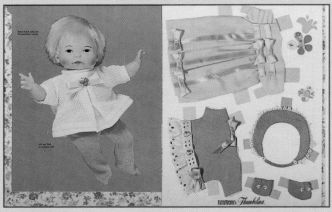

Patti   **Year: 1969**   **#4843**

Patti was drawn by Elsie Darien, and is a reprint of #3921. Other reprints of this set include #2759 and #9105. In this set, you will find one 11½" die-cut doll, Patti. The doll and the cover have Patti's dress and slip beautifully flocked in dark pink with specs of glitter. The set also comes with 26 press-out dresses and accessories with tabs.

Publisher: Lowe/James & Jonathan, Inc.
Original Price: 49¢   **Value: $8.00 – 15.00**

Little Miss Muffet   **Year: 1969**   **#2787**

Little Miss Muffet, a delightful Mother Goose character, is featured in this paper doll set that originates from set #1283, Cuddles and Rags. The expression on Miss Muffet is slightly different from that of the original. Miss Muffet has a redrawn smile; her pose however, remains the same as the doll in Cuddles and Rags.

This set includes one 10" die-cut doll, Miss Muffet, along with a 31-piece wardrobe to wear as she eats her curds and whey. All outfits have tabs and are ready to cut out.

Publisher: Lowe/James & Jonathan, Inc.
Original Price: 29¢   Value: $15.00 – 25.00

Courtesy of Edna Corbett

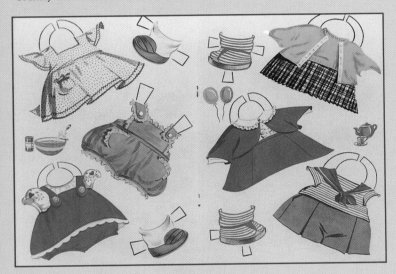

Rag Doll   **Year: 1969**   **#4626**

All throughout history, rag dolls have had a special place in little girls' hearts. In the early days, moms would sew their daughters these charming little stuffed dolls, often with buttons for eyes and yarn for hair. Not only did they serve little ones as friends and play toys, they were also practical. On Sundays, little girls could play with their dolls during the long church services; if a doll dropped, it would not disturb the other churchgoers.

This is a charming boxed set of paper dolls that includes two 6½" statuette rag dolls and a 32-piece press-out wardrobe with tabs.

Publisher: Whitman/Western
Original Price: unknown   Value: $10.00 – 20.00

Sugar n' Spice   Year: 1969   #3644A

This set was drawn by Jeanne Voelz and comes from set #4442. Included in this set are six die-cut dolls named Nancy, Heather, Jackie, Tinker, Sally, and Leslie. There are 41 punch-out outfits and hats with tabs. The tabs are printed with the name of the doll the outfit belongs to. The outfits are made from medium-weight cardboard.

Publisher: Saalfield
Original Price: 69¢   Value: $12.00 – 20.00
Courtesy of Edna Corbett

Sugar and Spice   Year: 1969   #N3961

This is another reprint of #4442 Sugar and Spice drawn by Jeanne Voelz. This sets differs from the above in that the outfits are printed on paper and are cut-outs, as opposed to lightweight cardboard punch-outs. Also the outfits in #3644A are brighter in color than those in #N3961.

Publisher: Saalfield
Original Price: 49¢   Value: $12.00 – 20.00
Courtesy of Edna Corbett

Mini Mopets   Year: 1969   #1320

This adorable set was drawn by Dorothy Grider and comes from set #4440 and shares the same name. Other reprints include #4234 and #5234.

In this set, you will find six die-cut dolls: Pam, Joy, Hank, Bobby, Tim, and Susie. There are 36 press-out outfits made of lightweight cardboard. The tabs have the first initial of the doll the outfit belongs to.

Publisher: Saalfield
Original Price: 29¢   Value: $12.00 – 20.00

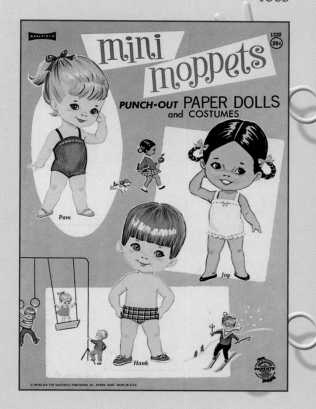

The Flying Nun   **Year: 1969**   **#6069**

This boxed set of The Flying Nun is very similar to the previous 1968 set, #4417 (pictured in this book). The stand-up dolls in both sets are identical, and include Sister Bertrille, Mother Superior, Sister Jacqueline, and Sister Sixto. Also included are five statuette dolls, Carlos and the four San Juan children. Set #6069 comes with the same 30 outfits and accessories as set #4417, but the clothes are made from lightweight cardboard as opposed to paper.

Publisher: Saalfield
Original Price: $1.29   **Value: $35.00 – 55.00**

White House   Year: 1969   #4475

This set of paper dolls was published one year after Richard M. Nixon, our 37th president, was elected. This set features the Nixon women, First Lady Patricia and daughters Trisha and Julie.

Richard Nixon had many ups and downs during his presidency, which ran from 1968 to 1974.

He was the only president to resign from office, after facing impeachment for his involvement in the ever-so-famous Watergate scandal.

However, Nixon also won great respect for his foreign policy. He ended America's involvement in Vietnam, eased tensions between the US, Russia, and China, and had the honor of being the first president to visit China,

Included in this set are three die-cut dolls, Pat, Trisha, and Julie Nixon, and 33 cut-out outfits with tabs.

Publisher: Saalfield Artcraft
Original Price: 29¢   Value: $20.00 – 40.00

Courtesy of Edna Corbett

Barbie Dolls and Clothes   Year: 1969   #1976

Another wonderful set of Barbie paper dolls! Barbie Dolls and Clothes includes two die-cut Barbie dolls, along with a 32-piece wardrobe that includes some favorite original outfits of Barbie doll's that were popular in the 1969 era, such as Red, White and Warm; Plush Pony, Shirtdressy, Little Bow Pink, and Cloud 9, to name a few.

Publisher: Whitman/Western/Mattel
Original Price: 59¢   Value: $40.00 – 65.00

Dolly Dears   Year: 1969   #1960

This Dolly Dears set was drawn by Neva Schultz, and is very similar to the 1967 #4701 Dolly Dears set that featured Cathy and Carolyn (pictured in this book). The dolls are the same except that the large doll in this set has auburn hair and green eyes. The smaller doll is identical to Carolyn in set #4701. None of the clothing in this set is a duplicate of that in set #4701.

In this set, you will find two die-cut dolls and a 44-piece cut-out wardrobe with tabs.

Publisher Whitman/Western
Original Price: 29¢   Value: $15.00 – 25.00

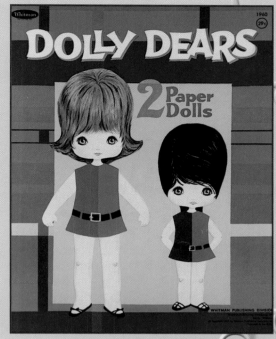

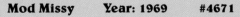

Mod Missy   Year: 1969   #4671

This mod set includes one 9½" statuette doll, Missy, along with 27 punch-out outfits and accessories with tabs, including wings, sunglasses, and a guitar.

Publisher: Whitman/Western
Original Price: unknown   Value: $8.00 – 15.00

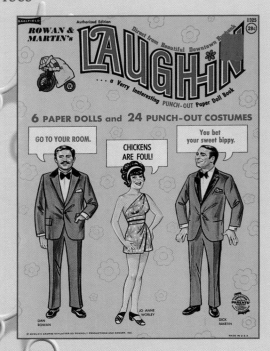

Laugh-in   Year: 1969   #1325

This set is based on the hit television comedy/variety show *Rowan and Martin's Laugh-In*. *Laugh-In* ran from 1968 to 1973, and enjoyed 124 episodes. The show was hosted by Dan Rowan and Dick Marin, and was full of one-liners, jokes, and skits. The shows regular cast included Goldie Hawn, Judy Carne, Arte Johnson, Lilly Tomlin, Ruth Buzzi, and announcer Gary Owens, to name a few.

Some of the memorable catch phrases included, "Sock it to me," "Here comes the judge," and "You bet your sweet bippy."

This paper doll set includes six die-cut dolls, Dan Rowan, Jo Anne Worley, Dick Martin, Judy Carne, Arte Johnson, and Goldie Hawn, with 24 punch-out costumes made of lightweight cardboard. Popular lines from the show are printed throughout the set.

Publisher: Saalfield
Original Price: 29¢   Value: $15.00 – 35.00

Daisy Darling Magic Doll   **Year: 1969**   **#4673**

The Daisy Darling boxed set includes one statuette doll, Daisy, along with 33 country-style outfits and accessories to cut out. Clothes stay on like magic by briskly rubbing the clothing over the doll. Scissors and a plastic stand complete the set.

Publisher: Whitman/Western
Original Price: 29¢   **Value: $8.00 – 15.00**

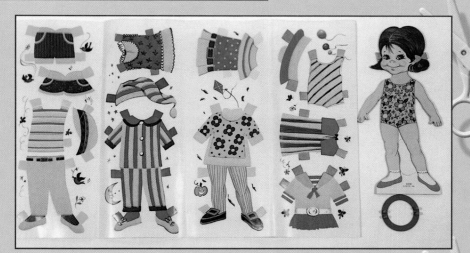

Eloise   **Year: 1969**   **#4672**

The Eloise set includes one 9½" statuette doll, Eloise, along with a 30-piece wardrobe flocked in pink. Clothes have tabs and are ready to press out.

Publisher: Whitman/Western
Original Price: unknown   **Value: $8.00 – 15.00**

Storybook Kiddles Sweethearts   **Year: 1969**   **#1956**

This set of paper dolls is based on the Liddle Kiddle line of dolls called Storybook Kiddles Sweethearts. These adorable 2" dolls come from our favorite fairy tale romances. They came packaged in their own storybook, complete with heart-shaped stands and a portrait pendant to slip a picture of the two lovebirds in.

This set includes four sets of fairy tale true loves, Romeo and Juliet, Robin Hood and Maid Marian, Rapunzel and the Prince, and the Queen and King of Hearts, along with a 62-piece wardrobe to cut out. Each outfit has tabs colored to match a doll stand.

Publisher: Whitman/Western/Mattel
Original Price: 39¢   Value: $30.00 – 50.00

Jackie & Caroline   #107

Jacqueline Kennedy was married to our 35th president, John F. Kennedy. She had two children, Caroline, born in 1957, and John Jr., born in 1960. Jackie defined her role as "to take care of the president" and felt strongly about motherhood. She once said, "If you bungle raising your children, I don't think whatever else you do well matters very much.

She was perhaps the most admired first lady in history, for her intelligence, beauty, grace, and her sense of culture. "Jackie," as she became known to the American public, took on her greatest task as first lady when she led the effort to restore the interior of the White House. In the end, the results reflected the elegance, splendor, and pride that was befitting "America's House."

The courage that she so visibly displayed in the aftermath of the tragedy that struck on Nov. 22, 1963, won her even greater respect and admiration. Jackie later married Aristotle Onassis, and after his death, she began a career in publishing and later became a senior editor at Doubleday. She died in New York City, on May 19, 1994. At her funeral, John Jr. described three of Jackie's attributes: "Love of words, the bonds of home and family, and her spirit of adventure."

In this set, you will find two statuette dolls, Jackie and Caroline, along with over 35 outfits and accessories to cut out, including one dress that shows Jackie's arms holding John Jr. as a baby. Clothes stay on with a rub of the magic wand.

Publisher: Magic Wand Corporation
Original Price: $1.00   Value: $25.00 – 45.00

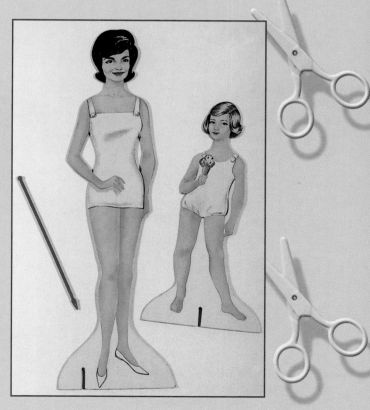

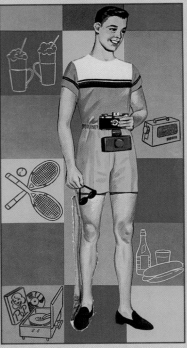

Date Time   #1754

The Date Time paper doll set originates from the 1954 #2740 set, Girl Friend–Boy Friend and was drawn by Jeanie Voelz.

This set has two lightweight cardboard dolls, Girl Friend and Boy Friend, along with a 6-piece cut-out wardrobe to with tabs.

Publisher: Saalfield
Original Price: 10¢   Value: $8.00 – 15.00

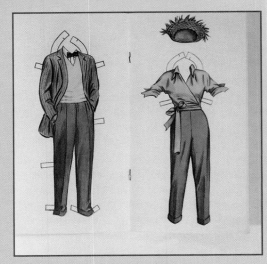

Tina   #4250

The Tina set is unique because the scene of Tina standing in front of a 3-way mirror is all one piece. Another unique feature is the inclusion of three different heads, with different faces and hairstyles, that slip around Tina's head and create different looks. Also included in the set are seven punch-out outfits made of lightweight cardboard. Tina's clothing is applied by inserting its tabs into the slots at the neckline, and then bending the tabs back behind the doll.

Publisher: Saalfield
Original Price: 39¢   Value: $10.00 – 20.00

Through the Year   **#1220**

Through the Year originates from set #1346, Pretty as a Rose, drawn by Lois Takatch. It Includes three die-cut dolls, Tina, Ellen, and Ann, along with a 29-piece cut-out wardrobe representing the different seasons of the years. The tabs have the name of the doll the outfit belongs to.

Publisher: Saalfield
Original Price: 39¢   Value: $15.00 – 25.00

Susan   **#1822**

   An adorable African American doll, Susan, is the main character in this set, one in a series of cut-out books. The book includes one doll and 27 outfits and accessories with tabs.

Publisher: Lowe
Original Price: 10¢   **Value: $6.00 – 18.00**

Cindy Book   **#1825**

   Cindy is another character in this series of cut-out books; she has blue eyes and dark hair, and an endearing smile. The book includes one doll and 27 cut-out outfits with tabs.

Publisher: Lowe
Original Price: 10¢   **Value: $6.00 – 18.00**

Courtesy of Edna Corbett

Sally   #1813

Sally is yet another character in this cut-out book series, which featured small books, a doll, and a complete wardrobe in each set, which was then sold at a very affordable price.

Sally's set includes one doll and 25 outfits with tabs.

Publisher: Lowe
Original Price: 10¢   Value: $6.00 – 18.00

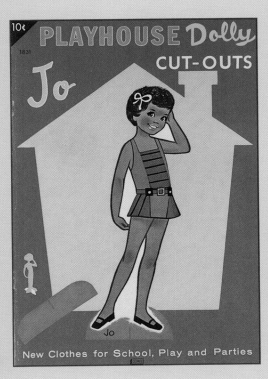

Playhouse Dolly Jo   #1831

Jo is an African American cutie and originates from set #2784, Little Girls (pictured in this book). She is ready to cut out and the set includes a 21-piece cut-out wardrobe with tabs.

Publisher: Lowe
Original Price: 10¢   Value: $6.00 – 18.00

Doll Time   #1844

This is a unique set, because it combines two sets of paper dolls by two different artists.

Queen Holden drew the larger doll and clothing in this set; these were originally featured in Peggy and Peter, set #9041, in 1962. Artist Nan Pollard contributed the two smaller dolls and outfits, originally from the 1950s set #1284, Toni Hair-Do Cut Out Dolls.

In this set, you will find three dolls, four hairdos, and a 30-piece cut-out wardrobe with tabs.

Publisher: Lowe
Original Price: 10¢   **Value:** $20.00 – 40.00

Baby   #1338

This adorable set originated from the 1950 set #2782, Baby Brother, and features one die-cut blue-eyed cutie with his own wading pool. There are also 20 cut-out outfits and accessories with tabs.

Publisher: Saalfield
Original Price: 29¢   Value: $18.00 – 35.00

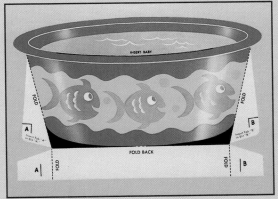

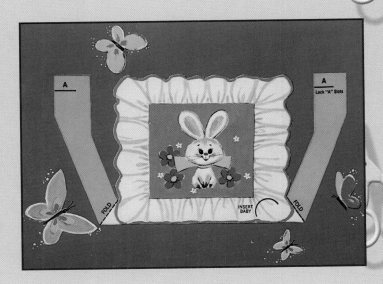

Julia   Year: 1970   #6055

Another set from the NBC television series *Julia*. This boxed set features four statuette dolls, Julia, Marie, Corey, and Earl J. Waggedorn, along with 49 outfits and accessories to cut out. The date on the clothing pages is 1968.

Note: In the chapter dealing with dolls of the 1960s, you will find another Julia set, #1335, dated "1968." It has 49 outfits and accessories identical to those in this set. However, for this set the dolls have been redrawn.

Publisher: Saalfield/Twentieth Century-Fox Film Corp.
Original Price: $1.50   Value: $40.00 – 55.00

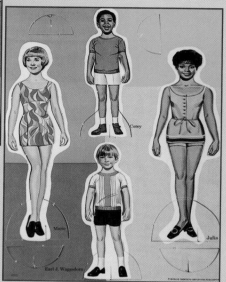

Buffy & Jody   Year: 1970   #4764

The Buffy & Jody set is based on the CBS television program *Family Affair* (read more about *Family Affair* in the 1960s section).

In this set, you will find two statuette dolls, Buffy and Jody, along with 36 outfits and accessories that stay on like magic when briskly rubbed over the dolls.

Publisher: Whitman/Western/Family Affair Company
Original Price: unknown   Value: $30.00 – 50.00

Beth Ann **Year: 1970** **#1995**

Kathy Lawrence, the daughter of Queen Holden, certainly inherited her mother's talents. This set shows it off.

Beth Ann's adorable face and outfits have captured the hearts of collectors everywhere. She is perhaps the most popular paper doll set that Kathy Lawrence has done.

In this set, you will find one die-cut doll, Beth Ann, along with 65 outfits and accessories to cut out. Beth Ann has her own high chair, bed, and stroller that she can slip into.

Publisher: Whitman/Western
Original Price: 39¢ **Value: $25.00 – 45.00**
Courtesy of Edna Corbett

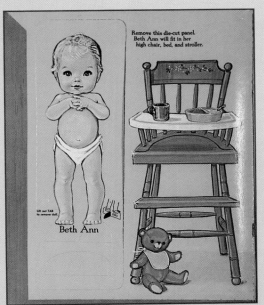

Tricia **Year: 1970** **#4248**

Tricia, the daughter of Richard M. Nixon, is featured in her own paper doll set drawn by Jeanne Voelz. This set has historical facts written throughout the book, and a pop-up White House complete with cherry trees and a fountain. The center of the book is a game board for the White House Tour Game. The set includes one die-cut doll, Tricia, and 15 cut-out outfits with tabs.

You can also find Trisha and many of her outfits in set #4475, published in 1969 and called The White House (shown in this book). Her mother, Pat, and sister, Julie, are also part of the set. It was also drawn by Jeanne Voelz.

Publisher: Saalfield Artcraft
Original Price: 39¢ **Value: $20.00 – 40.00**
Courtesy of Edna Corbett

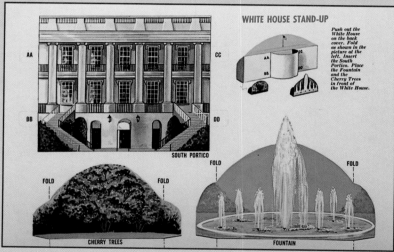

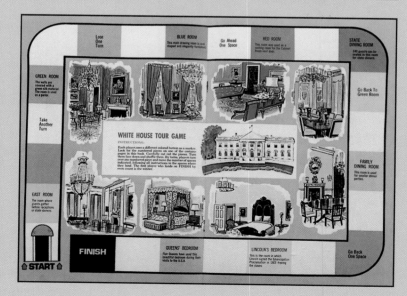

Goldilocks and The Three Bears   Year: 1970   #4211

This beautifully illustrated set is drawn by Belle Benoit, and is based on the very popular fairy tale of the same name. There is an adorable die-cut Goldilocks doll and also the three bears, Momma, Papa, and Baby Bear, along with a 29-piece cut-out wardrobe with tabs. This set was reprinted in 1970, with the same name, as #1211.

Publisher: Saalfield/ArtCraft
Original Price: 39¢   Value: $20.00 – 30.00

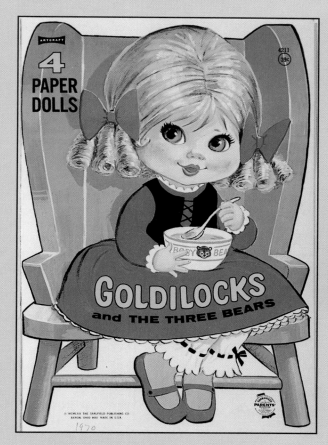

Little Dancers   **Year: 1970**   **#1946**

Here is one variation of the Little Dancers set. This set features two die-cut dolls named Rachel and Robin as little ballerinas, along with 32 press-out outfits and ballet costumes with tabs. (Set #1968 is pictured below.)

Publisher: Whitman/Western
Original Price: 59¢   **Value: $8.00 – 15.00**

Courtesy of Edna Corbett

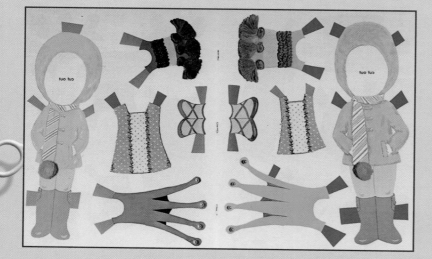

Little Dancers   **Year: 1970**   **#1968**

This set looks identical to the one above; however, the book is larger. Rachel and Robin, in a taller size, have the same 32 press-out outfits and ballet costumes as the preceding dolls. In both sets, Rachel's clothes have pink tabs and Robin's have orange tabs.

Publisher: Whitman/Western
Original Price: 59¢   **Value: $8.00 – 15.00**

Mrs. Beasley   Year: 1970   #1973

This set drawn by the Myers has an authorized edition of the lovable doll that became famous as on the hit TV show *Family Affair*. This doll became a popular paper doll and play doll for little girls in the late 1960s and 1970s. Mrs. Beasley came with 13 punch-out outfits with tabs.

Publisher: Whitman/Western
Original Price: 39¢   Value: $15.00 – 25.00

Courtesy of Edna Corbett

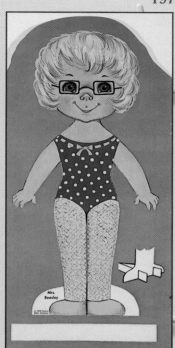

Raggedy Ann   Year: 1970   #1984

I find it interesting that a series of events can sometimes create a phenomenon. Johnny Gruelle found an old rag doll in the attic; the doll was worn and tattered, with no face. Johnny, a political cartoonist at the time, took his pen out and drew on the now-famous triangle nose, coal black eyes, and whimsical smile that we all know today as the face of Raggedy Ann. Gruelle ended up making up stories about the doll and her adventures to entertain his 13-year-old daughter, Marcella, who was sick from an infected small pox vaccine. Marcela would eventually die from her illness. In her memory, Gruelle later wrote *Raggedy Ann Stories* and began to sell Raggedy Ann rag dolls. Over the next 20 years, the stories would sell millions of copies, and even more Raggedy Ann and Andy dolls would be sold.

Included in this set is one 11½" die-cut doll, Raggedy Ann, and a 21-piece punch-out wardrobe with tabs.

Publisher: Whitman Book/Western/Bobbs-Merrill Company, Inc.
Original Price: 79¢   Value: $15.00 – 25.00

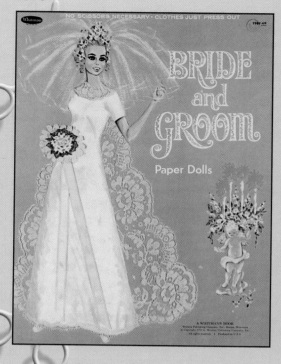

Bride and Groom   Year: 1970   #1989

Bride and groom paper dolls have always been a hit. Many little girls fantasize about their weddings. Paper dolls and imagination allow these girls to play out their dreams.

In this set, you will find four die-cut dolls, the bride, groom, maid of honor, and bridesmaid, along with a 28-piece punch-out wardrobe with tabs. The clothing includes a wedding dress, a veil, a tuxedo, and dresses for the maid of honor and bridesmaid.

Publisher: Whitman Book/Western
Original Price: 69¢   **Value: $15.00 – 25.00**

Mother and Daughter   Year: 1970   #4243

Jeanne Voelz drew this fabulous set. It incorporates two mother and daughter sets into one. One set of dolls and clothing comes from set #6078, published in 1963, and reflects a mother, daughter, and fashions from the 1960s.

A more contemporary set of dolls reflects styles from the 1970s.

The complete set comes with four die-cut dolls, two Mothers and two Daughters, and three pages of clothing for each fashion era; there are 46 outfits and hats to cut out.

Publisher: Saalfield
Original Price: 39¢   **Value: $20.00 – 55.00**

Barbie and Ken Dolls   Year: 1970   #1976

Another wonderful Barbie doll and Ken doll set, this one represents the Twist N' Turn Barbie doll and the Talking Ken doll.

There are two die-cut dolls, Barbie doll and Ken doll, along with 31 mod punch-out outfits with tabs.

A poster of Barbie doll and Ken doll completes the set.

Publisher: Whitman Book/Western/Mattel
Original Price: 69¢   Value: $25.00 – 45.00

Flatsy   **Year: 1970**   **#1994**

This paper doll set was published in 1970 and represents the popular Flatsy dolls by Ideal. They came with brightly colored hair and flat bodies, and were packaged in a picture frame. Each doll had a set of special accessories.

The complete set includes eight die-cut Flatsys, Dewie, Filly, Sandy, Cookie, Nancy, Rally, Bonnie, and Candy, along with 72 cut-out outfits and hats with tabs.

Publisher: Whitman Book/Western/Ideal Toy Corporation
Original Price: 69¢   Value: $20.00 – 35.00

Playmates   **Year: 1970**   **#1214**

This set is a reprint of set #4214. The cover on both sets is drawn by Dorothy Girder. However, the inside of the book originates from a foreign set.

This set includes four die-cut dolls, Christine, Paul, Robert, and Josephine, along with 50 cut-out outfits and accessories with tabs.

Publisher: Saalfield
Original Price: 39¢   **Value: $10.00 – 20.00**

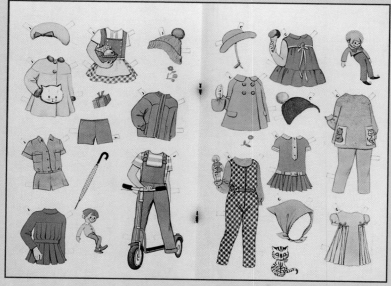

Babykins   **Year: 1970**   **#1982**

Babykins was one of my childhood treasures, and is very hard to find in excellent condition today.

This set includes two 9" die-cut babies, Ginny and Amy, along with 23 punch-out outfits, bonnets, and bibs. Ginny's outfits have pink tabs, and Amy's have yellow tabs.

Publisher: Whitman Book/Western
Original Price: 69¢   Value: $20.00 – 40.00

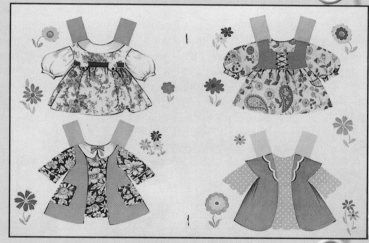

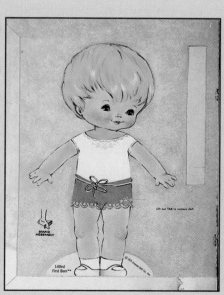

Littlest First Born   **Year: 1971**   **#1964**

Littlest First Born was drawn by Jack and Louise Myers and includes one 10" die-cut baby, Littlest First Born, with an 11-piece wardrobe to cut out. The folder has a handy pouch to carry the doll and clothes in.

Publisher: Whitman Book/Western/Uneeda
     Doll Co., Inc.
Original Price: 39¢   Value: $10.00 – 20.00

Courtesy of Edna Corbett

Baby Go Bye Bye   Year: 1971   #1988

How cute were the dolls put out by Mattel? Here is another little cutie? She came with big blue eyes, a round nose, and the happiest little upturned smile that showed off her two top teeth. Her most notable feature was her hairdo, which consisted of two little buns on each side. This 11" doll fit perfectly into her pink, four-wheeled, bumpety buggy.

The Baby Go Bye Bye paper doll set was drawn by Ruth Ruhman and includes one die-cut paper doll, her die-cut Bumpety Buggy to press out and assemble, and 39 press-out outfits and accessories, including sunglasses. Her folder doubled as a carry tote.

Publisher: Whitman Book/Western/Mattel, Inc.
Original Price: 69¢   Value: $10.00 – 20.00

Baby Tender Love   Year: 1971   #1960

Baby Tender Love was a popular line for Mattel during the 1970s. She was produced in several versions from the early-to-late 1970s, ranging from 11½ " to 19" high and with various expressions and hairstyles. There was a talking Baby Tender Love and even a Baby Brother Tender Love, along with an available line of outfits and accessories. Little girls were offered an assortment of Baby Tender Loves.

The paper dolls followed the same trend by offering many sets of Baby Tender Love paper dolls for little girls to enjoy.

In this set, you will find one die-cut toddler, Baby Tender Love, along with 25 outfits and accessories to cut out. The folder has a handy pocket to store your paper doll set in when it is not in use.

Publisher: Whitman/Western/Mattel, Inc.
Original Price: 39¢   **Value: $15.00 – 20.00**

Sleepy Doll   Year: 1971   #R4131

Sleepy Doll paper doll set is unique, because there is a sliding tab on the back of the doll's head; when the tab is pulled up or down, the doll's eyes open or close. This adorable Sleepy Doll set comes with one die-cut doll, Sleepy Doll, along with an 18-piece punch-out wardrobe and animal toy collection. The pieces are made of lightweight cardboard and have tabs.

Publisher: Saalfield/Horsman
Original Price: unknown   **Value: $15.00 – 25.00**

Baby Nancy   **Year: 1971**   **#4784**

Baby Nancy has a colorful history. It was created in the late 1960s, by an African American–owned company named Shindana (Swahili for *competitor*). This company was set up by Mattel, and it introduced many toys that had a multicultural theme. Baby Nancy has authentic features, wonderful kinky pony tails with pink bows, and a beautiful sleeveless sundress with white daisies. There is also a version of Baby Nancy with a natural hairdo. Baby Nancy's paper doll set has the same attention to detail that the doll itself has, with one 9½" statuette doll, Nancy, and a 23-piece punch-out wardrobe with tabs.

Publisher: Whitman/Western/Operation Bootstrap, Inc.
Original Price: unknown   **Value: $15.00 – 25.00**

Valerie   Year: 1971   #1965

Valerie is another doll in Mattel's long line of popular dolls, and it is quite rare to find her in mint condition. She has the same adorable head mold as Baby Small Talk. Valerie has a toddler body, though, and she can grow pretty hair. She was originally dressed in a beautiful yellow and white dress, and wore a big yellow bow in her hair.

Her paper doll set includes one die-cut toddler, Valerie, with three pop-out hair variations. One look is hair with curlers in, another is medium-length hair, and still another is hair that flows to the floor. There are 26 cut-out outfits and accessories with tabs.

Publisher: Whitman Book/Western/Mattel, Inc.
Original Price: 39c   Value: $12.00 – 20.00

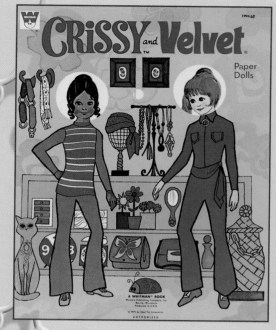

Crissy and Velvet   Year: 1971   #1996

Crissy made her debut in 1969 and was sold by the Ideal Toy Corporation though 1974.

This 18" beautiful redhead had pretty growing hair, and by pushing a button on her tummy and tugging on her hair, a child could make it flow down to her ankles. Turning the knob on her back would make her hair retreat back into her head, allowing little girls to decide what length Crissy's hair would be. (After the first year, Crissy's hair length changed to just above her knees.)

Crissy was so popular that a series of family and friends was created. Velvet, Crissy's cousin, arrived on the scene in 1970. She was 15" tall, with blonde hair and blue eyes. She also came in a beautiful African American version, which is hard to find today.

Many paper doll sets came from these wonderful dolls, including this set drawn by Leon Jason.

The set features two die-cut dolls, Crissy and African American Velvet. The set is unique, because there is a pinwheel with drawings of hairstyles for Crissy and Velvet. The wheel attaches to the front cover, allowing little girls to change Crissy and Velvet's hair styles with a spin of the wheel. There are 37 outfits and accessories to punch-out. Crissy's outfits have blue tabs, and Velvet's outfits have pink tabs.

Publisher: Whitman Book/Western/Ideal Toy Corporation
Original Price: 69¢   Value: $20.00 – 35.00

Crissy Magic Paper Doll   Year: 1971   #4774

This set of Crissy magic paper dolls comes with one 9½" statuette doll and a 48-piece magic stay-on wardrobe to cut out. Included is one plastic stand and a pair of scissors. There is more information about Crissy on the preceding page.

Publisher: Whitman/Western/Ideal Toy Company
Original Price: unknown   Value: $15.00 – 25.00

Dollikin   Year: 1971   #4776

Dollikin was Uneeda's fashion doll, and was perhaps made to compete with the popular Barbie, Tammy, and other fashion dolls of this time.

Dollikin was an 11½", fully possible doll with long straight hair that came in a variety of colors. She had her own clothing line that reflected the current fashion styles of the era.

The Dollikin paper doll set includes one 9½" statuette doll and a 32-piece cut-out wardrobe similar to the one for the Crissy set above. A plastic doll stand and a pair of scissors complete the set.

Publisher: Whitman/Western/Uneeda
Original Price: unknown   Value: $15.00 – 25.00

Dollikin   Year: 1971   #1958

Here is another set of Dollikins paper dolls. Even though this set and set #4776 share the same name, they are different in every way. This set comes in a folder as opposed to the box in set #4776. The die-cut doll in this set has a more whimsical look about her than the one in set #4776. Her long blonde ponytail looks like it's blowing in the wind. There is a 21-piece wardrobe to cut out that is completely different than the one in set #4776.

Publisher: Whitman Book/Western/Uneeda
Original Price: 39¢   Value: $15.00 – 25.00

Betsy McCall   Year: 1971   #4744

The character of Betsy McCall was first introduced in *McCall's Magazine* in May 1951. *McCall's* had a series of storylines about Betsy and her fashions that ran for 44 years. Because of Betsy popularity, dolls were produced by Ideal and other toy companies. She enjoyed a long stretch of popularity and is still well loved by some even today.

This boxed set of Betsy McCall includes one 9½" statuette doll, Betsy, along with a 26-piece wardrobe to punch out. A plastic stand is included.

Publisher: Whitman/Western/The McCall Publishing Company
Original Price: unknown   Value: $15.00 – 26.00

Betsy McCall   **Year: 1971**   **#1969**

Neva Schultz drew this beautiful set that has Betsy McCall's profile on the cover. This large book has one 11½" die-cut doll, Betsy McCall, and 27 brightly colored punch-out outfits and accessories with tabs. In this set, Betsy and her wardrobe do not resemble those in Betsy McCall set #4744 featured on the opposite page.

Publisher: Whitman/Western/The McCall Publishing Company.
Original Price: 39¢   Value: $15.00 – 25.00

Courtesy of Edna Corbett

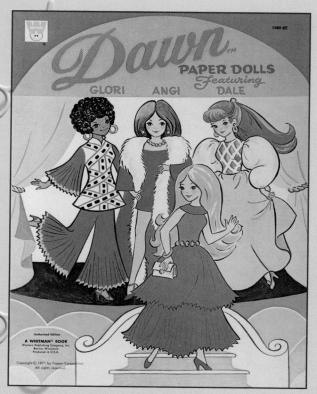

Dawn   Year: 1971

In 1970, Topper introduced Dawn. She was 6½" small, and had beautifully painted features, rooted hair, and eyelashes. Dawn and her friends Glori, Angie, and Dale were supermodels in the world of high fashion. The first year, Topper introduced more then 40 glamourous outfits that added to Dawn and her friends' huge success. As Dawn's popularity grew, new friends and outfits were added to the doll line.

This Dawn paper dolls set is based on Dawn and three of her friends, and includes four die-cut dolls, Dawn, Glori, Dale, and Angie, along with 44 outfits and hats to punch out. The clothing duplicates Dawn's and her friends' original wardrobes. There is a fabulous fashion stage so the doll can to have their own fashion show, and the dolls can be moved to different positions on the stage.

Publisher: Whitman Book/Western/Topper Corporation
Original Price: 39¢   Value: $20.00 – 35.00

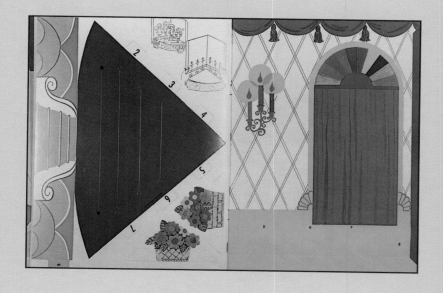

Playhouse Kiddles   Year: 1971   #1921

In 1970, Mattel introduced a new series of Liddle Kiddle cuties, called Playhouse Kiddles. They were 3½" tall and had fully posable bodies. There were three different Playhouse Kiddles: Cookin' Kiddle, Pretty-Parlor, and Good-Night Kiddle,

These Kiddles may look familiar to you, because they were made with the same head mold as the Skediddle Kiddles. Each Playhouse Kiddle came with her own room setting and with a set of snap-happy furniture. When all three Kiddles were collected, their playrooms could stack on top of one another to create a Liddle Kiddle playhouse, complete with a living room, kitchen, and bedroom.

Included in this Playhouse Kiddles set are three die-cut Kiddle dolls, Pretty Parlor, Good-Night Kiddles, and Cookin' Kiddle, and a playhouse and furniture set to press out and assemble.

Publisher: Whitman Book/Western/Mattel, Inc.
Original Price: 39¢   Value: $20.00 – 35.00

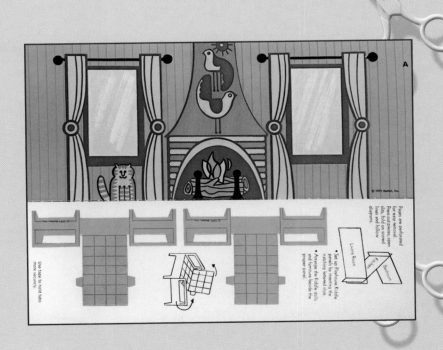

Kopy Kate   Year: 1971   #4618

Kopy Kate is an interactive set of paper dolls, drawn by Neva Schultz, that allows little girls to copy and color Kate. The directions instruct one (in a nutshell) to first remove the staples on the inside page, press out the dolls and bend them forward face-to-face at the center, which allows Kate to stand, and then fit an outfit on Dress Me Kate and color a fashion to match on Color Me Kate. The magic color would wipe off the doll with a tissue, so little girls could design new outfits repeatedly for Color Me Kate, having hours of fun.

This set includes two die-cut dolls, Color Me Kate and Dress Me Kate, along with 30 punch-out outfits for Dress Me Kate.

Outfits stay on with tabs.

Publisher: Whitman Book/Western
Original Price: 69¢   Value: $12.00 – 20.00

Dollies Go 'Round the World   Year: 1971   #4533

This delightful set drawn by Leon Jason features three die-cut dolls. Throughout the book, you will find 46 colorful outfits representing 24 countries, such as thoses of West Africa, Sweden, Burma, Israel, Spain, and Japan, to name a few. Clothes for each doll have color tabs to match the color of the doll's stand.

Publisher: Lowe
Original Price: 49¢   **Value: $10.00 – 20.00**

My Very Best Friend   Year: 1971   #4762

Do you remember your first best friend? I used to climb the fence to play with my best friend, even if we could only play for ten minutes. We spent hours playing together with only our paper dolls and our imaginations. We would role play and giggle until one of our moms told us to "quiet down." This adorable set, drawn by Tonda Rae Nalle, brings back all those wonderful memories. In this set, you will find Betsy and Tina, two statuette, big-eyed little girls that are best friends. A 7-piece magic stay-on wardrobe to cut out is included, as are plastic stands and a pair of scissors.

Publisher: Whitman/Western
Original Price: unknown   **Value: $10.00 –18.00**

Patchwork   Year: 1971   #3403A

This set drawn by Elizabeth Tedder originally came from set #6059. In the set, you will find three die-cut models named Mini Model Heather, Tini Model Anne, and Little Model Jill. There are nine punch-out outfits and accessories made of lightweight cardboard and 54 cut-out outfits and accessories to color; all outfits have tabs. The tabs on the outfits have the first initial of the doll that the outfit belongs to.

Publisher: Saalfield
Original Price: 89¢   Value: $10.00 – 15.00

Finger Dings   Year: 1971   #1993

These kickin' cuties came on the scene in 1969 and were popular through the early 1970s. A child could slip her fingers into their tights and let her fingers to do the walking, running, skating, or whatever else her heart desired. Finger Dings came with a head, torso, arms, and the outfits; the child's fingers provided the legs for the doll.

This paper doll set followed the spirit of the Remco dolls by providing a stand on each leg that looped around to fit the fingers, and allowed the three die-cut dolls, Millie Mod, Betty Ballerina, and Sally the Ice Skater, to walk forward or backward. There are 67 outfits and accessories to punch out. Each outfit has a colored tab to match a colored dot on a doll's stand. In addition, to complete the set, there are three Finger Dings doll scenes to punch out and stand up.

Publisher: Whitman/Western/Remco
Original Price: 69¢   Value: $10.00 – 18.00

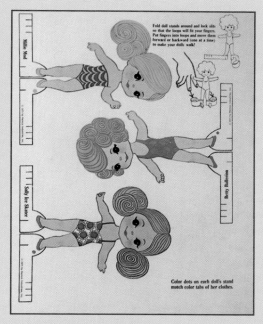

Bedknobs and Broomsticks   Year: 1971   #1999

This set of paper dolls is based on the endearing Walt Disney classic *Bedknobs and Broomsticks*. The movie premiered in December of 1971 and starred a young Angela Lansbury and David Tomlinson. The movie mixed visual effects with live action and animation, and created a family favorite. The plot was similar to that of *Mary Poppins*, because the story involved two orphan children that were on an adventure with two adults that were not their parents. *Bedknobs and Broomsticks* was nominated for five Oscars and won for Best Visual Effects. Later, Angela Lansbury won a Golden Globe for Best Motion Picture Actress in a Musical or Comedy.

This delightful set of paper dolls includes five die-cut dolls, Professor Emelius Brown (David Tomlinson), Miss Price (Angela Lansbury), Carrie (Cindy O'Callaghan), Charlie (Ian Weighill), and Paul (Roy Snart). The set also includes 40 outfits and hats to punch out. The color tabs on the outfits coordinate with each doll. The folder doubles as a pop-out of a London village.

Publisher: Whitman/Western
Original Price: 69¢   **Value: $35.00 – 55.00**
Courtesy of Edna Corbett

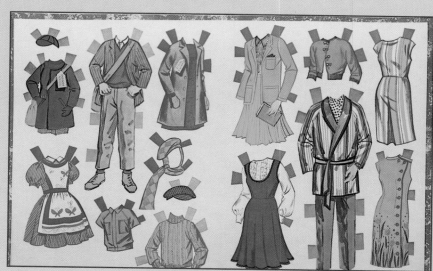

Nancy   Year: 1971   #1971

Nancy was created by Ernie Bushmile and made her debut in a newspaper comic strip in 1935. She started out with a small part and became so popular she wound up taking over the series. In 1971, Nancy had a brief encounter with television. She was in one segment of an *Archie* cartoon, and she never made it on television again.

In this Nancy paper doll set, you will find one 10" die-cut doll, Nancy, along with a 16-piece wardrobe that includes her ever-popular black, red, and white dress. Her outfits have tabs and press out.

Publisher: Whitman Book/Western/United Features Syndicate, Inc.
Original Price: 39¢   Value: $15.00 – 22.00

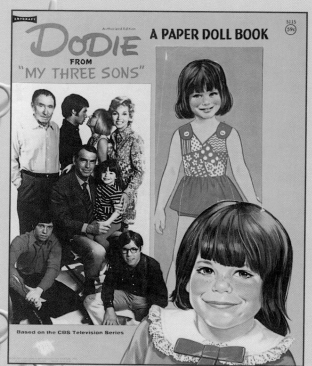

Dodie **Year: 1971** **#5115**

My Three Sons enjoyed 392 episodes (12 seasons) and aired from 1960 to 1972. It was one of the longest running sitcoms of all time.

In the 1969/1970 season, Steve Douglas (Fred MacMurray) fell in love with his son Ernie's (Barry Livingston) English teacher, Barbara Harper (Beverly Garland). They married, and Barbara's freckle-faced five-year-old daughter, Dodie (Dawn Lyn), joined the Douglas family. She was on the show from 1969 to 1972. As with most popular television characters, a set of paper dolls was modeled after her.

The complete Dodie set features two die-cut dolls, both Dodie, along with her dolly. On the back cover you will find a punch-out Dodie holding her doll. There are 25 punch-out outfits and hats for Dodie and her dolly, with tabs, and made of lightweight cardboard.

Publisher: Artcraft/Columbia Pictures Industries, Inc.
Original Price: 59¢ **Value: $25.00 – 45.00**

The Partridge Family   Year: 1971   #5143

In the fall of 1970, prime-time television introduced *The Partridge Family*. I remember sitting in front of my television every Friday night to watch this groovy family tour on their psychedelic bus and perform their favorite hits.

Shirley Jones was the star of the show and played Shirley, the hippest mom around. Her son Keith (David Cassidy) was the heart-throb of young girls everywhere (including me). There was Danny (Danny Bonaduce), who every week had a new money-making endeavor, and Laurie (Susan Dey), who was beautiful and represented the modern young woman of that time. The youngest of the group, Chris and Tracy, had minor roles in the show; Chris played drums and Tracy played tambourine. We must not forget Reuben Kincaid (Dave Madden), the family friend and manager. He was always being out-smarted by Danny. The Partridge Family also released many hit records in this era, including "I Think I Love You," perhaps its most popular hit. Because of the popularity of the Partridge Family, lunch boxes, toys, and paper dolls were produced and were met with instant popularity. Many sets of paper dolls based on this very popular show came on the scene.

The complete set features six die-cut dolls, Keith, Danny, Laurie, Chris, Tracy, and Shirley. On the back cover, there is punch-out of Keith playing his guitar. A 34-piece punch-out wardrobe, with tabs and made of lightweight cardboard, completes this set.

Publisher: Artcraft/Columbia Pictures Industries, Inc.
Original Price: 59¢   Value: $35.00 – 55.00

Nanny and the Professor   Year: 1970/1971   #5114

"Soft and sweet, wise and wonderful, oooh, our mystical, magical Nanny."

That was the opening line from the theme song for *Nanny and the Professor*, which aired as part of the Friday night lineup on ABC. The show was only on a year; however, it is a favorite of Baby Boomers.

A little bit of faith and love describes this television sitcom. *Nanny and the Professor* showed the softer side of family virtues. Juliet Mills was Phoebe Figalilly, better known as Nanny. One day, Nanny showed up on the doorstep of widower Professor Harold Everett (played by Richard Long) to be the nanny of his three children, Hal (David Doremus), Butch (Trent Lehman), and Prudence (Kim Richards). She instantly won their hearts. Each week, the show featured Nanny doing mystical, magical things. She had a fantastic ability to communicate with animals and to read minds. The children were constantly amazed by the things Nanny did and wondered, "Is it love or is it magic?" (This was the ending line of the theme song.)

This is one of three sets of paper dolls based on this television show. The complete set has five die-cut dolls, Nanny, Professor Everett, Hal, Butch, and Prudence, along with Waldo, the family dog. There is a 32-piece punch-out wardrobe made of lightweight cardboard. Tabs help the clothing stay on the dolls.

Note: This paper doll set is dated "1970" and "1971."

Publisher: Artcraft/Twentieth Century Fox Corporation
Original Price: 59¢   Value: $30.00 – 50.00

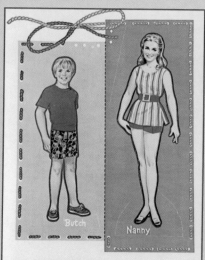

Magic Mary **Year: 1971** **#4010-1**

On this page are two of the 1970s versions of Milton Bradley's Magic Mary magnetic paper dolls. You can see that Mary has changed with the times; the sets reflects the hairstyles and clothing of the era.

This first set is the 1971 version, and it has one heavyweight statuette doll with a 15-piece wardrobe to cut out, along with magnets to tape on the backs of the outfits. The clothes stay on because the doll is magnetic.

Publisher: Milton Bradley Company
Original Price: unknown   **Value: $10.00 – 25.00**

1972

Magic Mary **Year: 1972** **#4010-1**

The box cover of the 1972 version features Mary in a different outfit from the one for the set above. The box cover is also smaller; however, Mary and her 15-piece wardrobe are identical to the 1971 set.

Publisher: Milton Bradley Company
Original Price: unknown   **Value: $10.00 – 25.00**

Magic Mary Ann   Year: 1972   #4010-2

If I were to guess, I would say that this Magic Mary Ann resembles a young girl at the age of about 12 or13 years old. She has a girl next door look with her long red hair, strawberry-colored cheeks, and freckles.

Magic Mary Ann comes with one heavyweight cardboard doll, Mary Ann, and 15 outfits and accessories to cut out. As with all Magic Mary sets, magnets for her clothing are included.

Publisher: Milton Bradley
Original Price: unknown   **Value: $10.00 – 25.00**

Magic Mary Lou   Year: 1972   #4010-4

The Magic Mary Lou set features a teenage girl and has a more mature wardrobe than the Magic Mary sets on the preceding page. This set also duplicates the fashion trends of this era, with brightly colored mod outfits.

Included in this set is one brunette statuette doll, Mary Lou, made of heavyweight cardboard. Also included is a 15-piece wardrobe to cut out. Like all of the previous Magic Mary sets, this one comes with magnets to tape on the back of the clothing pieces.

Publisher: Milton Bradley Company
Original Price: unknown   **Value: $10.00 – 25.00**

Rock Flowers   Year: 1972   #1956

Rock Flowers came rockin' on the scene in 1970, and were made by Mattel. They were 6½", and fully posable because each had a wire running throughout its body. They had mod rockin' outfits and their own 45 rpm record with an attachment that the dolls could be placed into, allowing the rockers to spin/dance around with the record as it played. The original three dolls were Heather, Lilac, and Rosemary Rock Flower. Later, more dolls were added to the line.

This Rockn' paper doll set includes three die-cut dolls, Rosemary, Heather, and Lilac, along with 45 mod outfits reflecting those 1970s fashions. The wardrobe is made to cut out and has tabs. The back of the folder has a three-colored disk that serves as a stage. The dolls slip into the colored disk by means of tabs on their bases. The Rock Flowers can then be positioned to give a concert.

Publisher: Whitman Book/Western/Mattel
Original Price: 39¢   Value: $8.00 – 15.00

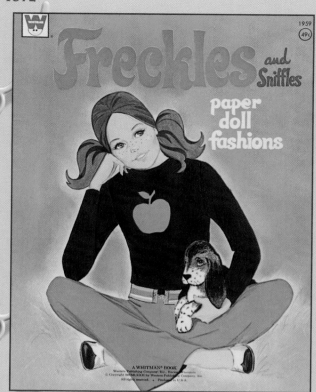

Freckles and Sniffles   **Year: 1972**   **#1959**

Neva Schultz drew a delightful set that includes one 10" die-cut doll, Freckles, and one cut-out doll, Sniffles. There are 31 cut-out outfits and accessories with tabs.

Publisher: Whitman Book/Western
Original Price: 49¢   Value: $8.00 – 15.00

Amy Jo   Year: 1972   #4231

Amy Jo, drawn by Jeanne Voelz, features one 13" die-cut doll, Amy Jo, along with her dolly and a highchair and cradle that dolly can fit into. Amy Jo and Dolly have 13 cut-out outfits and accessories with tabs. This set was also sold as #5231.

Publisher: Saalfield
Original Price: 39¢   **Value: $15.00 – 25.00**

Holly   Year: 1972   #2088

Holly is similar in her look to Amy Jo. However, Holly's artist was Irene Geiger. Holly, like Amy Jo, is a 13" die-cut doll. However, Holly's wardrobe is completely different than Amy Jo's. Saalfield also published this set in 1972 as sets #4232 and #5232. There are 23 cut-out outfits and accessories with tabs.

Publisher: Rand McNally & Company
Original Price: 98¢   Value: $15.00 – 25.00

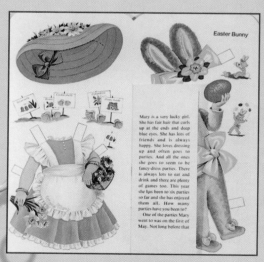

Mary and the Fancy-dress Parties
Year: 1972   No number

Mary is also a 13" die-cut doll and was drawn by Elizabeth Tedder. There are 13 outfits and accessories, Mary's doll, and five die-cut flowers from Mary's garden that fit together and stand upright. In addition, you will find a story in the middle of the book about Mary and her fancy-dress parties. Saalfield also published this set in 1972, under the name of Mary, Mary Quite Contrary, as sets #4230 and #5230.

Publisher: Award Publications Limited/Rand McNally
& Company
Original Price: unknown   Value: $10.00 – 25.00

Ballet Paper Doll   Year: 1972   #4233

Here is the last in the series of these similar-looking 13" dolls. Nan Pollard drew this adorable Betsy Ballerina. She comes with 21 cut-out costumes with tabs. Betsy also has her own stage and light setting, with a marquee that says, "Appearing Tonight/Betsy the Little Ballerina/in/Swan Lake/Curtain at 8:00."

Publisher: Saalfield/Artcraft
Original Price: 39¢   Value: $15.00 – 25.00

Bride   **Year: 1972**   **#1989**

It is exciting to go through these bride paper doll books to see the changes in wedding dress styles through the years.

In this bride paper doll set, you will find five die-cut dolls: the bride, groom, two bridesmaids, and the flower girl. There is also a 33-piece punch-out wardrobe that includes a 1970s-style wedding dress and a pin-striped tuxedo with bell-bottom pants. Clothing has colored tabs to match the colored dots on the dolls' stands. The folder doubles as a carry tote when the folder is flipped inside out and the handles are pulled up.

Publisher: Whitman/Western
Original Price: 69¢   Value: $15.00 – 25.00

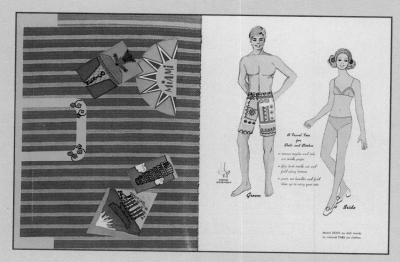

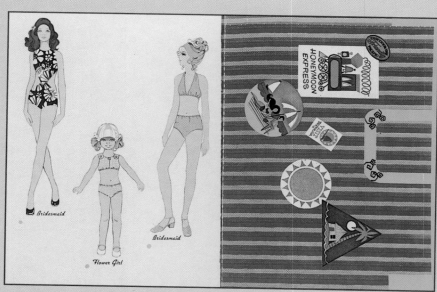

Malibu Barbie Doll Sun Set   Year: 1972   #1994

Malibu Barbie doll and friends inspired this paper doll set. Malibu Barbie doll came on the scene in 1971. She was so popular that virtually every one of Barbie doll's friends followed suit and became part of the Malibu series of dolls.

Malibu Barbie doll had the look of a suntanned California surfer chick, with her bleached blonde hair and brown sun-kissed skin.

This sunny set of paper dolls comes with four die-cut dolls, Barbie, Ken, Francie, and Skipper dolls, along with a 33-piece punch-out California wardrobe with tabs. The colored tabs match the base of the doll that the outfit belongs to.

Publisher: Whitman/Western Mattel, Inc.
Original Price: 69¢   Value: $15.00 – 30.00

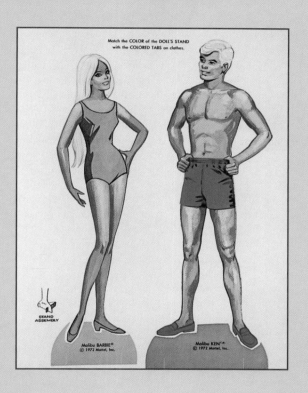

Malibu P.J. Magic Paper Doll   **Year: 1972**   **#4718/7418**

P.J. doll is another Malibu family member, and her boxed set includes one 9½" statuette doll, P.J. doll, along with a 53-piece press-out, magic stay-on wardrobe.

Publisher: Whitman/Western/Mattel
Original Price: unknown   **Value: $15.00 – 25.00**

Pos'n' Barbie Doll   **Year: 1972**   **#1975**

Pos'n' Barbie doll paper doll fashions are based primarily on Barbie doll's Best Buy fashion line, with favorites such as Picture Me Pretty, Glowin' Gold, and Perfect Purple, to name a few.

The complete set of Pos'n' Barbie doll features one die-cut Barbie doll and 38 punch-out outfits and accessories with tabs.

Publisher: Whitman/Western/ Mattel
Original Price: 39¢   **Value: $20.00 – 35.00**

1973

Hi! I'm Skipper   **Year: 1973**   **#1969**

This Skipper set features a large picture of the Pose 'n' Play Skipper doll on the cover and includes one die-cut Skipper doll and 38 punch-out outfits and accessories, all with tabs.

Publisher: Whitman/Western/Mattel
Original Price: 39¢   Value: $15.00 – 25.00

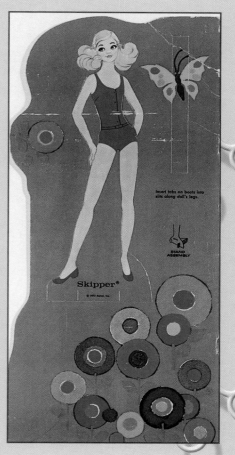

Francie Doll with Growin' Pretty Hair   Year: 1973   #1982

Francie doll entered into the 1970s with this stylin' set that features four different hairdos and fancy 1970s fashions.

In this set, you will find one die-cut doll with four different faces and hairstyles that attach by a tab that fits into a slit in the doll's body and covers the original face with a new one. There are approximately 38 punch-out outfits, accessories, and hair bows with tabs.

Publisher: Whitman/Western/Mattel
Original Price: 69¢   Value: $20.00 – 35.00

Quick Curl Barbie Doll   Year: 1973   #1984

In this set, the hairstyles go on the dolls differently than those in the above set. This set uses tabs on the wigs to hold them on the dolls. There are four die-cut dolls featured, Barbie, Francie, Kelley, and Skipper dolls, and eight wigs, all with different styles and colors. The set comes with six pages of outfits and accessories to punch out. Colored tabs on the outfits match colored dots on the dolls' bases.

Publisher: Whitman/Western/Mattel
Original Price: 79¢   Value: $20.00 – 35.00

Malibu Francie Doll   Year: 1973   #1955

This set is based on Mattel's highly successful series of dolls called Malibu Barbie and Friends. These dolls came with beach-tanned skin and blonde hair that gave them that California look. This Malibu Francie doll set features one die-cut doll and 37 cut-out outfits and accessories with tabs.

Publisher: Whitman/Western/Mattel
Original Price: 59¢   Value: $10.00 – 20.00

Courtesy of Edna Corbett

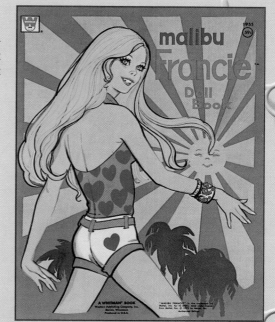

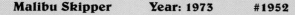

Malibu Skipper   Year: 1973   #1952

Here in this set we have another member of the Malibu family, Skipper doll. She is 10½" tall and larger than the other paper dolls in the Malibu series.

The complete paper doll set includes one die-cut Skipper doll, along with 29 cut-out outfits and accessories with tabs.

Publisher: Whitman/Western/Mattel
Original Price: 59¢   Value: $10.00 – 25.00

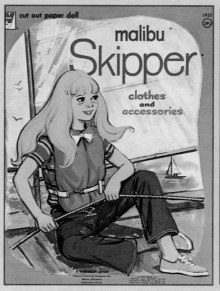

Barbie Doll's Boutique   **Year: 1973**   **#1954**

Because of Barbie doll's popularity in the 1960s and 1970s, there were many sets published that consisted of likenesses of the original dolls and clothing. However, some sets carried Barbie doll's name, but did not duplicate the original dolls or clothing line.

This is a beautifully illustrated set, but does not duplicate any of Barbie doll's original wardrobe pieces. The set features one die-cut Barbie doll and 29 cut-out outfits and accessories with tabs.

Publisher: Whitman Book/Western/Mattel
Original Price: 49¢   Value: $15.00 – 30.00
Courtesy of Edna Corbett

Dotti West   **Year: 1973**   **No number**

Dottie West was one of the most successful and controversial performers in country music. Despite a traumatic childhood, Dotty West started appearing on a local radio station when she was almost 13. In 1959, after numerous trips to Nashville to land a record deal, she was finally offered a contract. In the 1960s, '70s, and '80s, Dottie put out chart toppers and sold millions of records. Dottie was the first female artist to win a Grammy, for the hit single "Here Comes My Baby," which lead to an invite to join the Grand Ole Opry.

In 1991, the car Dottie was riding in on her way to an appearance at the Grand Ole Opry lost control. The singer died a couple of days later from injuries sustained in the crash.

This paper doll set features two die-cut dolls, both Dottie, one with short hair and one with long. There are 17 cut-out outfits and accessories with tabs, including a guitar, a microphone, a record album, and two wigs.

Publisher: Estelle Ansley Worrell
Original Price: $2.00   **Value: $8.00 – 16.00**

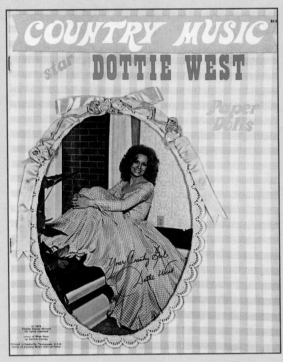

Lost Horizon   Year: 1973   #5112

This paper doll set, drawn by Dorothy Grider, comes from the 1973 musical fantasy remake of Frank Capra's classic movie *Lost Horizon*, by Columbia Pictures. In this set, you will find seven die-cut dolls: Catherine, Richard, Sally, Harry, Maria, Sam, and Chang. There are 22 punch-out outfits, with tabs and made of medium-weight cardboard.

Publisher: Saalfield/ArtCraft/Columbia Pictures
Original Price: 59¢   Value: $35.00 – 55.00

The Brady Bunch   **Year: 1973**   **#1976**

This set, drawn by Leon Jason, is based on the television show *The Brady Bunch,* which aired from 1969 to 1974. The show was on the cutting edge for its time, featuring a mother with three daughters who marries a man with three sons. The first year, the story centered around family conflicts and resolutions, dealing with the perils of blending two families. The next year, the show focused more on the wholesome family living common to middle-class folks who lived in the 'burbs.

The list of characters included Mike (Robert Reed), Carol (Florence Henderson), Marcia (Maureen McCormick), Jan (Eve Plumb) Cindy (Susan Olsen), Greg (Barry Williams), Peter (Christopher Knight), Bobby (Mike Lookinland), and — who could forget that nutty housekeeper? — Alice (Ann B. Davis). The show's ratings never made the top 25 during its original run. However, the reruns attracted millions of new viewers and are still popular today.

In this very Brady paper doll set, you will find six die-cut dolls, Mr. Brady, Mrs. Brady, Greg, Marcia, Jan, and Cindy, along with a 36-piece wardrobe to press out. The colored tabs on the clothes match a colored dot on a doll's stand.

Publisher: Whitman Book/Western Paramount Pictures Corporation
Original Price: 69¢   Value: $40.00 – 75.00

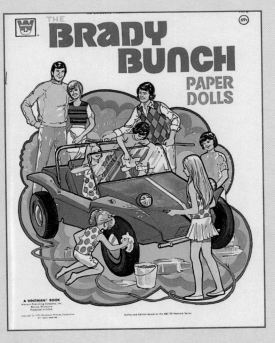

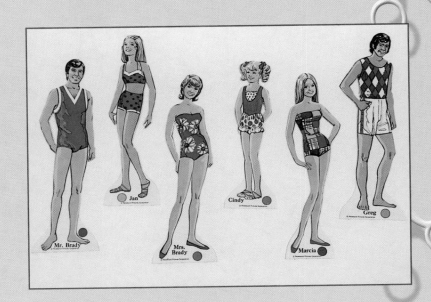

Mary Poppins   **Year: 1973**   **#1977**

This charming set features the characters in Walt Disney's *Mary Poppins*. It includes four die-cut dolls, Bert (Dick Van Dyke), Mary Poppins (Julie Andrews), and the two children Mary cares for, Michael and Jane. By removing the staples and turning the folder inside out, you create a magic tote bag to carry your dolls and clothes in. The set comes with 43 punch-out outfits and hats.

Note: Read more about Mary Poppins in the 1960s chapter.

Publisher: Whitman/Western/Walt Disney Productions
Original Price: 69¢   **Value: $25.00 – 45.00**

Courtesy of Edna Corbett

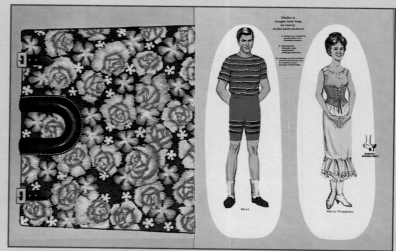

Mary Poppins   Year: 1973   #1967

    Mary Poppins went solo in this beautifully illustrated set of paper dolls. The complete set features one die-cut doll and 27 press-out outfits and accessories with tabs.
    Note: Read more about about Mary Poppins in the 1960s chapter.

Publisher: Whitman/Western/Walt Disney Productions
Original Price: 39¢   Value: $25.00 – 45.00

Courtesy of Edna Corbett

Baby Alive   **Year: 1973/1975**   **#1992**

Leon Jason drew this darling Baby Alive set. It was based on the vinyl doll produced by Kenner Products, the hightest selling doll of 1973. This little blonde baby doll, with her puffy cheeks, round little nose, and rosebud lips, had a battery-powered mechanism that allowed her mouth and nose to move when she was eating (much like Mattel's 1967 doll, Baby's Hungry). She came with colored food powder that little girls could mix with water and spoon into her mouth. They got to watch her eat, and they eventually had the task of cleaning up a messy diaper. Baby Alive was reissued by Kenner in 1990.

This paper doll set features one die-cut doll, Baby Alive, along with 21 outfits and accessories with tabs. Baby Alive comes with her own tote that holds her clothing when not in use.

Publisher: Whitman Book/Western/Kenner/General Mills
Original Price: 39¢   Value: $25.00 – 45.00

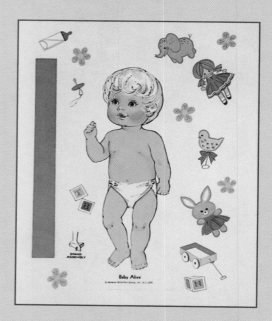

Sweet April   **Year: 1973**   **#1963**

This set was based on the 5½" doll Sweet April, by Remco. She can drink her bottle and cry real tears when a button on her back is pushed. She was sold with accessories such as a stroller, a swing, and lots of outfits.

Later, Miner Industries bought the rights to Remco dolls and produced Sweet April with straight legs instead of the original bent legs.

This set, drawn by Leon Jason, has one die-cut doll, Sweet April. The folder doubles as a swing that you can slide her into. There are over 15 cut-out outfits and hats with tabs.

Publisher: Whitman Book/Western/Remco
Original Price: 39¢   Value: $10.00 – 20.00

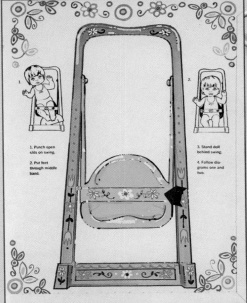

Lazy Dazy   **Year: 1973**   **#1958**

This is another paper doll set drawn by Leon Jason and based on a popular play doll. This original little cutie has a unique floppy body, so she can be placed in a sitting position. However, inside her body is a canister-type mechanism that causes her, when moved ever-so-slightly, to slowly fall down, closing her eyes and landing on her matching pillow as she does.

This complete set comes with one die-cut doll, Lazy Dazy, along with 20 cut-out outfits with tabs.

Publisher: Whitman Book/Western/Ideal
Original Price: 39¢   Value: $10.00 – 20.00

Drowsy   **Year: 1973**   **#1964**

In spite her of somewhat homely appearance, Drowsy won the hearts of millions of little girls when she made her appearance in 1964. She had sleepy eyes and a snuggly plush body design; she was made to look like she wore pink and white polka-dot sleepers. She had a pull string that allowed her to speak 11 toddler phrases. In 1974, some changes were made to Drowsy. Her hands were changed from vinyl to plush, and she went from 16" to 13" tall.

This Drowsy paper doll set features one 9" toddler die-cut doll, Drowsy, along with 24 cut-out outfits and hats with tabs.

Note: Read more about Drowsy in the 1960s chapter.

Publisher: Whitman Book/Western/Mattel
Original Price: 49¢   **Value: $12.00 – 20.00**

Little LuLu Paper Dolls   Year: 1973   #1979

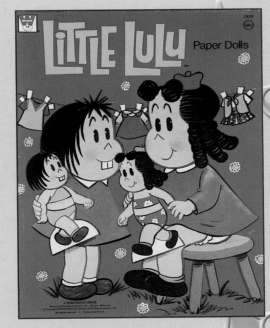

Leon Jason drew this wonderful Little LuLu paper doll set. Little LuLu originated as a magazine cartoon in 1935, and was created by Marjorie {Marge} Henderson Buell. By the mid-1940s, LuLu was a star of comic books and cartoons.
LuLu is very imaginative and can usually outsmart the "fellers," Iggy, Eddie,
Willy, and Alvin. She never starts anything with the boys, she just takes care of
things when they bother her and the girls. Then there is Annie, LuLu's best
friend and Iggy's sister. Younger than LuLu, Annie is always involved in her
friend's escapades when it's time to get even with Tubby and the fellers.

This complete set features two die-cut dolls, Little LuLu and Annie, along
with 25 outfits to press out. There are colored tabs; each matches a dot on the
base of the doll the outfit belongs to. LuLu and Annie also come with two
brightly colored die-cut doll babies to press out and assemble.

Publisher: Whitman/Western
Original Price: 69¢   Value: $15.00 – 25.00

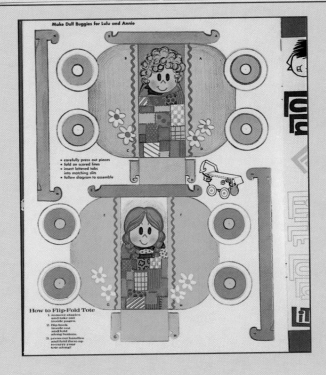

The Sunshine Family   **Year: 1974**   **#4337/7420**

In 1974, Mattel introduced the Sunshine family, father Steve, mother Stephie, and infant Baby Sweets. They were the 1970s version of the Nelson Family. The doll line included activity sets for the family, with themes like camping, bicycling, and growing veggies, to name a few. The Sunshine family was so popular that Mattel later added more family members to the line.

This boxed set comes with three statuette dolls, Steve, Stephie, and Baby Sweets, along with a 41-piece press-out wardrobe with tabs.

Publisher: Whitman Book/Western/Mattel
Original Price: 49¢   Value: $12.00 – 20.00

Tearful Baby Tender Love   **Year: 1974**   **#1957**

Tearful Baby Tender Love is one of many dolls in the Tender Love line by Mattel that was popular from the late 1960s through most of the 1970s. Baby Tender Love is a soft-bodied doll made to feel like a real baby. Because of her popularity, many different version were created to keep up with the demand. I will name just a few: Baby Tender Love, Talking Tender Love, Living Baby Tender Love, Tiny Tender Love, Newborn Tender Love, Sweet Sounds Tender Love, Baby Brother Tender Love, and Tearful Baby Tender Love. She came with her bottle and would drink, wet, and cry real tears.

This set of paper dolls includes one bouncy die-cut toddler, Baby Tender Love, and her little spotted dog. It also comes with a 27-piece cut-out wardrobe with tabs.

Publisher: Whitman Book/Western/Mattel
Original Price: 49¢   Value: $10.00 – 20.00

Baby Tender Love   Year: 1974   #4335/7411

Because of Baby Tender Love's popularity, there were many different paper doll sets of her, made by a variety of artists. This boxed Baby Tender Love set was not drawn by by the same artist that drew the previous sets.

Included is one statuette doll, Baby Tender Love, along with 27 outfits and accessories to press out.

Note: You can read more about Baby Tender Love at the beginning of chapter 2, Paper Dolls without Dates.

Publisher: Whitman Book/Western/Mattel
Original Price: unknown   Value: $8.00 – 20.00

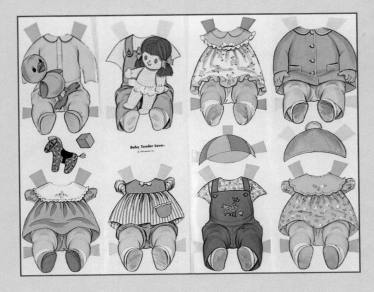

Hi! I'm Valerie   Year: 1974   #1974

This is another paper doll set based on a popular play doll. Valerie is a darling toddler with growing, pretty hair. The set includes one 13" die-cut doll, Valerie, along with 19 press-out outfits and accessories with tabs. Three of the accessories are pretty hairpieces for Valerie to wear.

Note: You can read more about Valerie in the beginning of chapter 2.

Publisher: Whitman Book/Western/Mattel
Original Price: 49¢   Value: $12.00 – 20.00

Peachy & Her Puppets   Year: 1974   #1966

This set was inspired by the taking vinyl doll Peachy & Her Puppets, by Mattel. This unique talking beauty came with four puppets. Peachy spoke three phrases in her own voice and eight phrases in the voiecs of her puppets.

Each puppet had a different size stem, and by inserting a stem into Peachy's hand and pulling her string, her operator could make her say two phrases that intelligently matched the persona of the particular puppet she was holding.

This paper doll set, drawn by Leon Jason, includes one die-cut Peachy doll and her four puppets: a dog, a girl, a clown, and a monkey. There are 30 cut-out outfits and accessories with tabs. Dress Peachy and have her put on a puppet show!

Publisher: Whitman Book/Western/Mattel
Original Price: 49¢   Value: $8.00 – 20.00
Courtesy of Edna Corbett

Wilma & Fred   **Year: 1974**   **#6688**

Yabba Dabba Doo! Who could forget that zany Stone Age family from Bedrock? *The Flintstones* was created by storyboard artist Don Gordon and produced by Hanna Barbera. The show enjoyed six seasons, 1960 – 1966. It was the first and longest (surpassed even now only by *The Simpsons*) animated prime-time television series, and it was big!

Fred (voice: Alan Reed) was the loud mouth in the leopard tunic. Every week he had a new outrageous scheme that went sour, and he would have to answer to his level-headed wife, Wilma (voice: Jean VanderPyl). Wilma was always in control of the situation and had the ultimate say in what Fred could and could not do. Even though Fred liked to think he was the head dude, Wilma ran the show.

When the show ended in 1966, it immediately went into syrdication. Today, we still get to enjoy Fred yelling with great enthusiasm, "Yabba Dabba Do!" *The Flintstones* has even been the inspiration for two feature films.

There are many different paper doll set based on this television show. This one is beautifully illustrated and has the theme of Fred and Wilma going on safari. There are two die-cut dolls, Fred and Wilma, along with 21 punch-out Stone Age safari outfits and accessories with tabs. On the back cover, there is a game to play.

Publisher: Wonder Books/Ottenheimer Publishers, Inc./Hanna-Barbera Productions

Original Price: 79¢   Value: $25.00 – 40.00

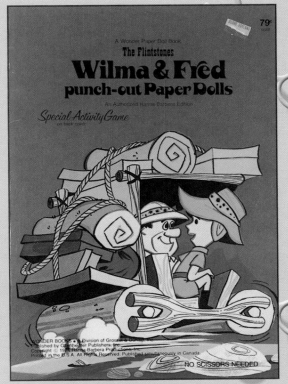

Pebbles   **Year: 1974**   **#6685**

On February 22, 1963, on the 84th episode, Hanna-Barbera introduced a new addition into the Flintstone's household — Pebbles (voice: Jean VanderPyl), nick- named Pebbly Poo. She would quickly become a much-loved favorite of fans of *The Flintstones*. That cute and cuddly Pebbles had the ability to melt the heart of her loud-mouthed, tough-guy father, Fred. He always became putty in her hands, and gave into her every whim. She loved to crawl around the dirt floor on Cobblestone Way making sounds of "Abb-gaba-goo," but perhaps her favorite thing to do was ride Dino, her pet dinosaur. He had the task of keeping her out of the trouble she would crawl into.

Included in this Pebbles paper doll set are two die-cut dolls, 10" Pebbles and 9½" Dino. There are 16 punch-out outfits and accessories with tabs, and a game on the back cover.

Publisher: Wonder Books/Ottenheimer/Hanna-Barbera
Original Price: 79¢   **Value: $25.00 – 40.00**

Bamm-Bamm   **Year: 1974**   **#6686**

My favorite cartoon as a child was *The Flintstones*. I would sit glued to the television every week to see what was rockin' in the town of Bedrock. My favorite characters were Pebbles and Bamm-Bamm; those two cuties were meant for each other. Bamm-Bamm (Voice: Don Messick) was the adopted son of Barney and Betty Rubble, the Flintstones' neighbors and best friends. Bamm-Bamm's most memorable trait was his incredible strength. He was always banging his club down, and when he did, the whole place would shake as though in an earthquake as he said the only two words he ever said for the entire run of the show: "Bamm-Bamm." Thus the name of Bamm-Bamm. During the long-running show, Pebbles and Bamm-Bamm watched, and sometime became caught up in, the adventures (or should I say misadventures?) of their parents, mainly Fred and Barney.

In their teenage years, Pebbles and Bamm-Bamm stared in their own animated series, which ran from 1971 to 1972.

In this wonderful paper doll set, you will find one 10" die-cut doll, Bamm-Bamm, with his Stone Age pet, Hoppy, and 17 punch-out adventure-type outfits with tabs. The back cover has a game called Hoppy's Trail.

Publisher: Wonder Books/Ottenheimer/Hanna-Barbera
Original Price: 79¢   Value: $25.00 – 40.00

Little Girls   Year: 1974   #6736

This set of three bubbly little girls drawn by Nan Pollard features three die-cut cuties, Jo, Jill, and Jane, along with a 50-piece cut-out wardrobe with tabs. This set is a reprint of set #2784, Little Girls, published in 1969. Each of these dolls are also featured separately in the Playhouse Dolly series; Jo is #1831, Jill is #1832, and Jane is #1833.

Note: You will notice Jo is featured in the 1960s chapter (chapter 1) of this book.

Publisher: Lowe/James & Jonathan, Inc.
Original Price: 69¢   Value: $10.00 – 20.00

Sunbeam   Year: 1974   #5235

These cute and cuddly babies are drawn by Belle Benoit and come from set #4235. This sunny set includes six adorable die-cut babies, Mark, Susie, Robbie, Vicki, Joy, and Patti, along with 45 outfits and hats to cut out. Each outfit has different colored tabs with the first initial of the baby the outfit belongs to.

Publisher: Saalfield/Artcraft
Original Price: 59¢   Value: $15.00 – 25.00

Courtesy of Edna Corbett

Dusty   Year: 1974   #1991

Dusty, the action fashion doll by Kenner, came swinging on the scene in 1974. She has an athletic build, tanned skin, platinum hair, a few freckles, and a great big smile. She is 11½" tall, with bendable knees and elbows, and she has a jointed wrist. When turned, it swivels back quickly, allowing her to swing her tennis racket as well as other sports equipment. Golf, volleyball, gymnastics, skiing, and other sports equipment sets for Dusty were all sold separately.

In this sportin' set drawn by Leon Jason, you will find one die-cut doll, Dusty, with her golf bag, volleyball, bat, and glove, along with 27 press-out athletic outfits with tabs. There is also a carry tote to keep Dusty and her outfits in when they are not in use.

Publisher: Whitman Book/Western/Kenner Products
Original Price: 79¢   Value: $8.00 – 10.00

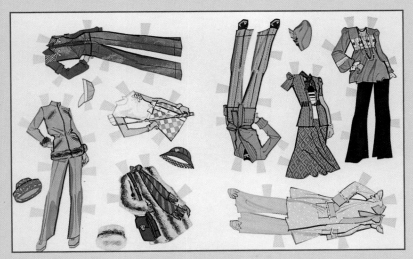

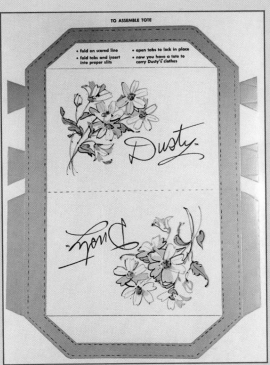

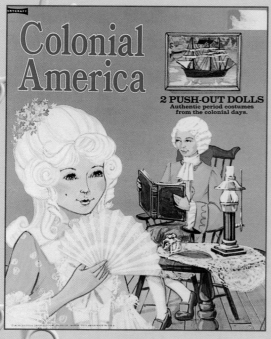

Colonial America   Year: 1974   #N4943

This historical set drawn by Linda Crockett is jam-packed with historically accurate period costumes of the colonial times. There is writing throughout the book documenting the dates and background of each outfit.

Two die-cut dolls are featured, a man and a woman, with 23 press-out outfits, hats, and wigs made of lightweight cardboard. A butter churn, spinning wheel, and many more accessories pertaining to colonial times can be cut out.

Publisher: Artcraft/Saalfield
Original Price: 89¢   Value: $15.00 – 30.00

Little LuLu and Tubby   Year:1974   #1987

Little LuLu always seemed to be matching wits with her friend and sometimes rival Tubby Topkins, the self-proclaimed leader of a group of "fellers" known as the East Side Club. The club's members included Iggy, Eddie, Willy, and LuLu's next door neighbor, Alvin. The humorous plots and storylines usually found LuLu at odds with Tubby, trying to outsmart him and put an end to his mischievous schemes and escapades, only to join forces with him later to thwart the devious plans of Mickey, Butch, and the rest of the West Side Boys.

The Little LuLu and Tubby paper doll set includes two die-cut dolls, Little LuLu and Tubby, and a 28-piece press-out wardrobe, with tabs, for the pair.

Publisher: Whitman/Western
Original Price: 79¢   Value: $15.00 – 25.00

Pippi Longstocking   Year: 1974   #1977

Created by famed Swedish children's author Astrid Lindgren (1907 – 2002) and named by her (then) seven-year-old daughter, Karin, free-spirited Pippi Longstocking seems to be ageless.

Published in Sweden in 1945, *Pippi Longstocking* told the story of the freckle-faced, redheaded (with horizontal pigtails), nine-year-old, mischief-making daughter of Efraim the Pirate. Wearing her homemade blue dress, long stockings (one blue, the other brown), and heavy, oversized boots, Pippi set out on whirlwind escapades, usually in the company of her friends, Annika and Tommy, and her monkey, Mr. Nilsson. Left on her own as her father sought treasure in far away places, Pippi used her incredible strength, cleverness, and the occasional big fib to make it through her many adventures and misadventures.

Just as popular today as they were some 50-plus years ago, when the book reached the shores of America, the tales of Pippilotta Longstocking continue to capture the hearts and imaginations of children worldwide.

This fabulous set includes three die-cut dolls, Pippi, Annika, Tommy, and Mr. Nilsson, Pippi's pet monkey, along with a 27-piece press-out wardrobe with tabs.

Publisher: Whitman Book/Western/G.G. Communications, Inc./Astrid Lindgren
Original Price: 79¢   Value: $15.00 – 25.00

Raggedy Ann and Andy Circus   Year: 1974   #1999

Raggedy Ann and Andy sets can't get any cuter than this one. The set is based on Johnny Gruelle's beloved rag dolls of the same names, and this adventure is taking Raggedy Ann and Andy to the circus!

There are two die-cut dolls, Raggedy Ann and her brother, Raggedy Andy. They have yarn hair and a 24-piece circus wardrobe.

Publisher: Whitman/Western/Bobbs-Merrill Company, Inc.
Original Price: 79¢   Value: $10.00 – 20.00

Paper Dolls of Early America   **Year: 1975**   **#1977-1**

This set was drawn by Mary McClain and includes two die-cut dolls, Sarah and Jane, along with an Early American butter churn and a carry tote. There are 28 Early American–style dresses, shawls, and hats to punch out. The colored tabs on the outfits each match the colored dot on a doll's base.

Publisher: Whitman Book/Western
Original Price: 89¢   **Value: $8.00 – 15.00**

Lydia   **Year: 1975**   **#1970**

I have always been a fan of African fabrics, and this is the only set that I know of in which the clothing pieces have been drawn to look like authentic African fabrics. That makes this set a real favorite of mine.

Included is one die-cut doll, Lydia, a stunning African American young woman who, by the look of the cover, is a singer. The set also comes with 34 cut-out outfits and hats with tabs.

Publisher: Whitman Book/Western
Original Price: 79c   **Value: $15.00 – 25.00**

Magic Mary Jane   Year: 1975   #4010-3

You may have figured out by now that I am a huge fan of Magic Marys. As I said earlier, I think the idea of magnetic dolls that came with magnets to tape inside their clothes was genius. The magnets allowed the clothes to stay on the doll no matter what kind of play a little girl might engage in.

These two sets follow in the footsteps of the earlier Magic Marys, with their beautifully drawn faces by Betty Campbell and brightly colored fashions reflecting the styles of the day.

The first set features blonde-haired, blue-eyed Mary Jane and 15 outfits to cut out.

The second set features an African American Mary Jane, again beautifully drawn. There are 15 outfits identical to those in the first set to cut out. Both sets include the magnets to tape on the backs of the clothing. Like magic — well, you know what I was going to say next.

Note: There is no box cover shown with the African American Mary Jane.

Publisher: Milton Bradley
Original Price: unknown   Value: $10.00 – 25.00

Barbie and Her Friends, All Sports Tournament
Year: 1975   #1981

Barbie doll and her friends are sportin a 'tude in this set of paper dolls. The set features the Free Moving Barbie doll and her friends, popular in the 1970s. (A lever on Barbie doll's back would swing her arms and upper torso.)

This winning set includes four die-cut dolls, Barbie, Ken, Cara, and Curtis, along with 20 punch-out outfits, including ones for golf, skiing, and tennis.

The colored tabs on the outfits match colored dots on the dolls' bases.

Publisher: Whitman/Western/Mattel
Original Price: 79¢   Value: $8.00 – 15.00

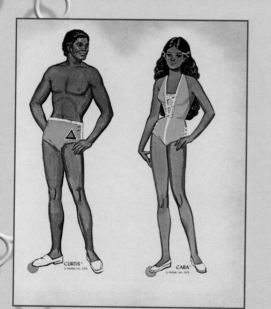

Yellowstone Kelley Doll   Year: 1975   #1956

Yellowstone Kelley doll is Barbie doll's outdoorsy friend, and is (like Barbie doll) made by Mattel. The 11½" doll comes with suntanned skin, long strait red hair, a twist/turn waist, and her sleeping bag and camping gear.

The paper doll set includes one die-cut doll, Yellowstone Kelley, and 26 cut-out outfits and accessories. The set also comes with press-out camping gear.

Publisher: Whitman/Western/Mattel
Original Price: 59¢   Value: $10.00 – 15.00

Courtesy of Edna Corbett

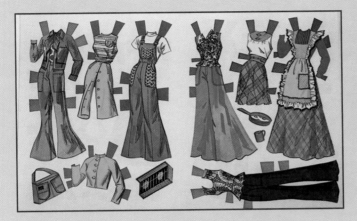

Jean Jeans   Year: 1975   #1961

Jean Jeans typifies a young teen from the 1970s. This set is jam-packed with fashions reflecting popular styles of the 1970s; many of the outfits have flowers, heart-shaped patches that say "Love" (remember those?), and other appliqués popular in this period.

This groovy set drawn by Leon Jason includes one die-cut doll, Jean Jeans, along with 32 far-out press-out outfits and accessories with tabs.

Publisher: Whitman Book/Western
Original Price: 79¢   Value: $7.00 – 15.00

Mods Matchin'   Year: 1973/1975   #1947

Groovy, *Far-out*, *Cool*, *Peace*, and *Man*. These four phrases sum up this set, Mods Matchin', drawn by Ruth Ruhman. Ruth has captured the essence of the 1970s with these way-out fashions.

Mods Matchin' paper dolls include two die-cut dolls, Renee (love those big hoop earrings) and Randy, along with 30 cut-out outfits and accessories with tabs.

Note: This set was printed in 1973 and 1975.

Publisher: Whitman Book/Western
Original Price: 79¢   Value: $7.00 – 15.00

A House Full of Dolls and Clothes   Year: 1975   #4507

Another delightful set drawn by Nan Pollard, this set comes from set #2723. The title of this set says it all; it is jam-packed with clothes, 55 outfits to be exact, all of them with tabs and ready to cut out.

There are four rosy-cheeked, big-eyed little cuties; two punch out and two must be cut out.

Publisher: Lowe/James & Jonathan, Inc.
Original Price: 49¢   Value: $7.00 – 14.00

Drowsy   **Year: 1975**   **#397/7408**

Mattel's Drowsy had a fabulously long run of popularity, starting in the 1960s and continuing into the 1970s. Even today, Drowsy continues to be a hit. As I have already said, when a play doll is in demand, the paper dolls will follow. Thankfully for us, the paper doll lovers, Drowsy's popularity produced many different sets of paper dolls.

Here is endearing boxed set that features one loveable statuette tot, Drowsy, and 29 punch-out outfits and accessories with tabs.

Publisher: Whitman/Western/Mattel
Original Price: unknown   **Value: $10.00 – 20.00**

Ankleidepuppe   **Year: 1975**   **#649-4195**

When I saw Ankleidepuppe, I instantly fell in love with her charming big blue eyes, rosebud mouth, and curly blonde hair. She is as beautiful as she is unique, and came all the way from West Germany.

Ankleidepuppe is a 12½" statuette doll, and she comes with eight realistic cut-out outfits with tabs.

Publisher: Siebert v Erlag Gmbh
Original Price: unknown   **Value: $20.00 – 35.00**

Itsy Bitsy Beans　　　Year: 1975　　　#1946-2

Mattel came out with several series of popular dolls called Baby Beans. Some talked, some cried, and some were just cuddly. They came with a beanbag body and vinyl head and hands. Itsy Bitsy Beans is the smaller version of the 11" Baby Beans; she is only 8" in size. Itsy has the same beanbag body as the other Beans, but her hands are stuffed and have Velcro sewn on, allowing Itsy to put her hands together or hold something.

Included in this floppy set are three die-cut dolls, Poofum, Piffle, and Pidgy, along with a 40-piece cut-out wardrobe with tabs.

Publisher: Whitman Book/Western/Mattel
Original Price: 59¢　　**Value: $5.00 – 10.00**

Baby Thataway   Year: 1975   #1997

"Baby Thataway, the doll you make walk and crawl, from Mattel," was the last line that accompanied one of the catchiest tunes for any doll in the 1970s. Baby Thataway is a 15" cutie that crawls, walks, and squirms. She has a soft vinyl head and a vinyl body.

This is my favorite paper doll set from the 1970s. It's a beautifully illustrated set, showing the charming and endearing little tot with her turned-up mouth, her blonde curls tied up in a pink bow, and her chubby little legs.

This fabulous set includes one 11" die-cut toddler, Baby Thataway, and 18 brightly colored outfits, along with her own bucket, shovel, and doll. There is a delightful pink carry tote to store Baby Thataway and her wardrobe in when you're on the go.

Publisher: Whitman Book/Western/Mattel
Original Price: 79c   Value: $9.00 – 20.00

Courtesy of Edna Corbett

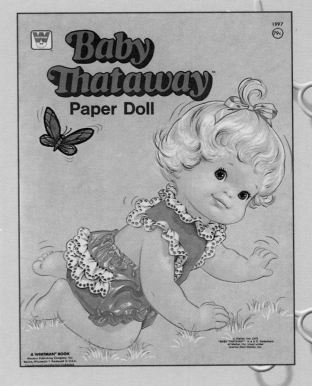

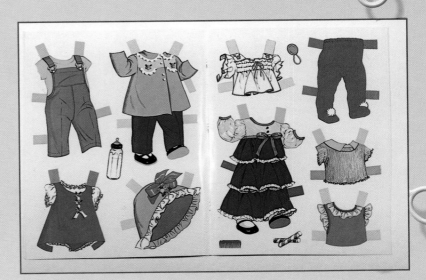

Cathy Quick Curl **Year: 1975** **#1998**

This is another charming paper doll set based on a popular doll by Mattel. Cathy Quick Curl was a darling 15" doll that came with her own curling wand, brush, and curlers. Her hair had fine cooper wires throughout that allowed her hair to easily hold a curl.

The complete set includes one 10½" die-cut doll, Cathy Quick Curl, along with three hairstyles that slip into the doll by tabs and give her new looks. There is also a 14-piece press-out wardrobe with tabs.

Publisher: Whitman Book/Western/Mattel
Original Price: 79¢ **Value: $10.00 – 18.00**

1976

Baby Dreams   Year: 1976   #1982

Baby Dreams, by Ideal Toys, were known as the "the dolls with the velvet skin." They had the sole distinction of being the only dolls that were flocked to achieve a velvety texture. Baby Dreams were some of the cutest dolls ever made, in my opinion, with their soft, velvety cheeks, big eyes, and those round faces outlined by their bonnets. They were definitely *dreamy*.

This wistful paper doll set includes one die-cut Baby Dreams, along with a 21-piece press-out wardrobe with tabs. Baby Dreams also has her own carry tote.

Publisher: Whitman/Western/Ideal
Original Price: 79¢   Value: $8.00 – 15.00

Courtesy of Edna Corbett

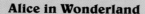

Alice in Wonderland   Year: 1976   #1948

The magical tale written by Lewis Carroll (Lewis Carroll was actually the pen name of Charles Dodgson) started out as the narrative *Alice's Adventures Underground*, invented for a young girl named Alice Liddell and her two sisters. The book became a literary classic.

First published in 1865, *Alice in Wonderland* spins fact into fantasy. While on an outing with the Liddell sisters and a friend, in and around Oxford, England, in the summer of 1862, Dodgson was persuaded to tell a story. Using Alice as the main character, Dodgson turned the day's activities into a whimsical tale that takes us along with Alice after she spots a white rabbit looking at his pocket watch as if he was late for something. Alice pursues the rabbit down his bunny hole and enters a magical world where she encounters strange and wonderful characters such as the Cheshire Cat, the Caterpillar, Tweedledee and Tweeedledum, the Mad Hatter, the March Hare, and of course, the regal Queen of Hearts.

This enchanting set includes four die-cut characters from the story, Alice, White Rabbit, Mad Hatter, and the Cheshire Cat, along with 51 magical cut-out outfits and accessories with tabs.

Publisher: Whitman Book/Western/Walt Disney Productions
Original Price: 59¢   Value: $15.00 – 25.00

Shirley Temple   **Year: 1976**   **#1986**

Born in 1928, in Santa Monica, California, Shirley Jane Temple displayed at an early age signs that she was of a tremendously gifted and talented child. It was her mother's love, nurturance, and dedication that helped direct Shirley on the path to stardom.

At the tender age of three, Shirley began taking tap dancing lessons at Melgin's Dance Studio, and it was here that a film producer named Jack Hays came looking for the next star to appear in his series of short films, called *Baby Burlesk*. After she was signed by Twentieth Century Fox, Shirley's career took off, and with her curly hair, dimples, and innocence, she captivated a nation and earned herself the title of America's Princess.

Shirley made 57 films during her career, including such titles as *The Runt Page*, *War Babies*, *Dora's Dunking Doughnut*, *Pardon My Pups*, *What To Do?*, *Out All Night*, *Stand Up and Cheer*, *Little Miss Marker*, *Baby Take a Bow*, *The Little Colonel*, *Poor Little Rich Girl*, *Stowaway*, *Heidi*, *Rebecca of Sunnybrook Farm*, *The Little Princess*, *Miss Annie Rooney*, *Fort Apache*, and *The Story of Seabiscuit*.

Shirley is now out of showbiz, but is still active. She has held posts in business and government, and is a very visible and recognizable spokesperson for health organizations and charities.

These next two pages show two sets of paper dolls featuring Americas Sweetheart.

The first set, shown here, has a beautifully illustrated cover, with a head shot of Shirley Temple and those famous curls and irresistible dimples. There is one 9½" die-cut Shirley Temple doll and a 19-piece wardrobe, many outfits representing costumes from her long movie career. There is also a handy carry tote to take Shirley and her clothes wherever you go.

All costumes have tabs and are ready to press out.

Publisher: Whitman Book/Western/Shirley Temple Black
Original Price: 79¢   Value: $10.00 – 20.00

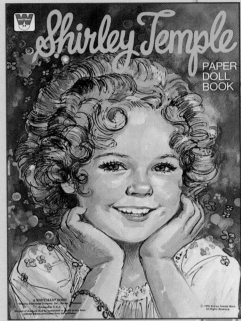

Shirley Temple   Year: 1976   #4388/7409

    This second set, featuring a charming 9½" statuette doll, comes boxed and has a 23-piece press-out wardrobe with tabs. This set also has many costumes from Shirley Temple's movies.

Publisher: Whitman/Western/Shirley Temple Black
Original Price: unknown   Value: $15.00 – 30.00

Wizard of Oz   Year: 1976   #1987

Click your hills three times and you'll be in Kansas. Okay, maybe not Kansas or anywhere else, but if you've ever picked up this L. Frank Baum classic, then you have traveled through one of the greatest novels ever written, in my opinion.

A good book should take you places, and when I first read *The Wizard of Oz* as a kid, I was whisked away along with Dorothy and her dog, Toto. An orphan, Dorothy lives a colorless life on her aunt and uncle's farm in Kansas, wishing for a better life and wondering if one exists somewhere over the rainbow. She doesn't have long to wait for an answer. A tornado hits the farm and Dorothy and Toto are whisked away, ending up in the colorful fairyland of Oz. Bewildered and wanting to go back home, she meets Glinda, the Good Witch of the North, who tells Dorothy it's always best to start at the beginning and follow the yellow brick road. So begins her journey, but before she reaches the Emerald City, Dorothy meets three very peculiar creatures: the Scarecrow, the Tin Man, and the Cowardly Lion. Their travels are filled with adventure, surprises, and self-discovery.

In 1939, Baum's classic was released as a motion picture by MGM studios, and this is how most people came to know the *Wizard of Oz*. I myself remember when *The Wizard of Oz* would make its yearly run on television (this was before videos and DVDs); I would excitedly anticipate getting to once again take a trip with Dorothy and the others down the Yellow Brick Road. The movie starred Judy Garland (Dorothy), Frank Morgan (professor Marvel/Wizard/Guardian of the Gate/Soldier), Ray Bolger (Hank Andrews/Scarecrow), Bert Lahr (Zeke/Cowardly Lion), Jack Haley (Hickory Twicker/Tin Man), Billie Burke (Glinda), and Margaret Hamilton (Miss Elmira Gulch/Wicked Witch of the West).

This delightful Wizard of Oz paper doll set, drawn by Mary McClain, includes five die-cut dolls, Dorothy, Toto, the Scarecrow, the Tin Man, and the Cowardly Lion, along with 24 whimsical press-out outfits with tabs.

Publisher: Whitman Book/Western
Original Price: 79¢   Value: $15.00 – 25.00

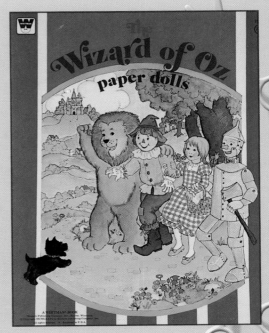

Tin Man

Cowardly Lion

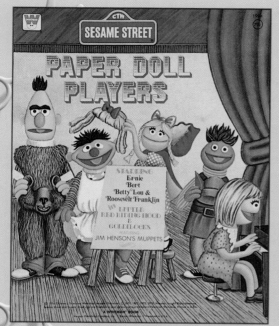

Sesame Street Players   **Year: 1976**   **#1994**

I was a little too old to watch it when in 1969, the Carnegie Corporation came up with the idea for a preschoolers' television show, but when Sesame Street aired that same year on National Educational Television (the predecessor of PBS), preschoolers were given a way to learn their letters, numbers, and social values, and have fun as they did.

A producer for PBS by the name of Joan Ganz Cooney offered master puppeteer Jim Henson the opportunity to showcase his Muppets (a combination of the words *marionette* and *puppet*) on Sesame Street. I'm sure many of you, like myself, had children who grew up sitting in front of the TV reciting their alphabets or counting along with such memorable characters as Kermit the Frog, Bert, Ernie, Big Bird, Grover, Oscar the Grouch, Count von Count, the adorable Sunffleupagus, and my personal favorite, Elmo (don't you just love that baby-talking red ball of fur?).

This paper doll set has a theme; the Muppets are performing *Little Red Riding Hood* and *Goldilocks*.

Included are four die-cut dolls, Ernie, Roosevelt Franklin, Betty Lou, and Bert, and a stage setting that consists of the beds and the chairs for Goldilocks and 17 costumes for the Muppets to wear as they perform their plays. All costumes are ready to press out and have tabs.

Publisher: Whitman Book/Western/Children's Television Workshop
Original Price: 79¢   **Value: $5.00 – 10.00**

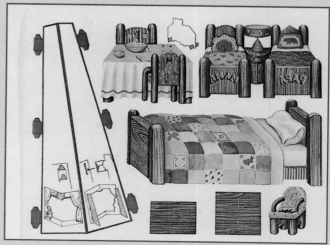

Polly Pal   **Year: 1976**   **#3730**

Leon Jason created Polly Pal, and this redheaded Gingham Gal became so popular that her image was used for an array of products. There were Polly Pal puzzles, Christmas ornaments, lunch boxes, and craft kits, as well as a 16" rag doll and, of course, this charming set of paper dolls.

Polly Pal's set includes one die-cut Polly Pal and 25 cut-out outfits and accessories with tabs.

Reprints of this set are #2730 and #4534.

Publisher: Lowe
Original Price: unknown   **Value: $10.00 – 20.00**

Courtesy of Edna Corbett

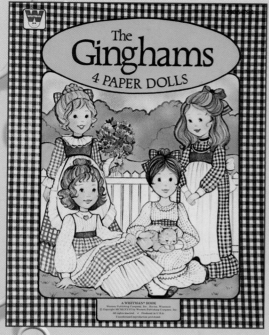

The Ginghams   Year: 1976   #1985

The Ginghams are charming little country girls named Sarah, Katie, Carrie, and Becky, there is a gingham theme in all they do.

The Ginghams started out as a Little Golden Book called *The Backwards Picnic*, written by Joan Chase Bowden and illustrated by JoAnne E. Koenig. Because of the book's popularity, another book followed: *The Ice Cream Parade*, also written by Joan Chase Bowden but illustrated by Kate Land. The Gingham girls quickly became a hit, so more books, as well as puzzles, coloring books, and paper dolls, were produced.

The paper dolls were met with instant success, so a series of two more paper doll books and 16 boxed sets were born. These were met with the same success.

In this first set of Gingham paper dolls, you will find four die-cut dolls: Sarah, Katie, Carrie, and Becky. A press-out picnic table (with a gingham tablecloth, of course), croquet set, park bench, bird bath, and baby doll with her old-time wicker buggy are included. There also are 39 press-out outfits and hats, each with color-coded tabs.

All of the Ginghams sets were drawn by Susan Morris, and all possess the charm and flair she is so well known for.

Publisher: Whitman/Western
Original Price: 79¢   Value: $8.00 – 18.00

Courtesy of Edna Corbett

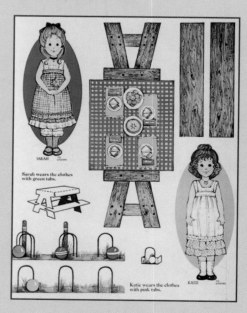

Wispy Walker   Year: 1976   #1944

Wispy Walker paper dolls, drawn by Leon Jason, were fashioned after the Uneeda life-size walking doll that stood a whopping 2' 7" from head to toe. She came in a variety of hairstyles and hair colors.

The set includes one 9½" die-cut doll, Wispy Walker, along with 34 delightful cut-out outfits and accessories with tabs.

Publisher: Whitman/Western/Uneeda
Original Price: 59¢   Value: $7.00 – 12.00

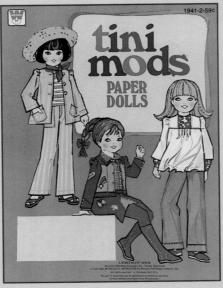

Tini Mods   Year: 1976/1978   #1941-2

Here we have another delightful set drawn by Leon Jason. Tini Mods originated from the 1968 set (#1988) with the same name. The cover is similarly illustrated and the set has six dolls instead of three. Other Tini Mods sets followed, #1945, #1983, and #1997.

The complete Tini Mods paper doll set features three die-cut dolls, Karen, Donna, and Cindy, and a 32-piece wardrobe reflecting those popular 1970s mod styles. The wardrobe is ready to cut out, and a colored dot on each doll's stand matches the colored tabs on her clothes.

Publisher: Whitman/Western/Uneeda
Original Price: 59¢   Value: $7.00 – 12.00

Pippi Longstocking   Year: 1976   #4390/7409

   Here we have a boxed set of Pippi and her friends. As is the case with the set previously featured in this book, this set of paper dolls is based on Astrid Lindgren's beloved children's books.

   Included in this fanciful set are three statuette dolls, Pippi, Annika, and Tommy, along with a 24-piece press-out wardrobe with tabs.

   Note: You can read more about Pippi Longstocking in the 1974 section of the book.

Publisher: Whitman/Western/G.G. Communications, Inc./Astrid Lindgren
Original Price: unknown   Value: $10.00 – 16.00

Malibu Francie Doll   Year: 1976   #4393/7420

Francie doll first came on the scene, as Barbie doll's modern cousin, in 1966. Since that time she, like Barbie doll and the rest of her family, has taken on many different appearances.

Malibu Francie doll was the first Francie to have an open-mouth smile. She had tanned skin and long blonde hair, and typified a California beach bunny. Mattel produced her from 1971 to 1977. Francie doll, like the other dolls in the Malibu series, had instant popularity.

In this boxed set, you will find one statuette doll, Francie, along with her 21-piece press-out wardrobe with tabs. None of the wardrobe items in this set come from original Francie fashions.

Note: There are many other Francie doll sets featured in this book.

Publisher: Whitman/Western/Mattel
Original Price: unknown   Value: $9.00 – 16.00

Skipper Doll   Year: 1976   #4395/7420

Here we have a boxed set featuring Barbie doll's little sister, Skipper doll, which includes a 9½" statuette doll with a charming smile, freckles, and two ponytails. There are 16 press-out outfits and accessories with tabs.

Note: There are many other Skipper sets featured in this book.

Publisher: Whitman/Western/Mattel
Original Price: unknown   Value: $9.00 – 16.00

Barbie's Fashion Originals   Year: 1976   #1989

The title of this set is fashioned after the series of clothing sets called Barbie's Fashion Originals. The set features a striking, die-cut Malibu Barbie doll with long straight blonde hair, and also includes a multi-colored mod carry tote with 22 punch-out outfits and hats with tabs. The fashions reflect 1970s styles.

Publisher: Whitman/Western/Mattel
Original Price: 79¢   Value: $10.00 – 20.00
Courtesy of Edna Corbett

Growing up Skipper   Year: 1976   #1990

Mattel came out with a new body style for its 1975 – 1977 version of Skipper doll. Getting this doll was like getting two dolls in one. When Skipper doll's arm was rotated in a counterclockwise position, she grew taller and developed small breasts, going from a young girl to a teenager in seconds. When it was time to play with the young Skipper doll again, her arm was turned clockwise.

This set has two die-cut Skipper dolls. One is the young version of Skipper doll, in a red swimsuit, and the other is a young teen version of Skipper doll, in a blue swimsuit. Each outfit has tabs that coordinate with the color on a doll's swimsuit. A multicolored, flowered carry tote is included, along with 25 outfits and accessories to press out.

Publisher: Whitman/Western/Mattel
Original Price: 79¢   Value: $10.00 – 20.00

Courtesy of Edna Corbett

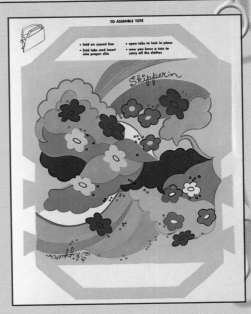

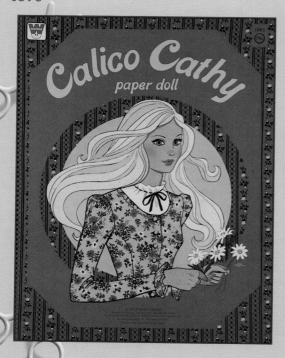

Calico Cathy   **Year: 1976**   **#1995**

   Calico Cathy represents a young country-style woman with long, flowing hair. The set has beautifully illustrated fashions that have a calico flair. The set includes one die-cut doll, Calico Cathy, with a calico print carry tote and 16 punch-out outfits and accessories with tabs.

Publisher: Whitman/Western
Original Price: 79¢   **Value: $8.00 – 15.00**

Courtesy of Edna Corbett

Big Jim and Big Jack   **Year: 1976**   **#1988**

Introduced by Mattel as a follow-up to the Major Matt Mason line and as a market rival to Hasbro's very successful G.I. Joe action figure, the original Big Jim line, which also included Jack, Josh, and Jeff, saw great popularity in the 1970s and 1980s in the US, Canada, Japan, and especially, Europe.

One of the most interesting facts in the competition between Big Jim and G.I. Joe was the difference in size. At only 8" Big Jim was a whole 4" shorter than G.I. Joe, yet market research and surveys of boys 8 – 13 showed that based on design features (biceps that actually bulged when the arm was bent) and a highly successful ad campaign, Big Jim was favored. Must be a guy thing!

This masculine set of paper dolls features Big Jim and Big Jack, with sports outfits. The complete set includes two die-cut dolls, Jim and Jack, along with 16 pieces of primarily sports attire, such as football, racing, and hunting outfits. All wardrobe pieces press out and stay on the dolls with tabs.

Publisher: Whitman Book/Western/Mattel
Original Price: 79¢   **Value $8.00 – 15.00**

Courtesy of Edna Corbett

Welcome Back Kotter   **Year:1976**   **#106**

These two sets come from the ABC television sitcom *Welcome Back Kotter*, with the extraordinary teacher, Mr. Kotter, and the memorable Vinny Barbarino. The show debuted in 1975 and aired for 95 episodes, ending in 1979.

The comedy starred Gabriel Kaplan (Kotter), Marcia Strassman (Julie Kotter), Robert Hegyes (Epstein), Lawrence Hilton Jacobs (Washingon), Ron Palillo (Horshack), and the future top-grossing, disco-dancing hunk John Travolta as the unforgetable Vinny Barbarino. (He still makes my heart skip a beat even today.)

Mr. Kotter, a Brooklyn-born teacher, returns to the inner-city high school from which he graduated, to teach a remedial academics group known as the Sweathogs. The Sweathogs are streetwise outcasts of the school systems who are just too much for most teachers. But when an equally sharp-witted, just as streetwise Mr. Kotter enters their lives and their class-room, and the Sweathogs have finally met their match! From that moment, it's laughter and comedy at James Buchanan High. I can still here Mr. Kotter shout, "They are not people they're sweathogs!" Mr. Kotter's complete set includes one 14" statuette doll, Mr. Kotter, along with 21 outfits and accessories to cut out. To attach the clothing to Mr. Kotter, you simply rub over the clothes with a hard object. When you're done, simply peel the clothing off.

Publisher: The Toy Factory/The Wolper Organization, Inc./The Komack Company, Inc.
Original Price: unknown   **Value: $20.00 – 35.00**

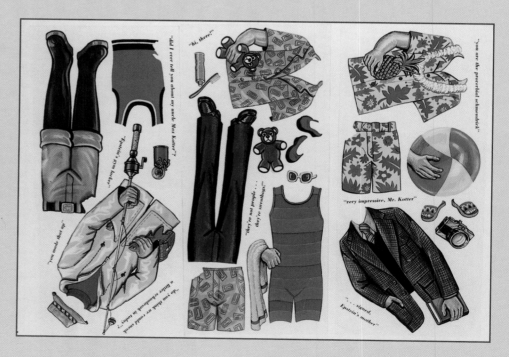

Vinny Barbarino   Year: 1976   #107

Welcome Back Kotter's Vinny Barbarino was a heartthrob who had all the girls mesmerized by his charisma, charm, and quick wit. He quickly became the focus of the show, and it became a launching pad for actor John Travolta's career. Who could forget such catch phrases as "Up your nose with a rubber hose," "Off my case, potato face," and "What? Where? When?"

This show was a favorite of mine and of numerous others who sat glued to the television to watch Mr. Kotter try to educate his Sweathogs. Thanks, Sweathogs, for the memories!

Vinny's set includes one 14" statuette doll and a 12-piece wardrobe in which, as in Mr. Kotter's set, the clothes rub on and peel off.

**Publisher: Toy Factory/The Wolper Organization, Inc./
    The Komack Company, Inc.**
Original Price: unknown   Value: $20.00 – 35.00

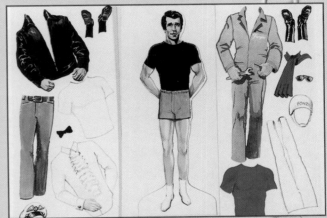

Fonzie   Year: 1976   #105

"AAAaaaaaaaaaayyyhhhh," I have to admit it, from 1974 to 1984, for half an hour every Tuesday night, I got a kick out of Arthur "Fonz" Fonzarelli and the rest of the *Happy Days* gang. I tuned in to watch the megacool, ultrahip Fonz in his leather jacket and Levis, as he kept an almost guardian angel–like presence over Richie, Potsie, Ralph Malph, and Joanie, and presided over his turf at Arnold's.

I suppose that as a young teen, I shouldn't have ever been so taken with a guy who at a snap of his fingers could have any group of girls flock to him, but come on, ladies, cool is cool. I grew up in the sixties, mesmerized by the likes of Dennis Hopper in *The Glory Stompers* or Peter Fonda in *Easy Rider*. We all loved the rebel, the ones who took a stand against the establishment. Let's face it, the guys wanted to be them, 'cause they were cool, and the girls wanted to date one, 'cause they were bad.

Maybe that's why The Fonz was and still is such a popular character. Thumbs up to the cool guy!

This ultracool set includes one 14" statuette doll, the Fonz, along with a 24-piece cut-out wardrobe including Fonzie's very cool black leather jacket and Levis. The clothes rub on and peel off.

Publisher: The Toy Factory/Paramount Pictures Corp.
Original Price: unknown   Value: $20.00 – 35.00

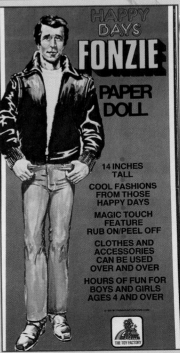

Donny and Marie   Year: 1977   #1991

Donny Osmond started as one of the Osmond Brothers, and went on to become a solo artist and shine in the limelight. Following him with acclaim of her own was his sister Marie. However, it was as a duo that they became super-stars.

Donny and Marie collaborated on a series of duets and enjoyed a trans atlantic Top 10 hit with a version of Dale and Griffin's "I'm Leaving It All Up To You." They followed this up with a cover of Tommy Edwards's "Morning Side of the Mountain." The duo's next move was into the country market, with a remake of Eddy Arnold's "Make The World Go Away."

In 1975, Donny and Marie guest co-hosted *The Mike Douglas Show*. Watching the show that night was the president of ABC TV, Fred Silverman. The brother and sister duo must have made quite an impression on Mr. Silverman, because in November of the same year, Donny and Marie starred in their first prime-time TV special. The special was a success, scoring some of the highest ratings in ABC TV history at the time. This led to the pair being given their own one-hour comedy/variety show, which debuted in January 1976. The show spawned a hit album and another US/UK hit with a revival of Nino Tempo and April Stevens's "Deep Purple."

After much success as a duo, both Donny and Marie headed off in separate directions, but in November of 1998, they reunited as co-hosts of their own talk show.

In this paper doll set, you will find two die-cut dolls, Donny and Marie, along with 20 press-out costumes and accessories with tabs. In the back of the book, you will find a stage to press out and assemble for the duo.

Publisher: Whitman/Western/Osbro Productions, Inc.
Original Price: 79¢   Value: $20.00 – 35.00

Denim Deb   Year: 1977   #1949

This set of teenage fashions reflects those hip 1970s styles and features one 9½" adolescent, Denim Deb, and 35 groovy' cut-out outfits and accessories with tabs.

Publisher: Whitman Book/Western
Original Price: 59¢
Value: $8.00 – 15.00

Little Ladies   Year: 1977   No number

Here we have a rare and charming set, Little Ladies. There are two die-cut dolls, Lorri, 9½" tall, and what looks to be her little sister, Leann, 8" tall. The pair comes with 19 cut-out outfits and accessories. Lorrie's tabs come outlined in green, and Leann's come outlined in blue.

Publisher: Childart
Original Price: 59¢   Value: $10.00 – 25.00

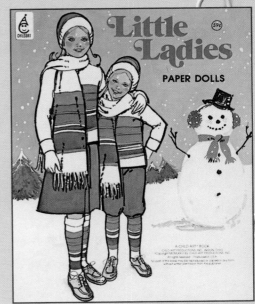

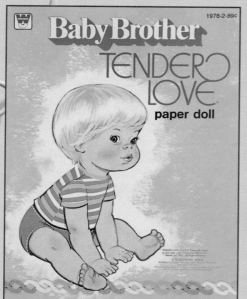

Baby Brother Tender Love   Year: 1977   #1978-2

Another doll based on the Tender Love line of soft vinyl dolls from Mattel, this 13" doll came in both an African American and a Caucasian version. It was very controversial because it was anatomically correct, which even in the free-spirited openness of the early '70s caused a quite a stir. Baby Brother Tender Love came with a one-piece soft body and rooted hair, and he could drink from his bottle and wet his diaper.

Other versions of Tender Love dolls were Baby Tender Love, Talking Baby Tender Love, and Tearful Baby Tender Love.

This set includes one die-cut doll and 16 punch-out outfits, along with a tote so you can carry Baby Brother with you wherever you go.

Note: Many Tender Love paper dolls are featured in this book.

Publisher: Whitman/Western/Mattel
Original Price: 89¢   Value: $8.00 – 18.00

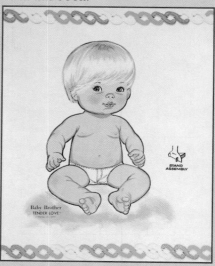

Rub-a-Dub Dolly   Year: 1977   #1941

Rub-a-Dub Dolly will take a bath with you! Her chubby little body was watertight, and she came with her own tugboat shower, allowing little girls to spend hours of playtime in the tub with their Rub-a-Dub Dollies. The bonus to moms was that when playtimes were over, they had squeaky-clean little girls.

Rub-a-Dub Dolly came with one 9½" die-cut tot and 35 cut-out outfits and accessories with tabs.

Publisher: Whitman/Western/Ideal
Original Price: 59¢   Value: $10.00 – 20.00

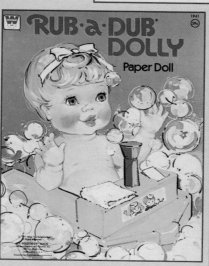

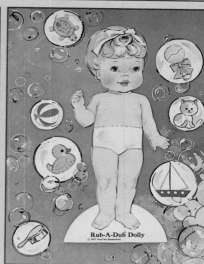

The Happy Family   Year: 1977   #1978-1

Hal, Hattie, and Hon are the Happy Family, made by Mattel, and are part of the Sunshine Family line of dolls. The Happy Family has vinyl heads, rooted black hair, and glass eyes. Mother and Father are jointed, and baby Hon has one-piece bent legs, and a vinyl body.

The Happy Family also has grandparents. Grandfather has gray rooted hair and a full beard and mustache; Grandmother has white rooted hair. They are truly endearing.

In this set, you will find seven wonderfully charming die-cut family members, Hattie, Hal, Hon, Grandfather, Grandmother, and the dog and cat, along with 42 punch-out outfits and accessories with tabs.

Note: Hon's clothing has both girl and boy styles.

Publisher: Whitman/Western/Mattel
Original Price: 89¢   Value: $10.00 – 18.00

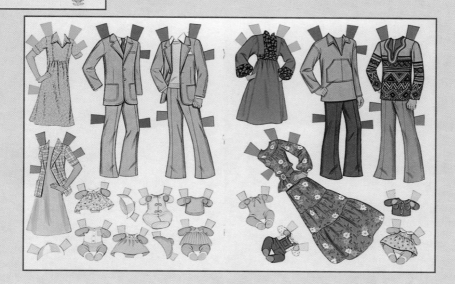

The Sunshine Family   Year: 1977   #1981

The Sunshine Family was a popular doll family made by Mattel. There were originally three members of the family, Steve, Stephie, and Baby Sweets. Shortly thereafter, Grandmother and Grandfather were added to the line. The Sunshine Family's paper dolls include seven die-cut dolls: Dad Steve, Mom Stephie, Baby Sweets, Grandfather, Grandmother, and the family dog and cat, and 33 press-out outfits with colored tabs that coordinate to the colored flowers on the dolls' bases.

Note: Read more about the Sunshine Family in the 1974 section of this book. Also, Sweet's wardrobe allows Sweets to be boy or girl.

Publisher: Whitman/Western/Mattel
Original Price: 89¢   Value: $8.00 – 18.00

Honey Hill Bunch   Year: 1977   #1976-1

Neighborhood friends introduced by Mattel in the mid-1970s, these 3" and 4" cloth dolls are truly adorable. If you ever had the chance to see or even own some of the Honey Hill gang, then you may remember the most notable features that these dolls possessed.

Some of these were their soft little bodies, their vinyl heads with rooted hair, and their hands with the small bits of velcro attached. The velcro allowed them to hold each other's hands or any of the felt accessories that they came with.

The Honey Hill Bunch included Battie, Solo, Sweetlee, Lil' Kid, I.Q., Slugger, Spunky, and Darlin'. Each was sold separately. Also available was the Honey Hill Bunch Clubhouse.

This friendly set includes seven of Honey Hill's finest: Battie, Spunky, Solo, Li'l Kid, Sweetlee, Darlin', and I.Q. In addition, also included is their trusty dog, Good Dog. There are 39 delightful punch-out outfits and accessories, with colored tabs that match the stand of the doll the clothes belong to. The back cover doubles as a clubhouse backdrop while you play with your Honey Hill Bunch.

Publisher: Whitman/Western/Mattel
Original Price: 89¢   Value: $10.00 – 18.00

Mickey & Minnie Steppin' Out   Year: 1977   #1986-41

In my opinion, there has never been a truer symbol of Americana than Mickey Mouse. He is without a doubt Disney's most recognizable and most popular character. From Asia to Europe, Mexico to Africa, and everywhere in between, Mickey is the quintessence of American culture, just as much so as Old Glory and apple pie.

Created by the late Walt Disney while he was on a train headed back to L.A., Mickey entered the world as Mortimer Mouse. Walt's wife Lillian was shown the drawings and promptly suggested to her husband that he should change the name of his new character to Mickey Mouse.

Mickey's career began with the May 15, 1928, release of *Plane Crazy*, a silent black and white in which Mickey builds a homemade airplane so that he can be like his hero, pilot Charles Lindbergh. At the same time, he has another motive — to entice Minnie, the girl of his dreams. With a little misfortune and a lot of determination, Mickey comes out successful in his endeavors. *Plane Crazy* is rarely credited with being the first Mickey Mouse cartoon, due to the lack of a soundtrack. However, it was rereleased a year later with an accompanying soundtrack, after *Steamboat Willie* and *The Galloping Gaucho*.

What is the magic of this little mouse? I think the answer can be found in the way that Walt Disney let his creation grow. As the years have passed, Mickey's demeanor has changed a great deal. He has gone from having a somewhat clumsy, rash, juvenile personality in his early days to having charm, purity, and modest shyness. His place as one of the worlds' most beloved characters has been rightfully secured. In this Steppin' Out set, you will find two 9" die-cut dolls, Mickey and Minnie, drawn in their earlier likenesses. Included are Mickey and Minnie's red Model T and 20 brightly colored press-out outfits with tabs.

Publisher: Whitman Book/Western/Walt Disney
Original Price: $1.29   Value: $20.00 – 35.00

1978

Daisy and Donald   Year: 1978   #1990-21

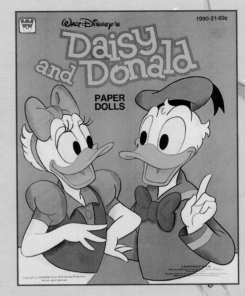

Donald Duck made his debut on June 9, 1934, in the Silly Symphony cartoon *The Wise Little Hen*. Hot-headed, stubborn, and temperamental, he has managed to endear himself to all of us as one of Disney's most cherished characters. He's tried so hard to be the man, but things never go his way, and being Donald, he's just a feather away from throwing a tantrum and blowing his lid. Try as he might to accomplish what he sets out to, trouble seems to be waiting for him.

Do you think Daisy was introduced to soothe the savage beast that is Donald? Just maybe! Making her debut as Donna Duck in 1937's *Donna Donald*, she was renamed Daisy three years later, in the 1940 cartoon, *Mr. Duck Steps Out*. Classy, sweet, and sophisticated, she seems almost too refined for a loose cannon like Donald. But with swinging tail feathers and a walk to rival that of Jane Mansfield, she seems to have a calming effect on ol' Donald Duck.

In this delightful and amusing set, Daisy is showing off her dazzling charm with those long lashes and a look that says she is using her womanly wiles on the unsuspecting Donald.

Both die-cut ducks are 9" tall and include a 24-piece brightly colored press-out wardrobe with tabs.

Publisher: Whitman Book/Western/Walt Disney Productions
Original Price: 89¢   Value: $6.00 – 20.00

Raggedy Ann and Andy   **Year: 1978**   **#19818-1**

This wonderfully charming set of Raggedy Ann and Andy features two 9½" die-cut dolls, Raggedy Ann and Andy, along with 20 fanciful press-out outfits with tabs.

Note: You can read more about Raggedy Ann and Andy in the chapter on the 1960s.

Publisher: Whitman/Western/Bobbs-Merrill Company
Original Price: 89¢   Value: $10.00 – 20.00

Teddy Bears   **Year: 1978**   **#1943-1**

Teddy Bears originates from set number #1967 and has a simplistic charm. The set features two 8½" die-cut country bears, along with 25 cut-out outfits, pets, and toys, all with tabs.

Publisher: Whitman Book/Western
Original Price: 59¢   **Value: $6.00 – 14.00**

Bridal Doll Book
Year: 1978   **#1983-1**

This is a wonderfully illustrated bridal set that originally comes from set #1986. This blissful set includes a complete playtime wedding, featuring the bride, groom, best man, maid of honor, and the flower girl, along with a 20-piece press out wardrobe with tabs, including a 1970s-style wedding gown and tuxedo.

Publisher: Whitman Book/Western
Original Price: 89¢   **Value: $10.00 – 20.00**

Courtesy of Edna Corbett

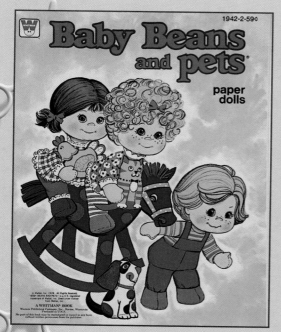

Baby Beans and Pets   Year: 1978   #1942

Launched by Mattel in the 1970s, these popular bean dolls were made with vinyl heads and hands, with their bodies and limbs having the bean (pellet) filling. Throughout the 1970s, there were several variations of these dolls (such as Mama Beans, Jeans Beans, and Biffy Beans) that had tiny holes in their eyes and would cry when they drank water. Bedside Beans featured faces with big yawns and sleepy eyes. Most Baby Beans came in African American or Caucasian versions.

This set includes three die-cut dolls and three pets, Dog, Chicken, and Cat, along with 26 cut-out outfits and hats and six toys to cut out. The colored tabs match the dolls the outfits belong to.

Publisher: Whitman/Western/Mattel
Original Price: 59¢   Value: $8.00 – 18.00
Courtesy of Edna Corbett

Rosebud   **Year: 1978**   **#1982**

Mattel came out with these adorable cuties in 1976. They came in a series of six diverse dolls with vinyl heads and hard plastic bodies, available in two sizes, 8" and 5".

In this wonderful paper doll set you will find three die-cut cuties, Silvie, Stella, and Marissa, along with 24 punch-out outfits, hats, and accessories with tabs.

Publisher: Whitman/Western/Mattel
Original Price: 89¢   **Value: $10.00 – 18.00**

Courtesy of Edna Corbett

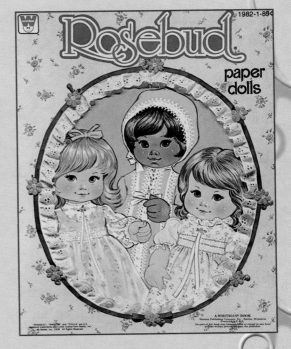

The Sunshine Fun Family   Year: 1978   #1995

The Sunshine Fun Family has a photograph of the Sunshine Family dolls on the front cover, as opposed to an illustration such as the previous sets featured in this book do. This set differs from the other sets because Sweets has grown up, becoming Big Sister to the new addition, Baby Bother. The family now has four members instead of three.

This complete paper doll set includes four die-cut dolls, Mom, Dad, Big Sister, and Baby Brother, along with the Sunshine Family pets, Dog and Cat.

There are 31 punch-out outfits with tabs. The tabs color coordinate to dots on the dolls' bases.

Publisher: Whitman/Western/Mattel
Original Price: 89¢   Value: $10.00 – 18.00

Courtesy of Edna Corbett

The Ginghams Paper Doll and Play Set
Year: 1978 #4214

On this page are featured two Gingham Paper Doll and Play sets drawn by Susan Morris. The first set highlights Katie and her country store, and includes one die-cut Katie, a pop-up country store, Katie's adorable dog, a mouse with cheese, a barrel of apples, and other items one would find in a country store. There are 11 press-out country dresses, with tabs, for Katie to go shopping in.

Publisher: Whitman/Western
Original Price: unknown Value: $8.00 – 15.00

Courtesy of Edna Corbett

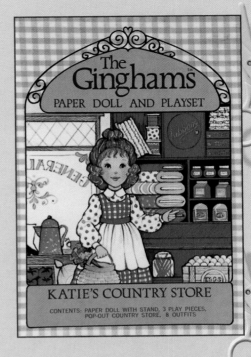

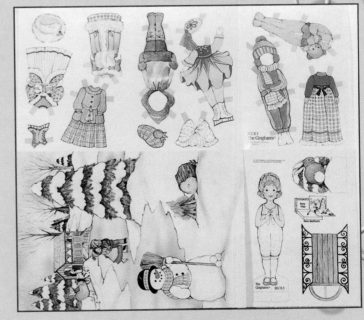

1979

The Ginghams Paper Doll and Play Set
Year: 1979 #7316A

This second set, Becky's Winter Carnival, features one die-cut Becky doll and a pop-out wintery wonderland scene complete with snowman, evergreen tree, and sled and bunny cottontail. There are 12 press-out warm winter outfits with tabs.

Publisher: Whitman/Western
Original Price: unknown Value: $8.00 – 15.00

Courtesy of Edna Corbett

Strawberry Sue   Year: 1979   #1976-2

This wonderfully illustrated set shows young teen fashions popular in the 1970s. You may have worn some of these styles, such as gauchos, midi skirts with high boots, or ruffled dresses. Many more familiar outfits are featured in this set.

This paper doll set includes a young redheaded die-cut teen, Strawberry Sue, along with 17 press-out outfits and accessories with tabs. A fabulous wheelbarrel to punch out and assemble is also included, and can be topped off with some die-cut strawberrys!

Publisher: Whitman Book/Western
Original Price: 89¢   Value: $8.00 – 15.00

Courtesy of Edna Corbett

Paper Doll Dancers   Year: 1979   #1981

This is a delightful, beautifully illustrated set of dancers. It features two die-cut ballerinas, Terri and Susan, ready to perform and complete with toe shoes. The set comes with 20 press-out costumes with tabs.

Publisher: Whitman/Western
Original Price: 89¢   Value: $15.00 – 30.00

Courtesy of Edna Corbett

Baby This 'n That   Year: 1979   #1980-2

Baby This 'n That was a 13" doll made by Remco. She was battery operated; by squeezing her feet, one could make her arms move. This caused her hands to rotate to her mouth as though she was eating. She came in both African American and Caucasian versions that also included her accessories: a spoon, a toothbrush, and a telephone. Her original box reads, "She does this 'n that with just a touch."

In this paper doll set, you will find one 11" die-cut doll, Baby This 'n That, and 14 adorable press-out outfits with tabs. There is also a toy box to punch out and assemble.

Publisher: Whitman/Western/Remco
Original Price: 89¢   Value: $5.00 – 12.00

Teddy Bears   **Year: 1979**   **#7409C-20**

Are these the cutest pair of bears? I love this set drawn by Susan Morris, which features two 9" cuddly statuette bears, Teddy and Tandy, along with a 32-piece press-out wardrobe with tabs.

Publisher: Whitman/Western
Original Price: unknown   **Value: $6.00 – 12.00**

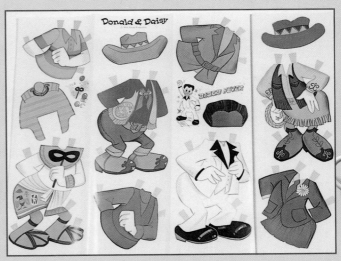

Donald & Daisy   **Year: 1979**   **#7409-A**

Here is a fabulous set of Walt Disney's favorite two ducks that features two 9" brightly colored statuette dolls, Donald and Daisy, along with a 28-piece press-out wardrobe with tabs.
Note: Read more about Donald and Daisy in the 1978 section.

Publisher: Whitman/Western/Walt Disney Productions
Original Price: unknown   **Value: $10.00 – 16.00**

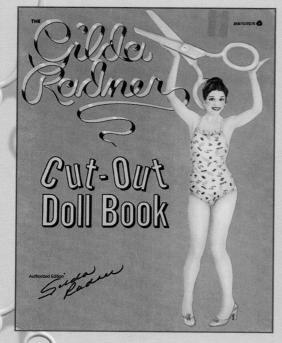

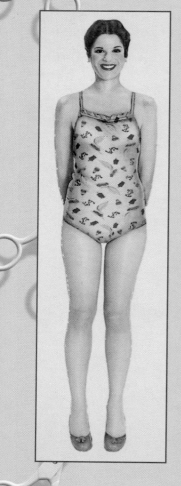

Gilda Radner   Year: 1979   #75127

Comedian Gilda Radner was one of the original cast members of the comedy show *Saturday Night Live*, and like other *SNL* members, Radner got her comedy start with the Second City comedy improv troupe. Named after the over-seductive vixen portrayed by glamour queen Rita Hayworth in the 1946 movie *Gilda*, the waifish, extraordinarily funny Gilda Radner seemed far from glamorous. Yet she captivated us with a power that made us all smile and laugh at ourselves. She was the 100-mile-a-minute, energetic, all-too-infectious goofball, and we loved her. Nope, she wasn't glamorous, she was just Gilda.

Radner met a very funny actor named Gene Wilder, whom she married in 1984. Within 18 months of her marriage, she began to experience flu-like symptoms and fever. After being told by her physician that her pain was imaginary, her illness began to grow worse. By the time it was discovered, the cancer had already taken its hold on her. For the next 2½ years, Gilda would fight to live her life and love Gene.

On May 20, 1989, at the age of 42, Gilda lost her fight. With many people still inspired by her suffering and her strength, today Gilda's legacy goes forward. Gilda was an extraordinary woman and fought an extraordinary fight. Gilda and her hilarious characters and comedy are greatly missed by her millions of fans and by those who knew and loved her.

This unique paper doll book includes one die-cut Gilda Radner, along with 56 costumes representing some of Gilda's most loved characters, such as Barbara Wawa, Roseanne Rosannadanna, Emily, and many more. All costumes have tabs and are ready to cut out.

Publisher: Avon
Original Price: $2.95   **Value: $9.00 – 18.00**

Marilyn Monroe   Year: 1979   #23769-9

We all know the tragic story of Miss Norma Jean Baker, who went on to find fame, fortune, and sadly, misfortune as Marilyn Monroe. This blonde bombshell was Hollywood personified. Glamorous, saucy, and mesmerizing, she was a '50s sex goddess.

In 1944, while on assignment for *Yank* magazine and taking photos of women contributing to the war effort, photographer David Conover spotted Norma Jean working on an assembly line at the Radio Plane Munitions factory in Burbank, California. She was quickly chosen as the subject of the shoot. Within two years of first appearing on the cover of *Yank* magazine, Norma Jean became a bona fide success as a model, and with a shining future ahead of her, she dyed her hair blonde, changed her name to Marilyn Monroe, and began her ascent to stardom.

Norma Jean enrolled in drama classes, which later paid off with a movie career.

Success came quickly for Marilyn, and she appeared in over 30 films and on numerous magazine covers. She garnered a variety of awards, a recording contract, and a star on Hollywood's Walk of Fame. Yet with success came misfortune. Her divorces were a matter of public record, and she was rumored to be involved in illicit affairs and to use drugs. She was also thought by some to be mentally unstable. She died in August of 1962.

She was and still is an American icon, admired and loved by many — so much so, that well into the mid-to-late 1990s, she was featured on a 32-cent US commemorative postage stamp, named the Number One Sex Star of the Twentieth Century by *Playboy* magazine, and voted the Sexiest Woman of the Century by *People* magazine. Along with that of the Beatles and of Elvis Presley, Marilyn Monroe memorabilia has become some of the most sought after and highly collected in the world.

This set is the first of many paper doll sets by Tom Tierney that will be featured in this book.

Marilyn Monroe's set includes one glamorous Marilyn Monroe doll and 46 cut-out replicas of some of Marilyn's most famous costumes, all made of lightweight cardboard and with tabs.

Publisher: Dover Publications, Inc.
Original Price: $4.95   **Value: $5.00 – 12.00**

Ladies of the Chorus, Columbia, 1948

Star Princess and Pluta **Year: 1979** **#1839**

This set is out of this world! It features space-age characters and comes complete with a North Star space base.

The cover of this set reads, "Space play for girls! Star Princess and Pluta have press-out space clothes, Starspeeder Spaceship plus a command center and outer planetary play scene!" This sums up this galactic paper doll play set.

The complete set includes two die-cut dolls, Star Princess and Pluta (the robot), along with 27 space-age costumes and helmets. The folder is tri-fold and opens to create a space command center. There are 30 pieces to assemble and fit into the command center.

Publisher: Whitman/Western
Original Price: $2.00 **Value: $10.00 – 20.00**

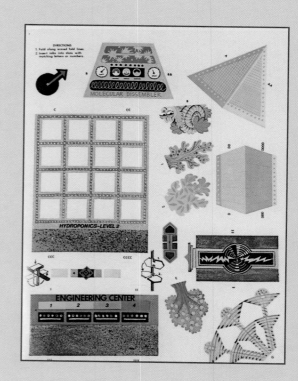

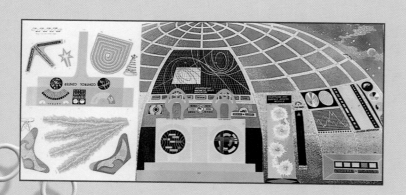

1980s

1980

Storybook Beans   Year: 1980   #1979-3

Baby Beans were the adorable little beanbag dolls by Mattel, and were popular in the 1970s. They were simply irresistible with their round vinyl faces, big, brightly colored eyes, and bodies that were full of beans, which allowed them to sit or melt into the arms of those who held them.

Mattel produced many variations of these little beanbag cuties, and this particular set of paper dolls represents the Storybook Beans collection, which is based on popular nursery rhyme characters such as Miss Muffet, Red Ridding Hood, and Bo Peep.

This set includes three 7" die-cut dolls, Little Bo Peep, Little Red Riding Hood, and Little Miss Muffet, each with her own Storybook stage to assemble. There are 34 press-out outfits and hats with tabs. Each colored tab matches a dot of the same color on a doll's base.

Publisher: Whitman/Western/Mattel
Original Price: 89¢   Value: $5.00 – 10.00

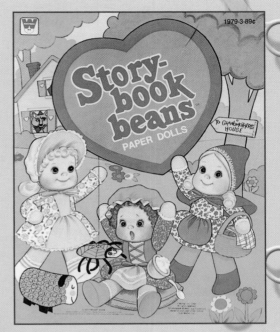

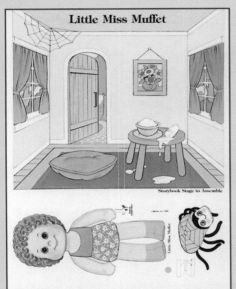

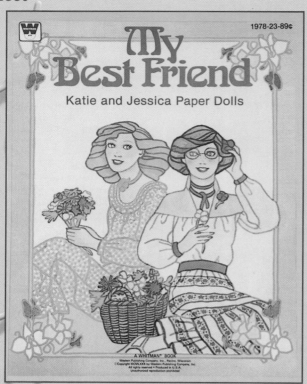

My Best Friend   **Year: 1980**   **#1978-23**

Remember your best friend? Sharing high school secrets that only she could understand, talking on the phone all night long after spending the entire day together? I remember.

This set captures the essence of best friends and features two 9½" die-cut friends, Jessica and Katie, along with a 22-piece wardrobe that shows off those 1980s fashions. Outfits press out and have colored tabs that match the color of a doll's base.

Publisher: Whitman Book/Western Publishing
Original price: 89¢   **Value: $5.00 – 10.00**

Raggedy Ann and Andy   Year: 1980   #1987-32

This is a delightful book of paper dolls that originates from set #1977-23 and features a whimsical Raggedy Ann with an impish grin and a bashful Raggedy Andy. This set is just too cute!

In this brightly illustrated set, you will find two 10" Raggedy Ann and Raggedy Andy die-cut dolls, and 17 press-out outfits with tabs.

Publisher: Whitman Book/Western/Bobbs-Merrill Company, Inc.
Original Price: 99¢   Value: $8.00 – 15.00

Miss America   Year: 1980   #7410D7-20

This set appeals to the little girl who dreams of one day being the next Miss America.

In this boxed set, you will find one 9½" statuette Miss America doll and a 31-piece wardrobe with tabs, including Miss America's winning gown and her crown.

Note: The cover features a photograph of Miss America 1972, Laura Lee Schaefer.

Publisher: Whitman/Western/Miss America Pageant
Original Price: unknown   Value: $5.00 – 10.00

Star Princess and Pluta   Year: 1980   #7410C-20

Here we have the boxed set of Star Princess and Pluta; you will find the book set #1839 featured in chapter 3 (1970s).

Princess and Pluta (the princess's trusty robot friend) are spotlighted as two statuette dolls, with 31 press-out out-of-this-world costumes with tabs.

Publisher: Whitman/Western
Original Price: unknown   Value: $8.00 – 12.00

Neighborhood Kid   **Year: 1980**   **#1985-32**

Aren't neighborhoods with lots of kids great? I can remember the neighborhood kids and me running through the yard playing freeze tag or hide-and-go-seek on warm summer nights, or a gang of us riding our bikes around the block. Those were the days, weren't they?

This set may just bring some of those memories rushing back as you flip through its pages. It has a melting pot of 12 die-cut children and 33 punch-out play outfits like Superman, a ballet tutu, a cowboy, and a clown, to name just a few.

Each outfit has color tabs that match a colored dot on a doll's base.

Note: This set comes from #1978-24.

Publisher: Whitman Book/Western Publishing
Original Price: unknown   **Value: $5.00 – 10.00**

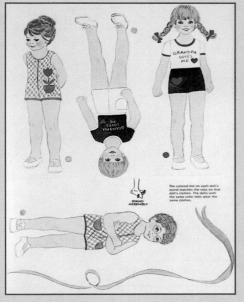

Winnie-the-Pooh   **Year: 1980**   **#1977-24**

During World War I, while on a train bound for eastern Canada, Lieutenant Harry Colebourn from Winnipeg bought a small female black bear cub for $20 from a hunter who had killed its mother. He named her Winnipeg, after his hometown — Winnie for short. After arriving in war-torn Europe and receiving his assignments, Lt. Colebourn decided to loan the young bear to the London Zoo for its safekeeping and care. Winnie remained there after the war, becoming a popular attraction and living until 1934.

While at the London Zoo, the bear was visited many times by Christopher Robin, son of author A. A. Milne. Christopher took such a liking to Winnie that he renamed his own teddy bear Winnie — Winnie-the-Pooh. The pair became the focus of a series of books, written by Milne, about their adventures in the 100 Acre-Wood (the surrounding area of Milne's country home in Ashdown Forest, Sussex). The book characters included Eeyore, Piglet, Tigger, and Kanga and Roo, all based on stuffed animals belonging to Christopher Robin.

Winnie-the-Pooh was published on October 14th, 1926, by Methuen. The Pooh books became favorites of both old and young, and have been translated into almost every known language. The Pooh books were also favorites of Walt Disney's daughters, inspiring Disney to release *The Many Adventures of Winnie-the-Pooh* as an animated film in 1977.

This delightful set includes 9 die-cut characters: Winnie-the-Pooh, Christopher Robin, Piglet, Owl, Tigger, Roo, Rabbit, Kanga, and we can't forget about that loveable donkey Eeyore. It also comes with five die-cut, what I call scene enhancers, and there is also a 58-piece wardrobe for Winnie and his friends. All outfits have tabs and press out.

Publisher: Whitman/Western/Walt Disney
Original Price: 89¢   **Value: $14.00 – 25.00**

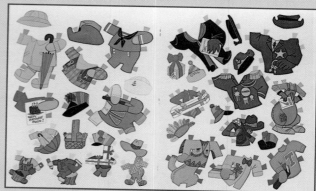

Super Teen Skipper Doll   Year: 1980   #19803

This set has a beautifully illustrated teenage Skipper doll on the cover and features one 9½" die-cut Skipper doll and a 30-piece press-out wardrobe with tabs. You will also find a brightly colored tote to carry Skipper along in when you are on the go.

Publisher: Whitman Book/Western Publishing/Mattel
Original Price: 89¢   Value: $8.00 – 15.00

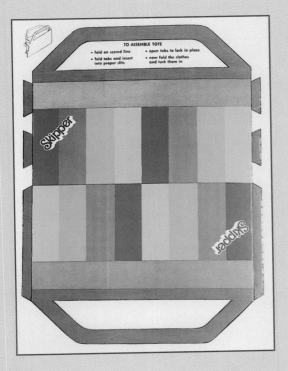

Starr and Her Friends   Year: 1980   #1982-31

In 1979, Mattel introduced Starr and her friends Tracy, Kelly, and Shaun. Mattel succeeded at capturing the spirit of high school teens and their extra curricular activities, and the dolls were met with instant popularity.

Starr and her friends attended the fictitious Springfield high, and all were involved in school activities. Starr, for instance, was homecoming queen and captain of the cheerleading squad; she also participated in the science club and was on the gymnastics team. Wow!

The dolls were 11½" and fully posable, with moveable shoulders, waists, heads, and wrists, and bendable knees and elbows. Each came with its own set of accessories such as guitars, tambourines, phones, and barrettes, and with its own yearbook.

Starr and Her Friends paper doll book includes four 9" die-cut teens, Starr, Shaun, Kelley, and Tracy, along with 20 school-time outfits such as homecoming queen, football, basketball, and cheerleading outfits, to name a few. All wardrobe pieces press out and have tabs.

Publisher: Whitman Book/Western Publishing/Mattel
Original Price: 99¢   Value: $6.00 – 10.00

Barbie Doll and Skipper Doll Campsite At Lucky Lake
Year: 1980   #1836

Barbie doll and Skipper doll have quite the camping setup in this extraordinary set. It is good for hours of fun, with an easy-fold-out campsite and camp furniture, and comes complete with Barbie doll and Skipper doll's very own boat dock and canoe. You will also find a tent, a hammock, backpacks, lanterns, trees, a waterfall, a deer, and a big yellow motor home to take them both to the Lucky Lake Campsite.

Also included are two die-cut dolls representing the Sun Lovin' Malibu line, Barbie doll and Skipper doll, complete with a 28-piece press-out outdoorsy wardrobe and a total of 33 press-out campsite accessories. The clothing has tabs.

Publisher: Whitman Book/Western Publishing/Mattel
Original Price: $2.00   Value: $10.00 – 20.00

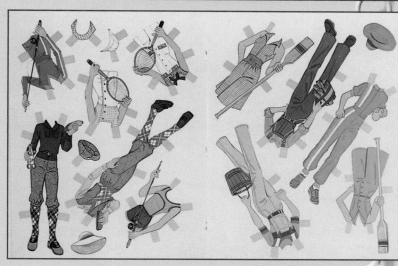

1981

Skipper & Scott   **Year: 1981**   **#7408c-1**

Based on the Super Teen Skipper doll and her pal Scott doll, this set features the pair on the go and ready for any activity.

There are two statuette dolls, Skipper doll and Scott doll, along with a 31-piece press-out active wardrobe with tabs.

Publisher: Whitman/Western Publishing/Mattel
Original Price: unknown   Value: $8.00 – 12.00

Pretty Changes Barbie Doll   Year: 1981   #1982-42

In my opinion, this set showcases a more sophisticated Barbie doll; she has a new, shorter hairstyle and an elegant wardrobe based on original Barbie doll outfits.

The Pretty Changes Barbie doll set includes one 10" die-cut Barbie doll, 25 classy fashions, and a variety of wigs. The wardrobe has tabs and is ready to press out. A carry tote to take Barbie along when you are on the go completes this set.

Note: The Whitman logo is printed on this particular set. There is a similar set published with the same name and number; however, the cover is illustrated a little differently and carries the Golden logo.

Publisher: Whitman Book/Western Publishing/Mattel
Original price: $1.29   Value: $10.00 – 20.00

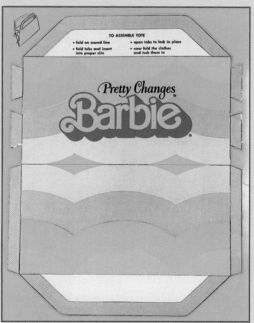

Fashion Show **Year: 1981** **#1939-42**

As a little girl, I would fantasize about being a model in a fashion show and walking down the runway in the most glamorous outfits made by the finest designers. I would walk with the utmost grace and style as cameras flashed all around me. I had outgrown paper dolls by the time this set made its debut, but had I had this set, it would have complemented my vivid imagination as I played out my fashion show fantasy.

This marvelous set is jam-packed with hours of fun for little girls, and the folder features a fashion show scene complete with curtains, a runway, and an audience. The other side of the folder becomes an apartment scene so the girls can change clothes and rest after a long day of modeling. Also included are two 9½" die cut models, Kristie and Nikki, and 22 sensational outfits for the girls to model down the runway. The wardrobe has tabs and is ready to press out.

Publisher: Whitman Book/Western Publishing
Original Price: $2.59   **Value: $4.00 – 10.00**

Trixie Belden and Honey Wheeler   **Year: 1981**   **#1987**

If you were a fan of mystery/detective stories as a kid, and grew up between the late 1940s and mid-1980s, you probably picked up a book written about this amateur detective. Trixie Belden, a freckled, spunky, and short-tempered teenager, was the main character in a series of 39 books originally started by Julie Campbell but later written by various writers at Western Publishing Company.

Beatrix "Trixie" Belden; her brothers, Mart and Brian; her best friend, Honey Wheeler (who came from an extremely wealthy family); and Honey's adopted brother, Jim Frayne, made up the Bob-Whites of the Glen Club and solved a host of mysteries.

If you were or are a fan of Trixie and Honey, then you might remember titles like *The Secret Mansion*, *The Mysterious Visitor*, *The Black Jacket Mystery*, or *The Mystery of the Missing Millionaire*. For those of you who thought that Trixie and the gang were gone for good, don't worry, because Random House Publishing has reprinted the first four books in the series. I think Trixie and her friends just might make a comeback!

This wonderful paper doll set includes two die-cut dolls, Trixie and Honey, along with 25 punch-out outfits and hats with colored tabs that match the dolls' undergarments.

Publisher: Whitman/Western
Original Price: $1.29   **Value: $8.00 – 15.00**

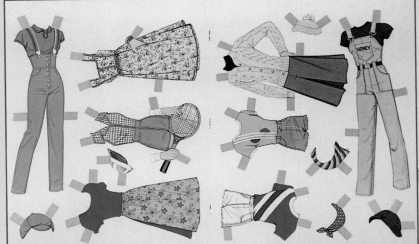

A PAPER DOLL PLAYBOOK

Bride and Groom

DOLLS AND CLOTHES   RECEPTION PLAY SCENE   GARDEN WEDDING SCENE

Bride and Groom   Year: 1981   #1837-32

You can almost hear the wedding bells ringing with this set.

There is everything you need to plan your own make-believe wedding; this set provides hours of fun for girls.

The folder folds out, creating a garden wedding scene complete with a covered gazebo, bridal walk, wedding bells, flowers, and family members.

The other side of the folder becomes a reception scene, complete with a spiral staircase, wedding cake, and a table with wedding gifts for the bride and groom, all made of medium-weight cardboard.

To top off this set, there is a beautifully drawn wedding party with six die-cut dolls: the bride, groom, flower girl, maid of honor, best man, and ring bearer. There are also 18 outfits, including a stunning wedding dress, veil, and tuxedo.

All wardrobe pieces come with tabs and are ready to punch out.

Publisher: Golden/Western
Original Price: $2.59   Value: $7.00 – 15.00

Courtesy of Edna Corbett

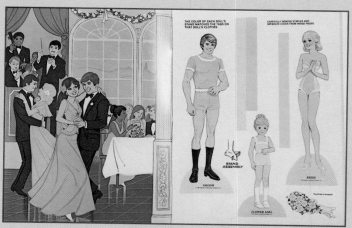

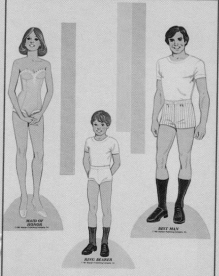

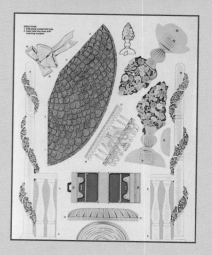

Peek-a-Boo Baby   Year: 1981   #1985-34

The 1980s saw a decrease in the production of paper doll sets featuring babies and toddlers. As the popularity of Mattel's Barbie doll rapidly grew, more and more paper doll publishers quickly turned their focus away from the cute cuddly babies, and began to publish the more in-style fashion paper dolls.

Here we have one of the few sets published in this era featuring a baby, and it is adorable!

This set includes one 8" die-cut baby, holding her rattle and baby bottles at her side, and a yellow gingham diaper bag and baby carrier to press out and assemble. There is a charming 13-piece press-out wardrobe with tabs.

Publisher: Whitman Book/Western Publishing
Original Price: 99¢   Value: $4.00 – 10.00

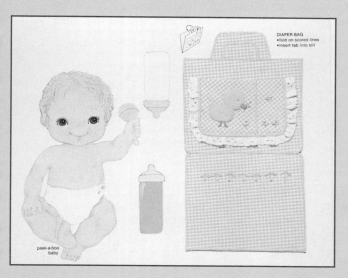

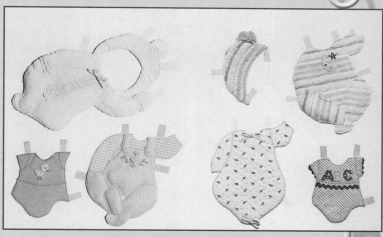

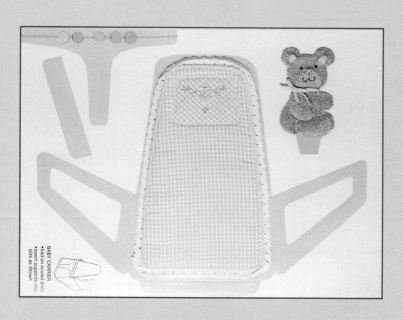

Annie and Sandy   **Year: 1982**   **#84979-5**

This set features the curly-headed, redheaded orphan and her dog, Sandy, from Harold Gray's 1924 *Little Orphan Annie*, which started in 1938 and ran as a daily and Sunday strip for several decades. Annie, an orphan, was taken in by "Daddy" Oliver Warbucks, a very wealthy capitalist. The comic strip included Warbucks' right-hand men, Punjab and the Asp. Every week, it seemed as though Warbucks was caught up in foiling evildoers out to harm Annie.

Little Orphan Annie was made into a movie in 1932 and adapted as a Broadway musical in 1977; the musical ran from April 21, 1977, to January 2, 1983. There have also been other productions, including of course, the highly praised big screen version in 1982 that starred Albert Finney as Daddy Warbucks, Aileen Quinn as Annie, and Carol Burnett as Miss Hannigan, the matron of the orphanage.

In 1967, Harold Gray was diagnosed with cancer, and in keeping with his practice of introducing political and social issues into his comic strip, Daddy Warbucks was also diagnosed with the same illness. But though Warbucks won his battle, Harold Gray died of cancer on May 9, 1968, after 45 years of drawing and writing one of the world's greatest newspaper comic strips.

In this set, you will find two die-cut dolls, Annie and Sandy, and 10 accessories, such as a leash and bone for Sandy and a ball and tennis racket for Annie. There are 22 cut-out outfits with tabs. On the back cover there is a trunk to press-out and assemble, so that when you are done playing with Annie and Sandy you can store their accessories in their trunk.

Publisher: Happy House/Tribune Company Syndicate, Inc.
Original Price: $1.79   **Value: $4.00 – 10.00**

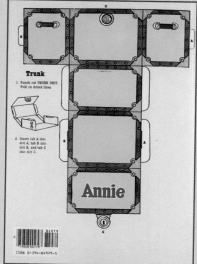

Rachel   Year: 1982   #A7554H-22

This Rachel set is a delightful and interactive paper doll set that includes a threader and thick strands of yarn, so little girls can create an easy-to-do hairstyle by threading the yarn through the already-punched-out holes in Rachel's head.

Rachel is one out of a series of eight paper doll friends with yarn hair; the others are Amy, Jennifer, Jessica, Kristin, Beth, Julie, and Peggy.

The dolls are made of heavyweight cardboard and measure 14" tall.

Rachel is the brunette of the group and comes with a 10-piece child's dress-up wardrobe, which includes fairy princess, nurse, space explorer, ballerina, and snake charmer outfits, to name a few. The clothes stay on when the clothing backs are rubbed with a wax crayon and then pressed firmly on the doll. The clothes can be peeled off and reapplied repeatedly.

Publisher: Whitman Book/Western Publishing
Original Price: unknown   Value: $5.00 – 12.00

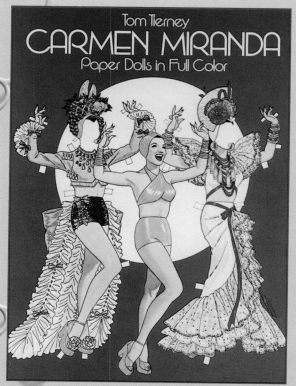

Carmen Miranda   Year: 1982   #24285-4

Carmen Miranda, the Brazilian Bombshell, was born Maria do Carmo Miranda da Cunha, on February 9, 1909, in Marco de Canavezes, Portugal. Not long after her birth, Carmen's family moved to Brazil and settled in the capital city of Rio de Janeiro. Carmen began singing on a local radio station and soon received a recording contract with RCA. By 1928, she was a genuine superstar in Brazil.

After much success in Brazil as a film and recording star, she was hired by Lee Shubert to star on Broadway in *The Streets of Paris*. As her fame in the US grew, she made what she thought would be a happy return home to Brazil, but upon arriving she was labeled as being "Americanized." Deeply saddened by this, Miranda flew back to the US, where she went under contract to Twentieth Century Fox and was cast in the musicals *Rosita* and *Chiquita*. However, it was for the 1943 film *The Gang's All Here*, that she donned the famous fruit basket headdress and sang samba numbers while dancing. Carmen's success was phenomenal for a Latina at that time, and although people would agree that most of her roles were indeed stereotypical, we can still be amazed at her popularity and acceptance by Hollywood and the rest of the country.

Carmen died of a heart attack on August 5, 1955, at home in Beverly Hills, California.

Tom Tierney has captured Carmen and her costumes beautifully in this set. Included is one Carmen Miranda doll (to cut out) and a 31-piece wardrobe representing many of the costumes of Carmen's career. All have tabs and are ready to cut out.

Publisher: Dover/Tim Tierney
Original Price: $4.95   Value: $4.00 – 10.00

Down Argentine Way
(20th Century-Fox, 1940)
Costume designer: Travis Banton

Something for the Boys
(20th Century-Fox, 1944/45)
Costume designers: Yvonne Wood & Kay Nelson

Doll Face
(20th Century-Fox, 1945/46)
Costume designer: Yvonne Wood

Two more costumes from Doll Face

Cabbage Patch Kids   Year: 1983   #641

Remember those irresistible Cabbage Patch Kids?

They were the brainchild of Xavier Roberts and a phenomenal success. I know many of us thought, "Wow, what a great idea! Why didn't I think of that?"

The original dolls came with pudgy faces and arms, were cloth from head to toe, and had yarn hair.

All dolls were born from the cabbage patch at Babyland General Hospital, 75 miles from Atlanta, in Cleveland, Georgia. They had thir own looks, names, birthdays, birth certificates, and adoption papers. Brilliant idea!

The hospital/museum is still in existence today and has thousands of visitors each year tour it to get a glimpse of those lovable, cuddly Cabbage Patch dolls.

In the hospital, you will find a fathers' waiting room with some original 1970s Cabbage Patch dolls, called Little People. There is also a nursery, complete with incubators, for the preemies who were born too early because of an unexpected frost.

Colonel Casey, "The Big Stork," watches over the preemies and waits for the next crop to arrive. There are school busses, schools rooms, a playground, a gift shop, and of course, the cabbage patch.

In 1982, Roberts sold his mass production rights to Coleco Toy Company; Coleco produced dolls similar to the originals, but they now had vinyl faces. Coleco could not keep up with the demand for these dolls the first year, and parents were left scrambling and waiting in endless lines at toy stores trying to get Cabbage Patch dolls for their daughters to adopt. (That year, I could not find the coveted doll in stock anywhere. My daughter had to have one, so a friend brought one all the way back from her visit to Ireland. I still have it!) The craze, however, was short lived, and sales declined. Coleco filed bankruptcy, and Hasbro took over production of the dolls in 1989. In 1994, Mattel purchased the rights from Hasbro and is still producing our little friends today.

This set features three statuette dolls made of heavyweight cardboard, one preemie and two toddlers. The two toddlers have holes punched in their hair, allowing little girls to loop in pieces of yard to crate their own hairstyles. There are 56 reproductions of original Cabbage Patch Kids outfits and accessories, including six hairstyles. All clothing pieces press out. They stay on the doll when rubbed with a wax crayon and pressed onto the doll.

Publisher: Avalon/Original Appalachian Artworks, Inc.
Original Price: unknown   Value: $8.00 – 15.00

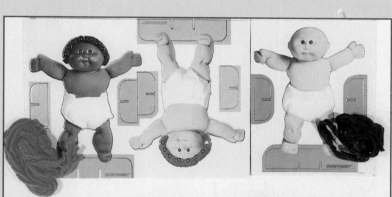
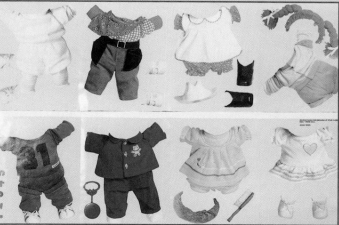
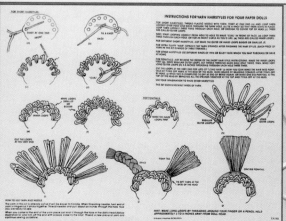

Pink & Pretty Barbie Doll
Year: 1983   #7411B

This set of paper dolls is based on the popular 1980s Pink & Pretty Barbie doll.

The set has an 11" statuette doll and a 17 piece-wardrobe, all with tabs and ready to press out.

Publisher: Whitman/Western Publishing
Original Price: unknown
Value: $6.00 – 12.00

Rainbow Brite   Year: 1983   #7407C

Rainbow Brite came on the scene in 1983, originally as a Hallmark greeting card character. That same year, Mattel produced her as a soft-bodied doll with a vinyl head and vinyl hands and a yellow yarn ponytail; the doll came in a variety of sizes. Her popularity grew, and soon Rainbow Brite was a character in movies and had her own television cartoon.

The cartoon premise went something like this: Rainbow Brite's original name was Wisp, and she was magically carried off to a place called Rainbow Land. Everything there was dull and dreary, and it was ruled by The Dark One. Rainbow Brite's main goal was to bring color to Rainbow Land, and she did just that, with the help of her friendly and fluffy sprite, Twink; her flying horse, Starlite; and her seven friends, the Color Kids. Each Kid represented a color of the rainbow, as shown by their names: Red Butler, Lala Orange, Canary Yellow, Patty O'Green, Buddy Blue, Indigo, and Shy Violet. After Rainbow Land was all brightly colored, Rainbow Brite stayed in the land to rule. She and her friends kept Rainbow Land and the universe draped in bright colors and free from their worst enemy, Murky Dismal, and his sidekick, Lurky.

This set is adorable and includes two 10" statuette dolls, Rainbow Brite and her buddy, Red Butler, along with an 11-piece brightly colored press-out wardrobe with tabs.

Publisher: Golden/Western/Hallmark
Original Price: unknown   Value: $5.00 – 10.00

Traditional Folk Costumes of Europe   Year: 1983   #7411B

I adore this charming set, drawn by Katy Allert and featuring authentic folk costumes that represent different parts of the world, such as Hungary, Poland, Rumania, France, Spain, and Greece. This set provides hours of fun and education for children by encouraging curiosity of different cultures.

This set includes two beautifully illustrated dolls to cut out named Margaret and Kristin, along with a 60-piece wardrobe, with tabs and rich in tradition. The tabs have the first initial of the doll the outfit belongs to.

Publisher: Dover
Original Price: $5.95   Value: $6.00 – 12.00

Joan Crawford   **Year: 1983**   **#2456-9**

Henry Fonda once said, "Joan was a star in every sense of the word..." Humphrey Bogart was quoted as saying, "Joan Crawford, as much as I dislike the lady, she is a star," and Bette Davis, well, what she had to say about Joan Crawford is unprintable for a paper doll book, but her words underscored the animosity the two women had for each other. In her tell-all book about her famous mother, daughter Christina shared with the world a dark side of Joan Crawford. Nevertheless, whatever one's opinion of her is, the woman sure did have an air of stoic dominance on the screen.

Born Lucille Fay LeSuer, in San Antonio, Texas, she left behind her turbulent life and headed to Hollywood to find the fame she craved. In 1925, she landed a bit role in *Pretty Ladies*. She struggled to make a name for herself for the next three years, until she was given the starring role in *Our Dancing Daughters*, which launched her career. As great an actress and big a star as she was, Joan only won a coveted Oscar once; that was for her performance in 1945's *Mildred Pierce*. With new stars rising in Hollywood, Joan started to find her career slowing. A saving grace for her should have been *What Ever Happened to Baby Jane?* in which she played opposite screen rival Bette Davis, but I guess the public had grown tired of Joan.

In 1970, she appeared in a very forgettable flop called *Trog,* and became a recluse soon after. She died on May 10, 1977, in New York City.

Tom Tierney illustrated a wonderful tribute to Joan in this set by representing three distinct phases of her incredible movie career. There are three Joan Crawford dolls and 28 cut-out designer fashions with tabs.

Publisher: Dover/Tom Tierney
Original Price: $4.95   **Value: $4.00 – 10.00**

Betty Boop Goes to Hollywood   Year: 1984   No number

"Boop-boop-a-doop," perhaps the most famous phrase spoken by a cartoon character of all time. Betty Boop, created by Grim Natwick and voiced by Mae Questral, started her successful career in 1930 in the animated cartoon *Dizzy Dishes*. Incredibly, she was not the star, and she had only one brief scene — as a dog, very different than the Boop that most of us know today. She remained a dog, as did her boyfriend, Bimbo, throughout more than half a dozen cartoons. Betty's popularity skyrocketed, and she was changed into a sexy Mae West–type character with pronounced curves, short skirts, and a baby doll voice. She was a hit, and soon every kind of item you could think of had her image — posters, t-shirts, dolls, and more.

Her last cartoon of this era was in 1939. Just prior to her retirement, censorship had swept through Hollywood and Betty Boop had lost her sexy look. She'd been altered to have less curves and a hemline that now went down to her knees. This look portrayed a more conservative, good girl image, and the sparkle that was Betty Boop was gone.

In 1980, Boop made a comeback with a bang! Furthermore, she is now one of the most collected cartoon characters of our time. You can find her anywhere and on any item. Welcome back, Betty Boop!

In this magnificent set, drawn by Trina Robbins, are a 9" die-cut Betty Boop and her little white dog, Pudgy. There are 24 outfits and accessories representing movie star costumes, such as Marilyn Monroe's famous airborne dress, Carmen Miranda's Tutti Frutti outfit, and Judy Garland's *Wizard of Oz* ensemble, complete with a basket for Pudgy. All outfits have tabs and are ready to cut out.

Publisher: Betty's Store LTD./Trina Robbins
Original Price: unknown   Value: $20.00 – 35.00

Courtesy of Edna Corbett

Cupie   Year: 1984   #24621-3

Cupid, or "Cupie," is the most famous love symbol of all time. We know him as a mischievous, chubby winged child with the cutest dimples, who aims his arrows at unsuspecting gods and humans and causes them to fall deeply in love. Throughout time, Cupid has played an important role in our celebrations of love, the most significant one being Valentine's Day. Cupid is a Roman god, the son of Venus, the goddess of love. (The Greak equivalents of these two are Eros and Aphrodite.)

This set by Tom Tierney possesses true charm and beauty, and yes, it is one of my favorites. (I do have a lot of favorites, don't I?) There are two charming and chubby Cupies with two separate pieces ment to be glued together to give him both a front side and a (literally) backside. There are also 14 delightful costumes such as a bee, a butterfly, a daisy, and a fairy, to name a few. All outfits have front and back sides. One attaches the clothes by folding them on the lines and then folding back the tabs. All dolls and costumes are ready to cut out.

Publisher: Dover/Tom Tierney
Original Price: $3.50   Value: $10.00 – 25.00

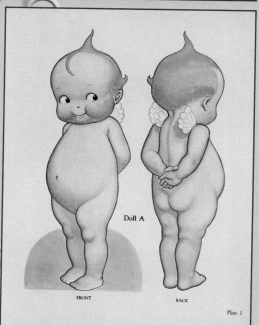

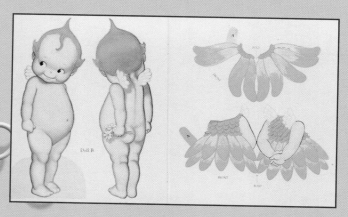

Stardancer   Year: 1984   #09052-6

This set reminds me of when my mother made me take dance lessons. I was never as good as the other girls, no matter how hard I tried. There is one recital in particular that comes to mind. I was all decked out in the fancy costume my mother hand made for this special occasion. The dance number our group was performing called for a 180-degree turn. I guess I didn't understand, because I turned only half way and ended up dancing with my back to the audience, while the other dancers correctly faced the crowd. Oops!

Stardancer includes two die-cut dancers, each posed differently, along with five die-cut accessories including ballet slippers, bags, and a radio. There is also a dance studio to press out and assemble, and there are 30 outfits and accessories to cut out. Tabs on the outfits are colored to match the colors on the dolls' bases.

Publisher: Rand McNally & Company/Morgan, Inc.
Original Price: $1.89   Value: $8.00 – 15.00

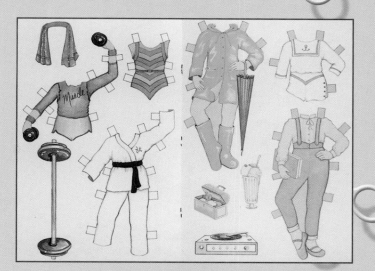

Puddin   **Year: 1984**   **#09052-6**

Puddin is an adorable little country girl with captivating big brown eyes, strawberry blonde hair, and a fanciful look on her face. This set comes with two 9½" die-cut Puddins. One Puddin is dressed in pink, and the other is dressed in blue and has a slightly different pose. There are nine die-cut accessories, including a fence, a birdhouse, and flowers. There are also 30 country-style outfits and accessories with tabs. Colored tabs on the clothing are green or blue, to match the appropriate doll's base.

Publisher: Rand McNally & Company/Morgan, Inc.
Original Price: $1.89   **Value: $8.00 – 20.00**

Charmkins   **Year: 1984**   **#86293-7**

In 1983, Hasbro introduced a new line of dolls, called Charmkins. Charmkins were simply charming at about 1" tall, and came scented with a flowery aroma. Each had a piece of jewelry, such as a hair comb, necklace, or ribbon, and all the dolls' jewelry pieces were interchangeable.

There were jewelry boxes that doubled as tiny dollhouses for the Charmkins; there you might find such characters as Popcorn the farmer, his wife, Blossom, and their children.

Those children, Brown-Eyed Susan and Willie Winkle, are featured in this paper doll set.

In this adorable set illustrated by Denise Fleming, you will find three die-cut dolls, the two children and their faithful dog, Buttercup. Also included is a 40-piece wardrobe with tabs that is ready to cut out.

Publisher: Happy House/Random House/Hasbro
Original Price: $1.29   **Value: $4.00 – 9.00**

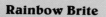

Rainbow Brite   **Year: 1984**   **#1534**

Here we have another Rainbow Brite set, which features four die-cut dolls, Rainbow Brite, Red Butler, Twink, and Starlite. It has a 17-piece press-out wardrobe with tabs. Also in this book is Rainbow Brite boxed set #7407C. The dolls in that set are 10" tall, and Twink and Starlite are not included. There are six more outfits in this set, but eleven are identical to the wardrobe for set #7407C

Note: You can read more about Rainbow Brite in the 1983 section of this book.

Publisher: Golden/Western Publishing Company/Hallmark
Original Price: $1.29   Value: $5.00 – 15.00

Barbie & Ken Dolls   Year: 1984   #1527

Ken doll and Barbie doll are all decked out for a night on the town in this set, based on the original Crystal Barbie and Crystal Ken dolls made by Mattel in the early 1980s.

In this set, you will find two die-cut dolls, Barbie doll and Ken doll, with a 12-piece glamorous wardrobe duplicating original formal wear of Barbie doll's and Ken doll's. All outfits have tabs and are ready to press out.

Publisher: Golden/Western/Mattel
Original price: 1.29   Value: $10.00 – 20.00

Barbie Doll Fantasy   Year: 1984   #1982-47

This is a favorite set of mine; it is beautifully illustrated and features the Pink & Pretty Barbie doll that was very popular in the mid-1980s.

Included in this paper doll set is one die-cut Barbie doll, along with an 18-piece wardrobe representing original Barbie fashions popular in 1983.

Publisher: Golden/Western/Mattel
Original Price: $1.29   Value: $10.00 – 20.00

Courtesy of Edna Corbett

Ginny   Year: 1984   #79002

Jeannie Graves founded the Vogue Doll Company in 1922; by 1951, she had created and introduced a little doll called Ginny, named after her daughter. Ginny enjoyed a great deal of popularity throughout the 1950s, and is a hot collector's doll today.

Ginny dolls were 8" tall and made of composition; later, in 1951, the material for them was changed to hard plastic. In the mid-1950s, the Vogue company added friends and family to Ginny's line. Some additions were Sparky, Ginny's trusty pooch (produced by the Steiff company); Jill, Ginny's sister; Jeff, Ginny's friend; and Ginnette, the baby of the family. There were fabulous outfits and accessories that could be purchased separately.

In this wonderful set done by Patti Chilbeck Meuler and Sue Nettleincham, you will find two stunning Ginny dolls and one Sparky to cut out, along with 100 beautifully illustrated cut-out outfits and accessories with tabs. Many are reproductions of the original Ginny wardrobe items.

Publisher: Meritus Industries, Inc./Vogue Dolls
Original Price: unknown   Value: $25.00 – 35.00

1985

Peaches 'n Cream Barbie Doll   Year: 1985   #1983-48

This set is based on Mattel's Peaches 'n Cream Barbie doll, and accurately depicts the original doll and her fashions popular in the mid-1980s. This set originated from set #1525 and is identical to it with the exception of its dark green cover.

Included is one 10¾" die-cut Peaches 'n Cream Barbie doll, along with a 16-piece press-out wardrobe with tabs. In addition, the set come with a handy carry tote to take Barbie doll and her outfits along in when you are on the go.

Publisher: Golden/Western/Mattel
Original Price: $1.29   Value: $8.00 – 15.00

The Heart Family   Year: 1985   #1526

In 1984, Mattel introduced the Heart Family dolls; these dolls weren't considered part of the Barbie family of dolls, but don't blink, you just might confuse the two. The Heart Family dolls had the same 11½", posable bodies as, and their faces possessed a remarkable family resemblance to, the popular Barbie and Ken dolls.

You could purchase a variety of Heart Family doll sets, for instance, one set consisted of Mom, Dad, and girl and boy twins. Other sets featured Mom and Toddler or Dad and Toddler, or even Mom and Newborn. There were also many cousins, representing many ethnic groups. Later, an adorable shaggy dog, a nursery for the baby, cars, and many other accessories were added to the Heart Family line, creating the opportunity for hours of fun and play for children.

This wonderful set features four die-cut dolls: Mom, Dad, twin Sister, and twin Brother; it comes with 25 press-out outfits and accessories with tabs.

Publisher: Golden/Western/Mattel
Original Price: $1.29   Value: $8.00 – 20.00

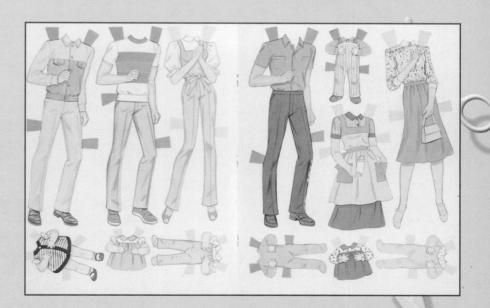

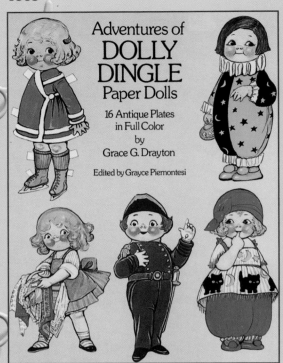

Dolly Dingle   **Year: 1985**   **#24809-7**

Grace Gebbie Drayton (1877 – 1936) was the creator and primary illustrator of the well-known Dolly Dingle character. Grace was also known for originating and illustrating the the famous Campbell's Soup Kids; who could forget the "Umm Umm Good" jingle?

Grace's paper dolls first appeared in 1913, in the women's magazine *Pictorial Review*. This charming set was reprinted from Drayton's original plates and represents the period from 1916 to 1923.

In this set, Dolly Dingle is able to make-believe that she is the lead character in various operas, plays, and children's fairy tales such as *La Boheme*, *Don Giovanni*, *The Mikado*, *Hansel and Gretel*, and *Little Red Riding Hood*.

Jam-packed with fabulous illustrations from the history of Dolly Dingle, this set comes with 38 dolls, 16 of which feature Dolly as various characters and enjoying many activities; she even joins the Red Cross. There is a 50-piece, colorful cut-out wardrobe with tabs.

Publisher: Dover
Original Price: $3.95   **Value: $4.00 – 8.00**

Princess of Power   Year: 1985   #1529

In 1985, the animated cartoon, *She-Ra, Princess of Power* was created as a spin-off to the popular cartoon *He-Man and the Masters of the Universe*. She-Ra was He-Man's twin sister. The show was targeted at young female viewers (but the boys watched too) and quickly became one of Filmation's biggest successes. Princess of Power enjoyed 93 episodes, but unfortunately, even though the series was very good, it was not as profitable as the He-Man series. The cartoon ended in 1986.

This set includes two die-cut dolls, She-Ra and Angella, and She-Ra's horse Spirit, who quickly becomes the unicorn Swift Wind when the set's die-cut wings and horned mask are added. There are 16 punch-out costumes and accessories with tabs.

Mattel created a popular series of action figures featuring She-Ra and her friends.

Note: You will also find this set as #1985 and #1984-54.

Publisher: Golden/Western/Mattel
Original Price: $1.29   Value: $4.00 – 8.00
Courtesy of Edna Corbett

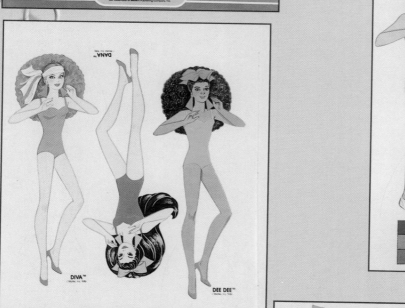

Barbie and the Rockers   **Year: 1986**   **#1528-1**

In 1986, Mattel introduced Barbie and the Rockers. Rock music was at the height of its popularity, so Mattel, in keeping with the times, marketed a Barbie doll with a full, curly hairstyle and glittery fashions. This Barbie doll was the leader of a rock band.

This paper doll set features Barbie and four of her Rocker friends, Dee Dee, Diva, Derek, and Dana. The die-cut dolls look as though they are ready to perform on stage, allowing little girls' imaginations to go wild!

There are 16 original Barbie doll outfits represented in this set; all have tabs and are ready to press out.

Note: Another Barbie and the Rockers set, #1528, is identical to #1528-1.

Publisher: Golden/Western/Mattel
Original Price: $1.29   Value: $8.00 – 15.00

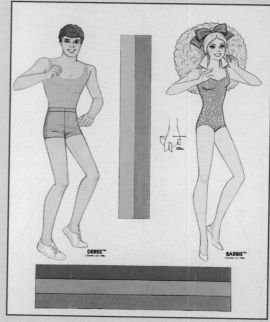

Jem   Year: 1986   #1524

Jem made her debut in the cartoon series *Jem and the Holograms*, which ran from 1985 to 1988. It was well-written and brilliantly animated, and combined adventure, fashion, and music with captions imitating MTV music videos. Jem (voiced by Britta Phillips) and the Holograms sang almost a hundred songs in their 65-episode run.

The premise went something like this: Jerrica Benton ran the Starlight Home for Girls, which she had inherited from her father. She also communicated with Synergy, a special computer that was the was brainchild of her late father. Through Jerrica's star earrings, and Synergy, she and her friends transformed into Jem and the Holograms, a rock band with fashion and flair. The Misfits and their greedy punk rock manager were the archrivals of the band, and week after week there were battles to be fought and won by Jem and the Holograms.

In 1986, Hasbro released 12½", fully posable dolls portraying Jem and her friends. Jem came with her star earrings; when a button on the back of her head was pressed, they would glow. The dolls came with their own line of high-quality fashions and a cassette tape of Jem and the Holograms singing.

This set includes six wonderfully illustrated die-cut dolls, Jerrica, Rio, Jem, Aja, Kimber, and Shana, along with a 21-piece press-out wardrobe with tabs. It also has three sets of earrings, including Jem's stars, for little girls to press out. The earrings can be attached to the paper dolls with string.

Publisher: Golden/Western/Hasbro
Original Price: $1.29   **Value: $7.00 – 12.00**

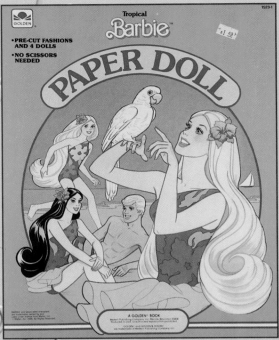

Tropical Barbie Doll   Year: 1986   #1523-1

Barbie doll and friends are ready for a tropical vacation in this set, based on the Tropical Barbie series by Mattel.

Of the four die-cut dolls featured in this book, Barbie doll, Miko doll, and Skipper doll have long, flowing hair; only Ken doll does not. All have original Barbie doll fashions swimsuits, and the set comes with a 27-piece cut-out tropical wardrobe with tabs. In this set, you will also find a Tahiti bird that slips onto an island perch.

Note: Another Tropical Barbie doll set, #1523, is identical.

Publisher: Golden/Western/Mattel
Original Price: $1.29   Value: $8.00 – 15.00

Punky Brewster   **Year: 1986**   **#1532**

David W. Duclon was the creator of NBC's hit television sitcom *Punky Brewster*, Punky (Penelope "Punky" Brewster), played by Soleil Moon Frye, was a spunky seven-year-old girl with a sunny disposition who had been abandoned by her mother at a Chicago shopping center. Punky and her dog, Brandon, then had to fend for themselves. After searching, they found an empty apartment to call home. Henry Warnimen (George Gaynest), a grumpy old bachelor, soon found the two trespassers and threatened to call the authorities. However, the funniest thing happened — he couldn't resist Punky's big brown eyes and winning smile; he fell head over heels for her, and somehow convinced the authorities to let Punky and her dog stay with him for a while. Punky had the ability to lift Henry's spirits, and she softened his heart, something no one had ever done before. Life, as Henry knew it, would never be the same.

Because of Punky's popularity (the show ran from 1985 to 1989), NBC aired an animated version of *Punky Brewster* that ran Saturday mornings; the show featured the adventures of Punky and her magical friend Glomer. Glomer could transport Punky and her friends to any part of the world in the blink of an eye. Punky was voiced by the original Punky, Soleil Moon Frye.

This set, based on the cartoon version of *Punky Brewster*, includes one die-cut Punky, as well as Brandon and Glomer. There are 25 Punky-style outfits with tabs for Punky and her two friends.

Publisher: Golden/Western/NBC, Inc.
Original Price: $1.29   **Value: $5.00 – 10.00**

Grace Kelly   Year: 1986   #25180-2

The Philadelphia-born star was an American movie princess long before capturing the heart of Prince Rainier and becoming Princess of Monaco. A star of film and television, Grace made her first screen appearances between the years 1950 and 1952, on the television shows *The Philco Television Playhouse Studio One* and the CBS production of *Don Quixote*, which starred Boris Karloff.

Making the jump to the big screen, she appeared with leading men Cary Grant, Gary Cooper, Bing Crosby, and Clark Gable. After starring in the critically acclaimed Hitchcock thriller *Rear Window*, Kelly took her place as one of Hollywood's greatest actors, and would be the director's choice in four of his classics. Her awards and accolades included an Academy Award Best Supporting Actress nomiation for *Mogambo* and an Academy Award for *The Country Girl*.

In 1955, Grace met and fell in love with Prince Rainier of Monaco, and in 1956, the two were married in a ceremony at Monaco's Cathedral of Saint Nicholas. With a life now based in this small coastal principality, it was now time for her to officially retire from the movies and turn her attention to her new role as Her Serene Highness Princess Grace of Monaco and to starting a family. She and Rainier had three children. Princess Caroline Louise Marguerite was born on January 23, 1957, Prince Albert Alexandre Louis Pierre, born March 14, 1958, and Princess Stéphanie Marie Elizabeth, born February 1, 1965.

On September 13, 1982, on a winding cliff road, she suffered a heart attack and lost control of her vehicle. Grace Kelly, movie star and princess, died 36 hours later in a hospital, at the age of 52.

Tom Tierney did a fabulous job portraying Kelly in three different eras of her life. The first is a young Grace in her 1955 *To Catch a Thief* swimsuit, the second is a middle-aged Grace, and the third is a more mature Grace. There are fabulous wardrobe pieces documenting many of Kelly's life milestones, such as the dress she wore at her Academy Award acceptance, her wedding gown, and many more. This set is rich with the history of a truly beautiful and sophisticated woman. The complete set features four dolls, three of Grace Kelly and one of Prince Rainier, along with 29 cut-out outfits and wigs with tabs, 11 of which are costumes from movie roles.

Publisher: Dover/Tom Tierney
Original Price: $4.95   Value: $5.00 – 12.00

The Hilda Toddler   Year: 1986   No number

Of all the German character babies ever produced, J. D. Kestner's Hilda is the most desirable to collectors and reproduction artists; she has delicate, realistic features that captivate all who see her.

Hilda was originally produced in 1914 and came with many variations. One of the most sought after Hildas was the bald (or painted hair) baby, which had a socket neck, bent limbs, a 23¼" bent leg, chubby body. Another variation came with a short mohair wig but the same baby body. In 1915, Kestner made a rare and stunning 15" Baby Hilda, with a molded-on blue and white bonnet. This baby had molded/painted curls, and like the Hildas before her, featured an open mouth, two front teeth, a molded tongue, and a chubby body. Hilda was also produced as a toddler; some toddler Hildas had short mohair wigs, while others had longer hairstyles with soft mohair curls. Hilda has universal appeal and continues to be a beloved classic.

Peck-Gandré has captured the essence of the Toddler Hilda in this paper doll set and has been producing extraordinary paper dolls sets, oftentimes replicas of vintage dolls and their wardrobes, with precise detail and beauty for years; all of its paper dolls come in their own folios.

This set features a 12" wonderfully illustrated Hilda Toddler, along with 12 authentic fashions and six outfits to color; all costumes have tabs and are ready to cut out.

Publisher: Peck-Gandré
Original Price: unknown   Value: $8.00 – 20.00

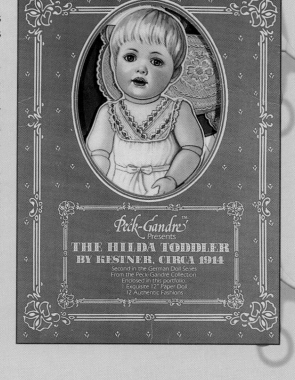

The Steiner Babe   Year: 1986   No number

In 1870, French doll maker Jules Nicholas Steiner produced a new baby doll. To distinguish his doll from the German dolls of that period, Jules called his baby the Steiner Bebe. She was an instant success, and soon other French doll makers were producing their own versions of the Bebe. Unlike the previous fashion dolls, the Bebe was molded to reflect the image of a middle-class French child, with huge eyes, delicate features, rosy cheeks and lips, and long ringlet curls. She had a painted bisque head and a molded composition body. Bebes were dressed in the richness of fashion dolls and the elegance of little children raised in middle-income families.

Jules accomplished what he went after with his Bebe; she was a favorite with children then, and she remains a favorite for collectors today.

Peck-Gandré does it again with this exquisite set that includes one 12" Steiner and 12 authentic fashions, and 11 black and white fashions to design and color. All clothes have tabs and are ready to cut out.

Publisher: Peck-Gandré
Original Price: unknown   Value: $8.00 – 20.00

American Family of the Victorian Era   Year: 1986   #25114

During Queen Victoria's long reign, particularly between the 1870s and the 1880s, middle-class families enjoyed a time of economic growth and leisure. Fashions in the Victorian era were ornate and somewhat prudish. Most women's fashions were impractical, so depending on a woman's activity, she may have had re-dress several times a day, almost always requiring help from a servant. To the Victorian women, appearance was more important than comfort. (I'm not sure times have changed all that much.) The Victorian idea of beauty encouraged the use of accessories like corsets. A corset would be tied so tightly that it created a disfiguringly sized waist; some women were known to faint from lack of oxygen. Other fashion accessories were bustles; these were made of materials like wire, steel springs, and even braided horsehair. There were hip, thigh, and calf paddings, bust enhancers, and posterior enhancers, all used to create a voluptuous, womanly body.

Women's fashions at this time were becoming more complicated, but men's fashions were being simplified. Men's fashions then were similar to what we see in men's fashions today; for instance, men were wearing shorter jackets, tweeds, stripes, and popular colors like black, browns, and greens.

Tom Tierney created this wonderful set depicting a middle-class American family of the Victorian era.

The set includes seven Victorian family members: Horace and Margaret (Grandparents), Diana and Hale (parents), and five children (Ronald, Helen, Erin, Piper, and Diana, all together as one doll). There are 36 costumes, richly detailed, that exemplify fashions of the Victorian era.

Publisher: Dover/Tom Tierney
Original Price: $4.95   Value: $5.00 – 8.00

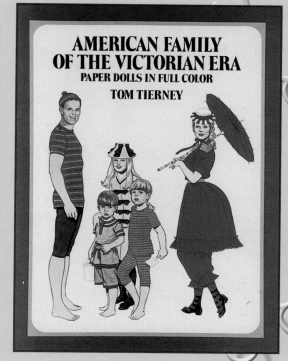

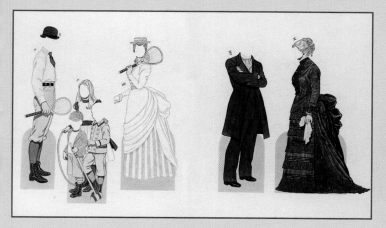

Moon Dreamers   **Year: 1987**   **#1542-1**

Moon Dreamers came on the dream scene in 1986, as a 15-minute television cartoon of the same name, and was part of the popular My Little Pony line. The job of the Moon Dreamers was to send people good dreams and protect them from bad dreams. The show had 16 episodes featuring such characters as Whimzee, Sparky Dreamer, Bucky Buckaroo, Dream Gazer, Dozer, Crystal Starr, and the evil Scowlene and Squawker. Hasbro then produced a series of adorable 6" vinyl dolls that glowed in the dark to help send children off to dreamland.

The complete Moon Dreamers set includes eight die-cut dolls, Crystal Starr, Bucky Buckaroo, Dozer, Whimzee, Dream Gazer, Sparky Dreamer, Squawker, and the evil Scowlene, and six stars children can put a string through and wear around their necks, all made of lightweight cardboard. There are also 46 dreamy press-out outfits with tabs that complete this set.

Note: This set originates from set #1542.

Publisher: Golden/Western/Hasbro, Inc.
Original Price: $1.29   Value: $3.00 – 8.00

It's fun to dress the dolls in colorful clothes and create imaginative play situations. Golden® Paper Doll books feature favorite characters and themes.

Look for other Golden® activity products, including Color/Activity books, Sticker Fun® books and Press-out books at stores near you.

Snow White   Year: 1987   No number

These next three sets are based on popular and charming fairy tale characters; they are all part of the Enchanted Forest series by Peck-Gandré. In this first set, Peck-Gandré has perfectly captured the enchanting beauty of Snow White. The back of the folio states that Peck-Gandré incorporated many early German clothing designs into this collection, which includes one statuette Snow White doll and 12 cut-out costumes (six in color and six to design and color on your own), all with tabs.

Note: Read more about the story of Snow White and Prince Charming in chapter 1, section 1967.

Publisher: Peck-Gandré
Original Price: unknown   **Value: $5.00 – 10.00**

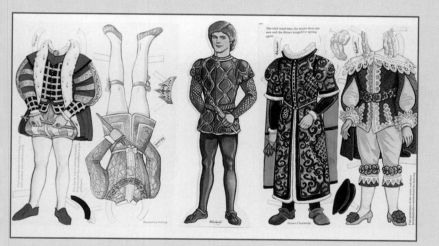

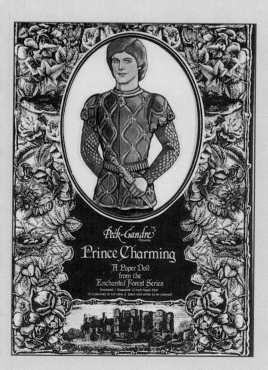

Prince Charming   Year: 1987   No number

Here we have the very handsome Prince Charming, again with Peck-Gandré's attention to detail. He is 12" tall and has 12 costumes (six colored and six to design to design and color), all with tabs and ready to cut out.

Publisher: Peck-Gandré
Original Price: unknown   **Value: $5.00 – 10.00**

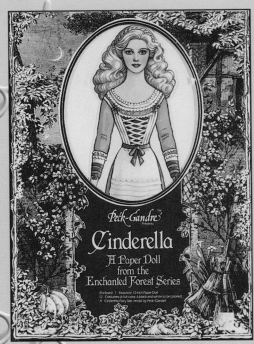

Cinderella   Year: 1987   No number

In this set, Peck-Gandré uniquely captures the beauty of both French and German designs for the charming Cinderella. This doll is both stunning and delightful, with bright colors and attention to detail. Her set includes one 12" statuette doll, Cinderella, and 12 costumes (six in color and six to color and design}, all with tabs and ready to cut out.

Note: Read more about the story of Cinderella in chapter 1, section 1965.

Publisher: Peck-Gandré
Original Price: unknown   **Value: $5.00 – 10.00**

Courtesy of Edna Corbett

This insert shows many of the paper dolls that are part of Peck-Gandré's line, and was included in each set.

Jewel Secrets Barbie Doll   Year: 1987   #1537-1

This set originates from set #1537; the two sets are identical with the exception of the stock number and the fact that this set does not display the price on the cover.

Both sets are based on Mattel's popular Jewel Secrets Barbie doll, and reflect original Jewel Secrets fashions.

This set includes four die-cut dolls, Barbie doll, Ken doll, Skipper doll, and Whitney doll, along with 13 glamorous press-out outfits with tabs. The back cover has a wonderfully illustrated jewel choker for little girls to press out and wear.

Publisher: Golden/Western/Mattel
Original Price: $1.29   **Value: $8.00 – 15.00**

Shirley Temple   **Year: 1988**   **#25461**

Shirley Temple was the enchanting little girl with ringlet curls who had dimples when she smiled, and who made life feel a little sunnier as she sang and danced her way into our hearts.

This wonderful set is a reproduction of the first original Shirley Temple paper doll set, drawn by Corinne and Bill Bailey and published by Saalfield. Saalfield acquired the exclusive rights to publish Shirley Temple items and published coloring books, storybook activity sets, and paper dolls featuring this delightful little sprite.

This set is a fabulous treasury of Shirley Temple history, and includes four different Shirley Temple dolls, along with a 30-piece wardrobe. Some of the costumes featured in this book were worn by the child star in her film roles. Included are her famous blue and white polka-dot dress from *Stand up and Cheer* (my personal favorite) and her pink ruffled dress and her yellow party dress from *Baby Take a Bow*. You will also find Shirley's baby doll inside of a 1930-model buggy, and a table and chair set.

The doll, outfits, and accessories all have tabs and are ready to cut out. The tabs are marked from one to four, to identify which Shirley doll the outfits belong to.

Note: Read more about Shirley Temple in chapter 3, section 1976.

Publisher: Dover/Children's Museum, Boston Mass.
Original Price: $4.95   **Value: $5.00 – 12.00**

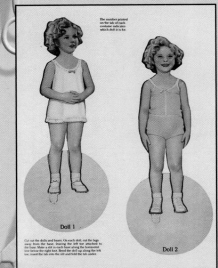

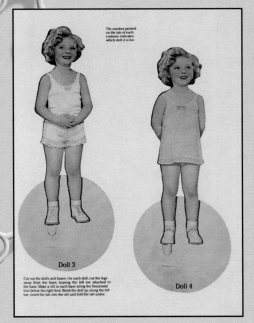

Bride and Groom   Year: 1988   #1501

Here we have a lovely bride and groom set, drawn by Virginia Lucia, that features a wedding party of four die-cut dolls: the bride and groom, the maid of honor, and an adorable flower girl. In addition, you will find a wedding table for a beautiful five-tiered wedding cake, with a basket of flowers and a wedding gift that slip into the table. All of these pieces are made of lightweight cardboard. There is an 18-piece press-out wardrobe, with tabs, that typifies 1980s fashions. It includes a stylish wedding dress and tuxedo. Each doll has a colored wedding bell on its base that matches the colored tabs on its outfits.

Publisher: Golden/Western
Original Price: $4.95   **Value: $4.00 – 8.00**

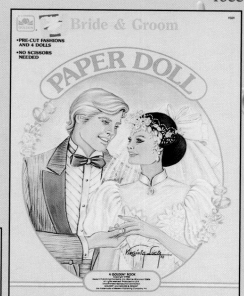

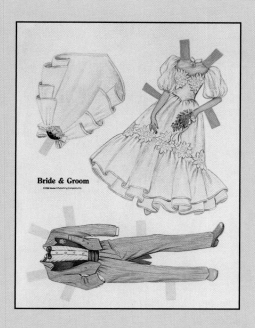

Goldilocks And The Three Bears   Year: 1988   No number

Goldilocks and the Three Bears is a great read for toddlers. It covers two important aspects of childhood interaction, respect and making choices. When my children were younger (before hip hop got to them), I would refer back to the story of Goldilocks when one would take something that belonged to the other, or jump off the bed or the couch and end up with a good-sized bump. To this day, I still have to remind them to respect their siblings' things and to make better choices. They don't seem to listen to Mama Bear, but when Papa Bear roars, now that's a different story.

Having read through much of this book, you may have realized by now that I am a big fan of Peck-Gandré's work. This exquisite set is no exception. With this 12" Goldilocks, Peck-Gandré has captured an enchanting innocence consistent with all of its paper dolls. There are six costumes in color and six in black and white to design and color, all with tabs and ready to cut out. The back cover features Mama, Papa, and Baby Bear.

Publisher: Peck-Gandré
Original Price: unknown   **Value: $5.00 – 10.00**

Courtesy of Edna Corbett

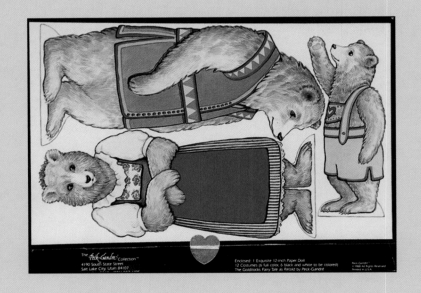

Little Red Riding Hood   Year: 1988   No number

When I read stories from the Brothers Grimm, it amazes me how they can draw me into the midst of one of their tales. There was a movement to have this story blacklisted in some schools here in the US, due to what some considered "overtly sexual content."

Well, I have pretty strong opinions when adults go looking to find sexual content in children's literature, but hey, that's a debate for another place and time. There were earlier versions of *Little Red Riding Hood*, two written and one oral, and all three were used as sources for the Grimm version of the tale about the young girl sent to her sick grandmother's house to take her a piece of cake and a bottle of wine.

Yeah, yeah, I know, a kid heading off with a bottle of wine, a grandmother who gets swallowed whole by a big bad wolf, a somewhat naïve Little Red Riding Hood who gets swallowed up by the wolf as well… But there is a happy ending. While the wolf sleeps off his meals, a huntsman comes along and cuts open the wolf's belly, and out jump Little Red Riding Hood and her grandmother. To think of it, hmmm… maybe it's not what you want your children to read. Just head to Blockbuster and rent the Disney short.

Peck-Gandré does it again with this charming set that includes one 12" Red Riding Hood, six costumes in color, and six costumes ready to be designed and colored. The back cover features the wolf, dressed in Grandma's nightie and waiting in the bed for the unsuspecting Red Riding Hood to arrive. Yikes!

Publisher: Peck-Gandré
Original Price: unknown   Value: $5.00 – 10.00

Courtesy of Edna Corbett

Beauty and the Beast   **Year: 1989**   **No number**

   This beautifully illustrated set reflects Peck-Gardré's vision of the beloved fairy tale, a story about the love between a young maiden and a prince who has been enchanted to appear as a beast.

   Peck-Gardré captured the essence of this enchanting fairy tale with a beautiful redheaded Beauty, the Beast, and a Handsome Prince. There are six color-printed Old European–style fashions and six fashions to design and color.

Publisher: Peck-Gandré
Original Price: unknown   **Value: $6.00 – 10.00**

Family Fun   Year: 1989   #89209

Here we have a happy family ready for family fun. This set includes four die-cut dolls: Mom, Dad, Big Sister, and Baby Brother. There are also a walker and bottle for Baby Brother and a Cabbage Patch look-alike doll for Big Sister, all made of lightweight cardboard. There are 25 color-printed fashions and eight more outfits to design and color. On the back cover, you will find a charming Victorian dollhouse for big sister to assemble.

Publisher: Checkerboard Press/Macmillan, Inc.
Original Price: $1.95   Value: $3.00 – 8.00

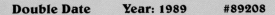

Double Date   Year: 1989   #89208

This delightful set features four friends, an African American couple and a Caucasian couple, ready to go out on a double date.

The set includes four die-cut dolls, along with six fashionable wigs for the girls and four hats for the fellas, all made from lightweight cardboard. Also included is a 64-piece wardrobe of night wear, active wear, and casual wear, plus more wigs and hats. All pieces have tabs and are ready to press out.

Publisher: Checkerboard Press/Macmillan, Inc.
Original Price: $1.95   Value: $3.00 – 8.00

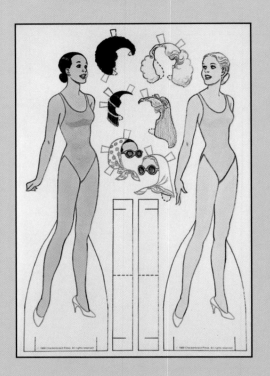

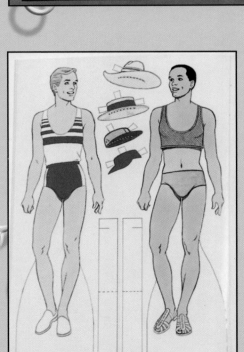

Friends at School   Year: 1989   #89210

Friends at School is a wonderful set featuring four school-aged children, and is filled with kidswear. Some of the outfits show the children holding books or lunch pails. In addition, you will find holiday wear such as Pilgrims and Indians (complete with headdresses), and a pumpkin Halloween costume. Little girls can have the paper doll children put on a school play.

The complete set features four 9" die-cut children, 15 color-printed outfits, and another half dozen outfits in black and white to design and color yourself. All outfits press out and have tabs. The back cover has the cutest little red wagon to press out and assemble.

Publisher: Checkerboard Press/Macmillan, Inc.
Original Price: $1.95   **Value: $5.00 – 10.00**

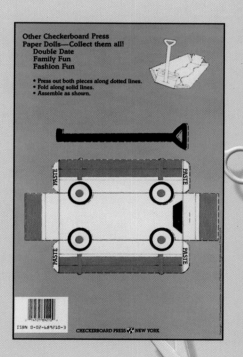

Cinderella   Year: 1989   #1545

This set, based on Walt Disney's timeless movie classic *Cinderella*, remains perhaps the most beloved Walt Disney fairy tale of all time.

This enchanting set includes five die-cut Walt Disney characters: Cinderella, Handsome Prince, Fairy Godmother, and two of Cinderella's mice friends, along with 13 costumes from the movie. All the outfits have tabs, and are ready to press out.

Note: Read more about Cinderella in chapter 1, section 1965.

Publisher: Golden Western/Walt Disney
Original Price: $1.29   Value: $5.00 – 10.00

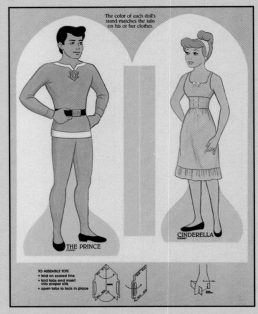

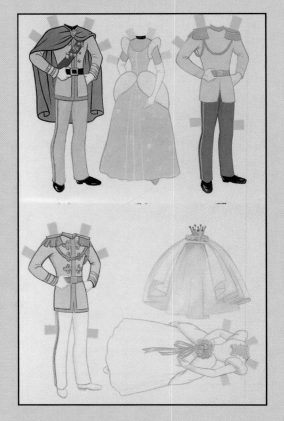

Nostalgic Barbie Doll (#1)   Year: 1989   No number

Since she came on the scene in 1959, Barbie doll has been fulfilling the fantasies and imaginations of little girls all over the world. She was advertised as a teenage fashion model, and she certainly had the wardrobe to prove it! Her beauty was unsurpassed, and she lived in the world of high fashion and glamour. In addition, she was a cheerleader and the prom queen, and she could ice skate and play tennis. There was nothing Barbie doll couldn't do.

She was 11½" tall, with a shapely figure, true red lips, and inverted V–shaped brows. Her eyes had white irises and black pupils, and she had a pert blonde or brunette ponytail. No other doll has enjoyed the same success as Barbie doll.

Peck-Gandré created a true work of art, while capturing the very essence of this first Barbie doll. She comes as a 12", exquisitely illustrated statuette doll. There is an eight-piece color wardrobe reflecting original Barbie doll fashions such as Gay Parisienne (1959), Solo in the Spotlight (1960), and Red Flair, to name a few. Also included are eight black and white outfits, so little girls can design and color their own Barbie doll fashions. All outfits have tabs and are ready to cut out.

Note: Read more about the Barbie doll throughout this book, beginning with chapter 1, section 1967.

Publisher: Peck-Gandré
Original Price: unknown   **Value: $10.00 – 20.00**

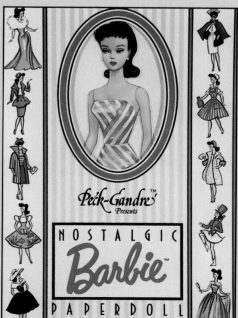

Nostalgic Barbie Doll (#5)   Year: 1989   No number

In the year following her debut, Barbie doll underwent some changes. The whites of her irises changed to blue, her eyebrows now had a soft curve, and she had a warmer flesh tone. By the introduction of Barbie doll #5 (she is considered by many to be the most beautiful of all the early Barbie dolls), she was being mass produced to keep up with growing demand. The rest is history.

Peck-Gandré features the popular #5 Barbie doll in this fabulous set; as in the above set, the statuette doll magnificently done at 12" tall. Barbie doll has seven original fashions, such as Enchanted Evening (1960), Friday Nite Date (1960), and Senior Prom (1963), and comes with nine black and white outfits to color and design that will inspire the designer in us all. All wardrobe pieces have tabs and are ready to cut out.

Publisher: Peck-Gandré
Original Price: unknown   **Value: $10.00 – 20.00**

Nostalgic Ken Doll   **Year: 1989**   **No number**

Ken doll made his debut in 1961, purely because of popular demand; Ruth Handler's vision of Barbie doll was that of an independent career woman. However, in the early 1960s, a woman was considered a failure without a male companion, so it became necessary to create Ken doll. He ended up being a huge success. He stood 12" and had short-flocked hair, dazzling blue eyes, and an aura of innocence. To create his image, the makers gave Ken doll the essential trappings of a well-bred male teenager, such as a high school letter sweater, a tuxedo for the prom, and a gray flannel suit for dating. Ken doll brought romance and adventure into the lives of little girls and opened a new door of possibilities in their imaginations. Girls had hours of fun dreaming up new adventures for Barbie doll and Ken doll.

This set done by Peck-Gandré captures the likeness of Ken doll in a 12" statuette doll and includes eight of Ken doll's popular wardrobe pieces, such as Rally Day, Ski Champion, and Touch Down, to name a few. There are also nine outfits in black and white to design and color. All have tabs and are ready to cut out.

Publisher: Peck-Gandré
Original Price: unknown   **Value: $15.00 – 25.00**

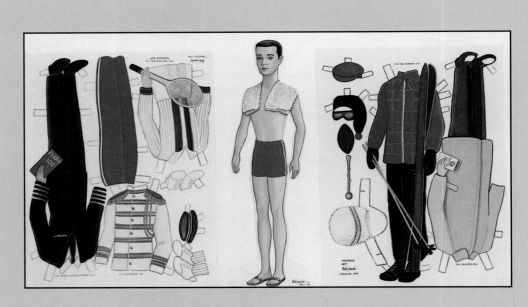

Index

Index